CATALOGUE OF BOOKS IN THE PRIVATE LIBARARY OF SHAMSUL ULMA

CATALOGUE OF BOOKS IN THE PRIVATE LIBARARY OF SHAMSUL ULMA

SYED ALI BILGRAMI

GYAN

Published by

GYAN

Gyan Publishing House
5, Ansari Road
Daryaganj, New Delhi-110002
Phone: 011-47034999, 9811692060
E-mail: books@gyanbooks.com

Distribution Network
gyanbooks.com
India, USA, Canada, UK, Australia

ISBN: 978-93-7447-452-5 (HB)

First Published, 1901

2nd Impression 2025

Printed at: Gyan Press, Delhi.

CATALOGUE OF BOOKS IN
THE PRIVATE LIBARARY OF SHAMSUL ULMA
Author: SYED ALI BILGRAMI

A CATALOGUE OF BOOKS

IN THE PRIVATE LIBRARY

OF

SHAMSUL ULAMA

SYED ALI BILGRAMI, B. A., L. L. B.,

ASSOCIATE ROYAL SCHOOL OF MINES, (LONDON,)

MEMBER OF THE ROYAL ASIATIC SOCIETY OF GREAT BRITAIN AND IRELAN[D]

MEMBER OF THE ASIATIC SOCIETY OF BENGAL AND BOMBAY,

FELLOW OF THE GEOLOGICAL SOCIETY OF LONDON,

MEMBER OF FEDERATED INSTITUTION OF MINING AND MECHANICAL ENGINEERS, LATE EXAMINER MADRAS UNIVERSITY,

&c. &c. &c.,

SECRETARY TO HIS HIGHNESS THE NIZAM'S GOVERNMENT,

PUBLIC WORKS DEPARTMENT, RAILWAYS AND MINES,

HYDERABAD, DECCAN.

MADRAS:

PRINTED AT THE A. L. V. PRESS, 149, POPHAM'S BROADWAY.

1901.

LIST OF ABBREVIATIONS.

1. A. S. S.—Ânandâśrama Sanskrit Series.
2. A. C. E. R.—Ancient Classics for English Readers.
3. An. Ox.—Anecdota Oxoniensia.
4. Auc. San.—Auctores Sanscriti.
5. Bib. Cl.—Bibliotheca Classica.
6. Bib. Con.—Bibliotheqne Contemporaine.
7. Bib. Ind.—Bibliotheca Indica.
8. Bib. It.—Bibliotheca Italiana.
9. Bib. Na.—Bibliotheque Nationale.
10. Bib. Pos.—Bibliotheqne Positiviste.
11. Bib. San.—Bibliotheca Sanskritica.
12. B. B. C.—Bohn's British Classics.
13. B. S. S.—Bombay Sanskrit Series.
14. C. N. Sc. M.—Cambridge Natural Science Manuals.
15. Can. Po.—Canterbury Poets.
16. C. N. L.—Cassell's National Library.
17. Ch. Cl.—Chandos Classics.
18. C. P. S.—Clarenden Press Series.
19. C. S.—Classical Series.
20. Cl. Wr.—Classical Writers.
21. C. A. Sc. S.—Collin's Advanced Science Series.
22. C. E. Sc. S.—Collin's Elementary Science Series.
23. C. Sc. S.—Contemporary Science Series.
24. Eng. Cit.—English Citizen Series.
25. E. M. L. S.—English Men of Letters Series.
26. Eng. Phi —English Philosophers.
27. Eng. Wor,—English Worthies.
28. For. St.—Foreign Statesmen.
29. G. O. L. S.—Government Oriental Library Series.
30. G. Sc. T. B.—Griffin's Scientific Text-Books.
31. H. F. S.—Hachette's French Classics.
32. H. I. F. P. R.—Hachette's Illustrated French Primary Readers.
33. H. V. W.—Handy Volume Waverly.

34. H. S. Sc. S.—Hehir's Sanitary Science Series.

35. He. Na.—Heroes of the Nations.

36. His. Pr.—History Primers.

37. I. Sc. S.—International Scientific Series.

38. J. A. O. S.—Journal of the American Oriental Society

39. K. M.—Kâvya Mâla.

40. L. S. E. F.—Les Grands Ecrivains Français.

41. L. E. L. S.—Library of English Literature Series.

42. L. U. S.—Library of Useful Stories.

43. L. P S. Literary Primer Series.

44. Lit Pr.—Literature Primers.

45. L. Sc. C. B.—London Science Class-Books.

46. L. H. B.—Lubbock's Hundred Books.

47. M. C. L. S. { Macmillan's Colonial Library Series.
Methuen's Colonial Library Series.

48. M. S. S.—Madras School Series.

49. M. E. Sc.—Manuals of Elementary Science.

50. M. L. S —Masterpiece Library Series.

51. M. L. F. B.—Minerva Library of Famous Books.

52. N. S.—Nature Series.

53. P. T S.—Pâli Text Society.

54. P. P. S.—Pitt Press Series.

55. R. T. S —Religious Tract Society.

56. R. Sc. S.—Romance of Science Series.

57. Rul. Ind.—Rulers of India Series.

58. S. B. E.—Sacred Books of the East.

59. Sc. Pr.—Science Primers.

60. S. N.—Story of the Nations.

61. T. L. L.—Tagore Law Lectures.

62. T. B. Sc.—Text Books of Science.

63. Th. Fr.—Theatre Français.

64. T. O. S.—Trübner's Oriental Series.

65. U. C. C. T. S.—Universal Correspondence College Tutorial Series.

66. U. E. M.—University Extension Manuals.

67. U. E. S.—University Extension Series.

68. V. S. S.—Vizianagaram Sanskrit Series.

TABLE OF CONTENTS.

ERRATA.

In Page	No.	Line	for	read
2,	18,	1,	Julius	Julius.
8,	117,	1,	Madhthara's	Mahîdhara's.
13,	46,	2,	Pcona	Poona.
21,	15,	1,	Rhishîkesa	Hrishîkesa.
22,	33,	1,	Londen	London.
23,	36,	1,	Edited	Edited by.
28,	27,	1,	Pandti	Pandit.
29,	39,	1,	Edited	Edited by.
30,	61,	2,	Millinâtha	Mallinâtha.
32,	94,	2,	Dargâprasâda	Durgâprasâda.
37,	12,	2,	Dentchland	Deutchland.
39,	54,	1,	Introduotory	Introductory.
62,	2,	1,	Omit *Romanised.*	
76,	79,	2,	Edlted	Edited.
80,	30,	2,	Tranclated	Translated.
81,	40,	1,	Pronunciatiou	Pronunciation.
81,	42,	2,	Daffield	Duffield.
82,	49,	1,	Rook	Book.
103,	65,	3,	Introdution	Introduction.
111,	41,	3,	hy	by.
113,	76,	2,	Read in the end (Th. Fr. No. 42.)	
121,	213,	2,	76	75.
138,	155,	1,	Dyee	Dyce.
139,	174,	1,	Essays	Essay.
141,	206,	1,	Anthors	Authors.
141,	206,	1,	Biogoaphical	Biographical.
147,	302,	2,	Authr's	Author's.
150,	345,	2,	J. W. Timbs	J. Timbs.
150,	345,	2,	Add in the end	4 Vols.
163,	24,	1,	Compbell	Campbell.
177,	72,	2,	ond	and.
181,	25,	2,	ond	only.
196,	56,	3,	Mad	Map.
231,	1,	1,	Vede	Vade.
240, read line 3 of No. 39 as line 3 of No. 37 of the same page.				
249,	8,	1,	Medical	Medica.
243,	8,	1,	Kriechthere	Kriechthiere.
251,	42,	1,	Principles	Principal.
257,	7,	1,	Manaal	Manual.
260,	30,	2,	Blow pepe	Blow pipe.

A.

SANSKRIT LANGUAGE AND LITERATURE.

I.—*Vedas, Brâhmanas, Sûtras and Vedic Exegesis.*

1. AITAREYA ÂRANYAKAM—By Râjendralâla Mitra, (Bib. Ind.) 1876, (out of print).
2. ——————— With the Commentary of Sâyanâchârya—Edited by Bâbâ Śâstri Padke, and published by Hîranârâyana Apte, (A. S. S. No. 38).
3. ———BRÂHMAṆA—Text and Translation—By Martin Haug, 2 vols. Bombay, 1863 (rare).
4. ——————— Text—With extracts from Sâyanâ's Commentary (Romanised)—By T. Aufrecht Bonn. 1879.
5. ——————— Text—Bombay, 1891.
6. ——————— Part I—with the Bhâshya of Śrîmat Sâyanâchârya (the first four Panchikas only)—Edited by Pandit Kâśinâth Śâstri Agâse. Poona, 1896, (A. S. S. No. 32).
7. ——————— Part II—(the last four Panchikas only), with the Commentary of Sâyanâcharya—Edited by Pandit Kâśinâth Śâstri Agâse. (A. S. S. No. 32).
8. ÂPASTAMBA GRIHYA SÛTRA—With extracts from the Commentaries of Haradatta and Sudarśanârya—Edited by M. Winternitz. Vienna, 1887.
9. ——————— With a Commentary of Sudarśanârya, (G. O. L. S.) Bib. San. No. 1 Mysore, 1893.
10. ———SRÂUTA SÛTRA.—Belonging to the Taittirîya Saṃhitâ with Rudradatta's Commentary. Edited by Dr. R. Garbe vols. I and II. Calcutta, 1882, (Bib. Ind.)
11. ÂRSHEYA BRÂHMAṆA.—Edited by A. C. Burnell, Mangalore 1876 (rare).
12. ÂŚVALÂYANA GRIHYA SÛTRA.—With Gârgya. Nârâyaṇa's Commentary—Calcutta 1869, (out of print). (Bib. Ind).

13. Âsvalâyana Śrauta Sûtra.—With Gârgya Nârâyaṇa's Commentary. Calcutta 1874, (Bib. Ind.)

14. Atharva Veda Samhitâ.—Hymns of the—By M. Bloomfield. (S. B. E. Vol. XLII). Oxford, 1897.

15. ———— Seven hymns of the—By Maurice Bloomfield. Baltimore, 1886.

16. ———— Index Verborum to the—By W. D. Whitney. (Vol. XII of J. A. O. S.). New Haven, 1886.

17. ———— Das seschste Buch der, übersetzt und erklärt von Carl Adolf Florenz—Gottingen, 1887.

18. ———— Hundert Lieder des—By Julins Grill, 2nd Edition. Stuttgart, 1888.

19. ————Prâtisâkhya—By W. D. Whitney. (Vol. VII, J. A. O. S.). New Haven, 1862.

20. ————Samhitâ—Text.—Edited by R. Roth and W. D. Whitney. Berlin, 1856 (rare).

21. ———— Bombay 1881. Reprint of above.

22. ———— With Sâyanâ's Commentary, Kândas I to X —Edited by Śankar Pândurang Pandit, M. A., Bombay Govt. Central Book Depôt, 1895.

23. Barthalémy Saint Hilaire M. J.—Des Vedas. Paris, 1854.

24. Benfey, M.—Die Quantitätsverschiedenheiten des Samhitâ und Pada Texten der Veden. Göttingen, 1874-81.

25. Bergaigne, A.—La Religion Vedique—3 vol., Paris, 1883.

26. Do. and V. Henry—La Sanskrit Vedique. Paris 1890.

27. Delbrück, B.—Altindische Syntax—Halle, 1888.

28. ———— Altindische Tempuslehre—Halle, 1887.

29. ———— Vedische Chrestomathie—Mit Anmerkungen and Glossar. Halle, 1874.

30. Gaedicke Carl—Der Accusativ im Veda. Breslau, 1880.

31. Gaṇapati Atharvashîrsam—Edited by Pandit Vâmana Śâstri Islâmpurkar, (A. S. S. No. 1).

32. Gobhila Grihya Sûtra—with a Commentary—By Chandrakânta Tarkâlankâra, (Bib. Ind.). Calcutta, 1880.

33. ———— Das—Romanized Text with Translation—By F. Knauer. Leipzig, 1881.

34. Gopâla Tâpani—Calcutta 1870, (out of print). (Bib. Ind.)
35. Gopatha Brâhmaṇa—Calcutta 1872, (out of print). (Bib. Ind.)
36. Grihya Sûtras—The—Rules of Vedic domestic ceremonies. Translated by H. Oldenberg and F. Max Müller (S. B. E. Vol. XXIX. Part I containing Śânkhâyana, Âsvalâyana, Pâraskara and Khâdira—Vol. XXX, Part II. Gobhila, Hiraṇyakesin and Âpastamba). Oxford, 1886 and 1892.
37. Haug, M.—Ueber Das Werth und Wesen des Vedischen Accents. Munchen, 1873.
38. Hillebrandt, A.—Varuna und Mitra. Breslau, 1877.
39. ——— Das Altindische Neu and Vollmondsopfer. Jena, 1879.
40. ——— Über die Göttin Âditi. Breslau, 1876.
41. ——— Veda Chrestomathie. Berlin, 1885.
42. Hiraṇyakesin Grihya Sûtra.—With extracts from the Commentary of Mâtridatta—Edited by J. Kirste. Vienna, 1889.
43. Hirtzel A.—Gleichnisse und Metaphoren in Rig Veda. Leipzig, 1890.
44. Kaegi A.—The Rig Veda—The oldest literature of the Hindus—Translated from the German by M. Bloomfield. Boston, 1886.
45. Kâtyâyana Śrauta Sûtra—With extracts from the Commentaries of Kârka and Yâjnikadeva—Edited by A. Weber. Berlin, 1859, (very rare, present from the Secretary of State for India).
46. ———Sarvânukramaṇi—With extracts from Shadguru Sishya's Commentary—By A. A. MacDonell (An. Ox., Vol. I, Part VI). Oxford, 1886.
47. ———Śukla Yajur Veda Prâtisâkhya—With Uvvata's Commentary. Benares, 1888.
48. Kaushîtaki Brâhmaṇa—By B. Lindner. Jena, 1887.
49. Kauśika Sûtra—With extracts from the Commentaries of Darila and Kesava—Edited by M. Bloomfield, (Vol. XIV J. A. O. S.). New Haven, 1890.

50. Lanman C. R.—Noun inflection in the Veda (from J. A. O. S. Vol. X). New Haven, 1880
Delbrück B—Das Altindische Verbum. Halle, 1874.
Avery J.—Contributions to the history of noun inflection in Sanskrit (from J. A. O. S. Vol. X), New Haven 1880. (Three Volumes in one).

51. LÂṬYÂYANA SRAUTA SÛTRA—Bib. Ind. Edition. Calcutta, 1872, (out of print).

52. Lindner, B.—Die Altindische Nominalbildung. Jena, 1878.

53. Ludwig, Alfred.—Anschauungen des Veda. Prag., 1889.
——————Die Kritik des Rig Veda Texts. Prag. 1889.

54. MAITRÂYANI SAMHITÂ—By Dr. Leopold Von Schroeder, 4 vols. in two. Leipzig, 1881-86, (Stenzler's copy).

55. NRISIMHA TÂPANI of the Atharva Veda—Bib. Ind. Edition. Calcutta, 1871 (out of print.)

56. PARIBHÂSHÂ SÛTRAM—With the Commentary of Kapurdaswâmi. Mysore, 1893.

57. PINGALA CHHANDASSÛTRA—With Halâyudha's Commentary. Bib. Ind. Edition. Calcutta, 1874 (out of print).

58. PURUSHA SÛKTAM—Sri—With Sâyana's Commentary. Poona, 1888, (A. S. S. No. 3).

59. RIKSAMHITÂ.—First Ashtaka—Bombay Edition.

60. RIGVEDÂDI BHÂSHYA BHUMIKA.—Edited by Dayânanda Sarasvati. Ajmere, 1893.

61. RIG VEDA PADA TEXT—Edited by F. Max. Müller. London, 1873.

62. RIG VEDA—Siebenzig Lieder des—By Karl Geldner and Alf. Kaegi. Tübingen, 1875.

63. ——————Die Hymnen des (Romanized).—Edited by Theodore Aufrecht, 2 vols., Bonn, 1877, (Vols. VI and VII of Weber's Indische Studien).

64. ——————A Selection of Hymns from the—By P. Peterson. Bombay, 1880. (Extract from Sâyana's Commentary on the Selection bound in the same volume.)

65. ——————Zwolf Hymnen des—Mit Sâyana's Commentary. Von. E. Windisch Leipzig, 1883.

66. ————Hymns from the—By Peter Peterson. Bombay, 1888. (B. S. S. No. 36).

67. ————Die Hymnen des—Vol. I., Metrische and Textgeschtliche Prolegomena—By H. Oldenberg Berlin, 1888.

68. ————Handbook containiug Sâyanâ's Preface and first Anuvâka of the first Mandala—By P. Peterson. Bombay, 1899, (B. S. S No. 41).

English Translation of Sâyana's Preface.

69. ————Prâtisâkhya—Edited by F. Max. Müller. Leipzig, 1856 (scarce).

70. ———— Samhitâ—Liber Primus Edit Fredericus Rosen. London, 1838 (rare).

71. ————and Pada Texts of the first Mandala—By F. Max. Müller. London, 1869.

72. ———— English Translation Vol. I Hymns to the Maruts—By F. Max Müller. London, 1869.

73. ———— With Sâyana's Commentary—Editio Priceps—By F. Max. Müller, 6 vols. London, 1874 (rare).

74 ———— 1st and 2nd Adhyâyas of the 1st Mandala—by Rev. K. M. Banerji. Calcutta, 1875, (rare).

75. ———— Samhitâ and Pada Texts—Edited by F. Max. Müller 2 vols. London 1877.

76. ———— With Sâyana's Commentary—Edited by Tukâram Tâtya, 8 vols. Bombay, 1878–90.

77. ———— Index to Sûtras quoted in the Commentary.

78. ———— With Sâyana's Commentary, Second Edition—By Max. Müller, 4. vols. London, 1892.

79. ———— With Sâyana's Commentary, first Mandala. Calcutta Edition.

80. ———— English Translation by H. H. Wilson, 6 vols., London, 1866–1888 (rare).

81. ———— German Metrical Translation—By H. Grassmann, 2 vols. Leipzig, 1876.

82. RIG VEDA—German Translation with Commentary and Introduction, 6 vols.—By Alf. Ludwig. Prag., 1876—88.

83. ———Hymns of the—English Metrical Translation—By R. T. H. Griffith, 4 vols. Benares, 1889—92.

84. ———The Bengâli Translation—By Romesh Chunder Dutt, 2 vols. Calcutta.

85. RIKSANGRAHA, or a University Selection of Vedic Hymns with the Commentary of Sâyanâchârya—Edited by Vishnu Govind Bijapurkar, M.A. Bombay, 1895.

86. Roth, R—Literatur und Geschichte des Veda—Stuttgart, 1846, (rare.)

87. RUDRÂDHYÂYA, ŚRÎ—With Sâyana Mâdhavâchârya and Bhatta Bhâskara's Commentaries. Poona 1888, (A.S.S. No. 2)

88. SÂMA VEDA SAMHITÂ—English Translation—R. T. H. Griffith. Benares, 1893.

89. ——— Die Hymnen des Mit Ubersetzung und Glossar—By Theodor Benfey. Leipzig, 1848 (rare)

90. ———With Sâyana's Commentary, 5 vols., Bib. Ind. Ed. Calcutta, (rare and out of print). 1874–78.

91. SAMHITOPANISHAD BRÂHMAṆA—By A. C. Burnell. Mangalore, 1877, (rare.)

92. SAMSKÂRARATNAMÂLA—By Hari Nârâyaṇa Apte. (A. S. S. No. 39) Poona 1899.

93. SANDHYA—3 small tracts, (bound in one).

94. ŚÂNKHYÂYANA ŚRAUTA SÛTRA—With Varadatta Suta Ânartîya's Commentary, Vol. I and parts, Bib. Ind. Edition. Calcutta, 1888.

95. SANSKRIT TRACTS one volume containing—

1. Roth. Abhandlungen über den Atharva Veda.
2. Roth. Der Atharva Veda in Kaschmir.
3. Haug. Brahma und die Brahmanen.
4. Stein. Zoroastrian Deities on Indo—Scythian coins.
5. Kellner. Einleitende Bemerkungen zu dem indische Drama Mrichhakatika.
6. Rosen. Rig Veda Specimen.
7. Weber. Zwei Vedische Texte über omina und Portenta.

8. B. Müller. Kâlidâsa's Śakuntala und ihre quelle.

96. Sarasvati (Dayânanda)—Atha Samskâra Vidhi—Allahabad, 1891.

97. SARVÂNUKRAMA SÛTRA, SIKSHA and ANUVÂKA SÛTRA of the Śukla Yajur Veda. Bombay, 1888.

98. ŚATAPATHA BRÂHMAṆA—With extracts from the Commentaries—Edited by A. Weber, Berlin 1855, (very rare and present from the Secretary of State for India.)

99. ———— According to the text of the Mâdhyandina School. Translated by Julius Eggeling (S. B. E. Vols. XII, XXVI, XLI and XLIII. Parts I, II, III and IV). Oxford, 1882, 1885 and 1894.

100. Scherman, L.—Philophische Hymnen aus der Rig und Atharva Veda. Strassburg, 1887.

101. Simon, A.—Vedischen Schulen. Kiel, 1889.

102. Stenzler A. F.—Index to the Grihya Sûtras of Asvalâyana, Pâraskara, Śânkhyâyana and Gobhila. Leipzig, 1886.

103. ———— Indische Hausregeln—Text and Translation of Asvalâyana and Pâraskara Grihya Sûtras. Leipzig, 1864 (scarce).

104. TAITTARÎYA ÂRANYAKA—Bib. Ind. Edition. Calcutta 1872, (out of print).

105. TAITTARÎYÂRANYAKAM—of the Black Yajor Veda—with the Commentary of Sâyanâchârya—Edited by Hari Nârâyaṇa Âpte, Parts I and II, (A. S. S. No. 36). Poona, 1897.

106. TAITTARÎYA—Brâhmaṇa—Bib. Ind. Edition, 3 vols. Calcutta, 1859-62 (out of print).

107. ———— With the Commentary of Sâyanâchârya—Edited by Hari Nârâyaṇa Âpte (A. A. S. No. 37(Parts I, II, & III. Poona, 1898.

108. ———— PRÂTIŚÂKHYA—Edited by W. D. Whitney, (Vol. IX J. A. O. S.). New Haven, 1871.

109. ———————— Bib. Ind. Edition. Calcutta, 1872 (out of print).

110. ————————Samhitâ—With Sâyana's Commentary, Bib. Ind. Edition, 4 vols., (all published). Calcutta, 1860-61 (early numbers out of print).

111. ———————— With extracts from the Pada Text—By A. Weber, (Vols. XI and XII of Indische Studien). Leipzig, 1871.

112. ———————— Text. Bombay, 1888.

113. Tândya Mahâbrâhmana—Bib Ind. Edition, 2 vols. Calcutta 1870-74, (out of print).

114. Vaidika Kośa—By N. B. Godabole. Bombay, 1889.

115. Vaitâna Sûtra—Text and Translation—By R. Garbe, 2 vols., Bib. Ind. Edition. Calcutta, 1869 (out of print).

116. Vâjasaneyi Samhitâ—The White Yajurveda—Text—Bombay, 1888.

117. ———————— With Mahdîhara's Commentary—Edited by By A. Weber. Berlin 1852 (very rare. Present from the Secretary of State for India in Council).

118. ———————— With Mahîdhara's Commentary—Edited by Jîvânanda Vidyâ Sâgara. Calcutta, 1893.

119. Vedângas—The six—Texts only. Bombay, 1893.

120. Vedârthayatna—An attempt to interpret the Rig Vêda—By S. P. Pundit, 4 vols., (and loose parts so far as published) Bombay, 1876-81.

121. Vedic Hymns.—Hymns to the Maruts, Rudra, Vâyu and Vâta—Translated by F. Max Müller (S. B. E. Vol. XXXII. Part I.). Oxford, 1891.

122. Vedische Studien—By R. Pischel and Karl Geldner, 2 vols. Stuttgart, 1889 and 1897.

123. Wallis, H. D.—Cosmology of the Rig Veda. London, 1887.

124. Yâska's Nirukta—With Introduction and Notes—By R. Roth. Göttingen, 1847 (scarce).

125. ————————With Durga's Commentary. Bib. Ind. Edition, 4 vols. Calcutta, 1882-86.

126. Zimmer, H.—Altindische Leben. Berlin, 1879.

II—*The Upanishads and Hindu Philosophy.*

1. Aitareyopanishad—With Śankarâchârya's Bhâshya and a Commentary by Śrîmat Ânandagnâna. Poona, 1889. (A. S. S. No. 11).
2. Appayadîkshita.—Siddhantalesa—with extracts from the Śrîkrishṇâlankâra of Achyutakrishṇânandatîrtha—by Gangâdhara Śâstri Mânavallî—Vol. I. Part I. (V. S. S.). Benares. 1890.
3. Atharvaṇopanishads (Eleven)—Edited by Colonel G. A. Jacob. (B. S. S. No. 40). Bombay, 1891.
4. ———————(A. S. S. No. 29).
5. Âtmabôdha—Of Śankarâchârya with Mâdhavânanda's Commentary. Bombay, 1889.
6. ——— and Prabodha Chandrodaya Nâtaka—(English Translation)—By J. Taylor. Bombay, 1886.
7. Ballantyne, J. R.—Lectures on the Nyâya Philosophy being an exposition of the Tarka Sangraha. Allahabad, 1849.
8. ——————— A lecture on the Vedânta—being an exposition of the Vedântasâra. Allahabad, 1850.
9. Bhagavat Gîta—in red silk binding.
10. ———————or the Sacred lay in the original Sanskrit by J. Cockburn Thomas. Hertford, 1855.
11. ———————Die—übersetzt und erlaütert von Dr. F. Lorinser. 1869.
12. ———————or Song Celestial, from the Mahâbhârata—By Edwin Arnold, London, 1885.
13. ———————or Dialogues of Krishṇa and Arjuna—Translated from Sanskrit—By Charles Wilkins Bombay, 1887.
14. ———————With two Sanskrit and one Hindi Commentary. Lucknow, 1888.
15. ——————— Notes on the—By T. Subba Rao, Bombay, 1888.

16. ——————With Śrîdhara's Commentary. Bombay, 1891.
17. ——————Second Edition. Bombay, 1895.
18. ——————Śrîmat—With the Commentary of Śankarâchârya—Edited by Pandit Kâśinâth Śastri Agâse. Poona, 1897. (A. S. S. No. 34.)
19. ——————English Poetical Translation with Notes and Introductory Essay—By Kâśinâth Trimbak Telang. Bombay, 1875.
20. ——————With the Sanatsujâtîya and the Anugîta—Translated by K. T. Telang (S. B. E. Vol. VIII.). Oxford, 1882.
21. ——————or Hindu Philosophy, being a translation and exposition of—By John Davies, M. A., (Cantab) London, 1882. (T. O. S.).
22. Bhâmati—By Vâchaspati Miśra, Edited By Pandit Bâla Śastri. Benares, 1880. (rare). (Bib. Ind.)
23. Bhâsha Parichheda—With Siddhânta Muktâvali. Calcutta, 1877.
24. Bose. Râmachandra,—Hindu Philosophy, the Orthodox Systems, London, 1884.
25. Brihadâranyakam—Katha, Kena, Îsa and Mundaka Upanishads. —By L. Poley. Bonn, 1844.
26. Brihadâra Nyakopanishad—With Commentary—By Dr. E. Roer. Calcutta, 1856.
27. ——————With Sankarabhâshya and Ânandagiri's Gloss—By Jîvânanda Vidyâsâgara. Calcutta, 1876.
28. ——————By Otto Böhtlingk. St. Petersburgh, 1889.
29. ——————With Śankarabhâshya and Ânandagiri's Gloss. Poona, 1891. (A. S. S. No. 15).
30. ——————Bhâshya Vârtika of Sureśvara, 3 vols. Poona 1891-1894. (A. S. S. No. 16).
31. ——————Mitâkshara—By Śrîman Nityânanda Muni—Edited by Pandit Kâśinâth Śâstri Agase. Poona, 1896. (A. S. S. No. 31).
32. Chhandogyopanishad of Sâma Veda—(English Translation). By R. Mitra. Calcutta, 1862.

33. ————————By Otto Böhtlingk. Leipzig, 1889.

34. ————————With Śankarâchârya's Bhâshya and Ânandagiri's Gloss. Poona, 1890. (A. S. S. No 14).

35. Deussen—Dr. Paul—Das System, des Vedânta. Leipzig, 1888.

36. English works of Râja Râmmohan Roy, Vols. I and II—By Jogendra Chunder Ghose, Calcutta, 1885.

37. Gymnosophista—Being the text of the Sânkhya Kârika. By Chistianus Lassen, 1832.

38. Hall, F.—A contribution towards an index to the Bibliography of the Indian Philosophical systems. Calcutta, 1859.

39. Hindu Philosophy examined by a Benares Pandit. Two vols. in one (in Hindi). Allahabad, 1886.

40. Îsa, Kena, Katha, Praśna, Munda and Mândûkya Upanishads, with Śankara Bhâshya and Ânandagiri's gloss—By Dr. E. Röer. Bib. Ind. Calcutta, 1850. (rare).

41. Îsopanishad, with Śankarabhâshya and other glosses. Poona, 1888. (A. S. S. No. 5).

42. ———————— With Sanskrit and Hindi Commentary—By Bhîmasena Śarma. Allahabad, 1892.

43. Jacob, Major, G. A.—A Manual of Hindu Pantheism (English Translation of the Vedântasâra). London, 1881. (T. O. S.).

44. Jaiminîya Nyâyamâlâ Vistara of Mâdhavâchârya—Edited by Theodor Goldstücker and E. B. Cowell. London, 1878, Vol. I of Anc. San. (very rare).

45. ———————— Poona, 1892 (A. S. S. No. 24).

46. Kathopanishad—With Śankarâchârya's Bhâshya and other glosses. Poona, 1889, (A. S. S. No. 7).

47. ————————With Sanskrit and Hindi Commentary.—By Bhîmasena. Allahabad, 1893.

48. Kaushîtaki Brâhmanopanishad—With the Commentary of Śankarânanda—By E. B Cowell, M.A., Calcutta, 1861. (Bib. Ind.)

49. Kesavamisra.—Tarkabhâshâ—with the Commentary of Govardhana—Edited with introduction and notes by S. M. Paranjape—Poona, 1894.

50. Mahânârâyanopanishad, The—With Dîpika—Edited by Col. G. A. Jacob. Bombay, 1888. (B. S. S. No. 35).

51. Maitrâyanîyopanishad—With the Commentary of Râmatîrtha—By E B. Cowell, M.A., London, 1870. (Bib. Ind.)

52. Mândûkyopanishad—With Sankarabhâshya and other glosses. Poona, 1889. (A. S. S. No. 9).

53. ——— With Sankarâchârya's Bhâshya and other glosses. Poona, 1890. (A. S. S. No. 10).

54. ——— With Sanskrit and Hindi Commentary—By Bhîmasena. Allahabad, 1891.

55. Max. Müller—Three Lectures on the Vedânta Philosophy. London, 1894.

56. Mîmâmsa Darsana—Vols. I & II,—By M. Nyâyaratna 1873 & 1875 (very rare). Bib. Ind.

57. Mundakopanishad—With Sanskrit and Hindi Commentary—By Bhîmasena Sarma. Allahabad, 1891.

58. Naishkarmya Siddhi—of Surêswarâchârya, with the Chandrika of Jnânottama, edited with notes and index—By Colonel G. A. Jacob, (B. S. S. No. 38). Bombay, 1891.

59 Nrisimhatâpanîyopanishad—(A. S. S. No. 30). Poona, 1896.

60. Nyâyabindutîka of Dharmottarâchârya—Edited by P. Peterson. (Bib. Ind). Calcutta, 1890.

61. Nyâya Darsana—With the Commentary of Vâtsyânana—By Pandit J. Tarkapanchânana (Bib. Ind.). Calcutta, 1865, (very rare).

62. Nyâya Kusumânjali—Edited by Harachandra. Calcutta, 1888

63. ——— Sûtra—With Viswanâtha's Commentary in Hindi—By Pandit Sukhdayal Sastri, Lithograph Edition. Lahore, 1883.

64. ——— PHILOSOPHY.—Categories of the—With a commentary by Viśwanâtha Panchânana. Edited and Translated by Dr. E. Roer. (Bib. Ind.). Calcutta, 1850. (very rare.)

65. PANCHADAŚI of Mâdhavâchârya—With Commentary—By Govind Śastri. Bombay, 1881.

66. ————————(English Translation)—By N. Dhole. Calcutta, 1886.

67. PRAŚNÔPANISHAD—With Sankarâchârya and other glosses. Poona, 1889. (A. S. S. No. 8).

68. ————————With Sanskrit and Hindi Commentary—By Bhîmasena. Allahabad, 1894.

69. RÂJA YOGA PHILOSOPHY—A Compendium of the—Bombay Edition. Bombay, 1888.

70. Regnaud, P.—Materiaux pour servir A L'histoire de la philosophie de L'Inde. Paris, 1876.

71. Śândilya—Aphorisms of—With the Commentary of Swapneśwara—By J. R. Ballantyne, L.L.D., Calcutta, 1861.

72 ————————(English Translation.)—By E. B. Cowell, M.A. Calcutta, 1878.

73. ŚANKARADIGVIJAYA—By Vidyâraṇya with Commentary. Poona, 1891. (A. S. S. No. 22).

74. SANKARA SIVE DE—Theologumenis Vedânticorum—With the text of Bâlabodhini, F. H. H. Windischmann, Bonnae, 1833.

75. SÂNKHYA KÂRIKÂ—The——By Îswara Krishna—Translated by H. T. Colebrooke. Bhâshya of Gaudapâda—Translated by H. H. Wilson. Oxford, 1837. (very rare.)

76. ————————With Gaudapâda's Commentory and an Exposition called Chandrika—By Pandit Bechanarâma Tripâthi Benares, 1883.

77. ————————or Hindu Philosophy—Translated into English by John Davies M.A., London, 1881 (T. O. S.)

78. ——————of Îswarakrishna—By Henry Thomas Colebrooke, also the Bhâshya of Gaudapâda—By H. H. Wilson M.A., F.R.S., (reprint.) Bombay, 1887.

79. Śânkhya Philosophy of Kapila—Aphorisms of—With Commentaries and English Translation—By Ballantyne, J. R. Benares, 1852.

80. ——————Pravachana Bhâshya—With Vijnânabhikshu's Commentary and a Preface—By Fitz-Edward Hall, M.A. Calcutta, 1856.

81. ——————Darśanam—By Pandit Kripârâma. Benares, 1890.

82. ——————Sâra—a treatise of Sânkhya Philosophy—Edited by Fitz-Edward Hall, D. C. L., Calcutta, 1862 (very rare). (Bid. Ind.)

83 ——————Sûtra Vritti—By Dr. Richard Garbe. Calcutta, 1888. (Bib. Ind.)

84. SARVADARŚANA SANGRAHA—Edited by Mâdhâvâchârya, Part I only. Calcutta, 1858. (Bib. Ind.)

85. ——————Edited by Târânâtha Tarkavâchaspati Calcutta, 1872.

86. —————— (English Translation)—By. A. E. Gough and E. B. Cowell. London, 1882. (T. O. S.)

87. ŚATAŚLOKA of Śankarâchârya—Bombay, 1886.

88. ŚWETÂŚWATAROPANISHAD—With the Bhâshya of Śrîmat Śankarâchârya and Dîpikas of the same by Śrîmat Śankarâchârya and Nârâyaṇa. Poona, 1890. (A. S. S. No. 17).

89. TAITTIRÎYOPANISHAD—With Śankarâchârya's Bhâshya and the Gloss of Ânandgiri. Poona, 1889. (A. S. S. No. 12.)

90. ——————Bhâshya Vârtikta. Poona, 1889. (A S.S. No. 13.)

91. —————— With Sanskrit and Hindi Commentary—By Bhîmasena. Allahabad, 1892.

92. ————————(English Translation)—By Dr. E Röer. Calcutta, 1853.

93. TALAVAKÂRA OR KENÔPANISHAD—With Sankarâchârya's Bhâshya and other glosses. Poona, 1888. (A. S. S. No. 6).

94. ————————With Sanskrit and Hindi Commentary—By Bhîmasena. Allahabad, 1893.

95. TARKA KAUMUDI—Edited by M. N. Dvivedi. Bombay, 1886. (B. S. S. No. 32).

96. TARKA SANGRAHA—With two Commetaries, Bombay, 1888.

97. ————————With Dîpika and English Translation. Bombay, 1889.

98. TATVÂVALI—By Śrî Chandra Kânta Tarkâlankâra, with Author's Commentary. Calcutta, 1870.

99. UPANISHADS—The ten—With Commentary and Bhâshyas of Śankara and Ranga Râmânujamuni. 1869. (Very rare.)

100. ————————Philosophy of the—By A. E. Gough London, 1882. (T. O. S.)

101. ————————The ten—Bombay, 1887.

102. ————————The ten—Bombay Edition. Bombay, 1891

103. ————————The text of 108—By TukârâmTâtya. Bombay, 1893.

104. ————————The Theosophy of the—Part I, London, 1896.

105. ————————Translated by F. Max Müller (S. B. E. Vols. I. and XV, Parts I and II). Oxford, 1879 & 1884.

106. ————————English Translation of—Reprinted by Tukâ Râm Tatya. Bombay, 1891.

107. VAIŚESHIKA APHORISMS of Kanâda—Archibald E. Gough, B.A. Benares, 1873.

08. VAIŚESHIKA DARŚANAM—With the Commentary of Chandrakânta Tarkâlankâra. Calcutta, 1887.

19. Vaiyâsika Nyâya Mâla—of Bhâratîtîrthamuni. Poona, 1891, (A. S. S. No. 23).

10. Vedânta Darśanam or Brahma Sûtrâs—With Śankarâchârya's Bhâshya and the Gloss of Ânandagiri. Jivânanda Vidyâsâgara's Edition. Calcutta, 1876. (rare).

111. ———— or ———— With Sankarabhashya and other Glosses, 2 vols. Poona, 1890 & 1891 (A. S. S. No. 21).

112. ———— or Vedânta Sûtras—(German translation), by Dr. Paul Deussen. Leipzig, 1887.

113. ———— English Translation by G. Thibant, 2 vols., 1890 & 1896 (S. B. E. Vols. XXXIV and XXXVIII.)

114 ———— Paribhâsha—With Commentary—Edited by Pandit Jîvânanda Vidyâsâgara, B.A. Calcutta, 1875.

115. ———— With Commentary (Lithograph Edition). Benares, 1886.

116. Vedântasâra—Edited by Dr. Othmar Frank. München, 1835.

117. ———— Edited by Pandit J. Vidyâsâgara, Calcutta, 1875.

118. Vidyâraṇyaswâmi.—The Jîvanmukti Viveka—Edited by Vâsudeva Sâstri Paṇasîkara. (A. S. S. No. 20). Poona, 1890.

119. Visishṭâdvaita Philosophy—By N. Bhâshyâchârya. Madras, 1887.

120. Yoga Aphorisms of Patanjali—With the Commentary of Bhoja Râja—By R. Mitra, Calcutta, 1883.

121. —— Philosophy—A treatise on the—By N. C. Paul, Bombay, 1888.

122. —— Sûtra of Patanjali—By Manilâl Nabhûbhai Dvivedi. Bombay, 1890.

III.—*Purâṇas, Itihâsas and Nîti Literature.*

1. Agni Purâṇa—Edited by R. Mitra, 2 vols., in one volume. (Bib. Ind.) Calcutta, 1873 (rare).
2. Arnold, Edwin, c.s.i.—The Indian Idylls from the Sanskrit of the Mahâbhârata. London, 1883.
3. Bâṇa—Harshacharitra—Edited by Jîbânanda Vidyâsâgara. Calcutta, 1876.
4. ——— With the Commentary of Śankara—Edited by K. P. Paraba and D. P. Vaze. Bombay, 1892.
5. ———Uchchvâsa V.—Edited by Barada Kânta Vidyâratna. Calcutta, 1884.
6. ———Pârvatîpariṇayanâtaka—Transliterated, with notes in German by Prof. K. Glaser.
7. ———Kâdambarî—Pûrvabhâga with the Commentary of Bhânu Chandra—Bombay, 1858.
8. ———Edited by Târânâtha Tarka Vâchaspati. Calcutta, 1871.
9. ———By Pandit Nobin Ch. Vidyâratna. Calcutta, 1884 (a key).
10. ———Parts I and II—Edited by Peter Peterson, b.a., 1885-89 (B. S. S. No. 24.)
11. ———Selected portion for B. A., 1888-89, Text and Commentary—Edited by Pandit Nobin Ch. Vidyâratna, 1886.
12. Ballala, Bhoja Prabandha—Edited by Jíbânanda Vidyâsâgara b.a., Calcutta, 1872.
13. Bhâgavatam—Srîmat—Bombay, 1884.
14. Brahma Purâṇa—The—By Srîmat Vyâsa—Published by Hari Nârâyaṇa Âpte (A. S. S. No. 28). Poona, 1895.
15. Brihannâradîyâ Purâṇa—The—Edited by Pandit Rhishîkesa Śâstri. Fasciculi I—V. Calcutta, 1886–88.
16. Châṇakya Nîtidarpaṇa—Edited by Pandit Hari Shankar. Benares, 1888.
17. Daṇḍin—Daśakumâracharîtra—Edited by Jibânanda Vidyâsâgara, b.a., Calcutta, 1870.

18. ——————Part I—By George Bühler, PH.D., (B. S. S. No. X), Bombay, 1873.

19. ——————With the Commentaries of Kavîndra Sarasvati and Śivarâma—Edited by N. B. Godabole, B. A., and K. P. Paraba. Bombay, 1883.

20. DVÂTRIMŚATA PUTTALIKA—Edited by Jibânanda Vidyáságara, B.A., Calcutta, 1881.

21. HARIVAMŚA—(Vyâsa)—Edited by Pandit Nimaichandra Siromani, 1839, (rare). Calcutta Edition.

22. ——————French Translation by M. A. Langlois, Parts I and II. Paris, 1834–35.

23. HITOPADEŚA—(Sanskrit Text)—by Francis Johnson. Hertford, 1847.

24. ——————Sanskrit Text—With interlinear translation—Edited by Max. Müller, M.A., London, 1864—65. Books I to IV.

25. ——————Edited by K. P. Paraba. Bombay, 1885.

26. ——————Nârâyaṇa's—Edited by P. Peterson. Bombay, 1887, (B. S. S. No. 33).

27. ——————With Pûrnânanda's Commentary—Edited by Pandit Durga Dutt Śâstri, Lahore, 1888.

28. —————— English Translation—By Francis Johnson, London, 1848.

29. KADAMBARÎSÂRA—By Mâhâdeva Shivarâm Âpte B.A., Poona, 1885.

30. KALHANA—RÂJATARANGINÎ—(French Edition with Translation). By M. A. Troyer, 3 volumes. Paris, 1842 (rare and presentation from Translator.)

31. KALKI PURAṆA—Edited by Jaganmohana Tarkâlankâra, Calcutta, 1878.

32. Kâmaudaki—Elements of Polity—(Bib. Ind.)—Edited by Râjendra Lâla Mitra. Calcutta, 1861.

33. Mahâbhârata—Selections by Francis Johnson, Londen, 1842

34. ——————Âdi Parva and Sabha Parva—Edited by Protâp Chendra Roy, (Sanskrit Text). Calcutta, 1884.

35. ——————Vana Parva and Virâta Parva—Edited by P. C. Roy (Sanskrit Text). Calcutta, 1886.

36. ——————Vana, Virâta, Udyôga, and Bhîshma Parvas—Edited P. C. Roy (Sanskrit Text). Calcutta.

37. ——————Âdi Parva and Sabha Parva—Edited by P. C. Roy, (English Translation). Calcutta, 1884.

38. ——————Vana Parva—Edited by P. C. Roy (English Translation). Calcutta, 1884.

39. ——————Virâta Parva and Udyoga Parva—Edited by P. C. Roy (English Translation). Calcutta, 1884.

40. ——————A Prose English Translation from the Original Sanskrit—Edited by Manmatha Náth Dutt (Vol. I Âdi to Udyoga Parva). Calcutta, 1896.

41. ——————The same. Drona Parva. Calcutta, 1898.

42. Merutungâchârya—Prabandha Chintâmaṇi. Bombay, 1888.

43. Nalopâkhyânam—Sanskrit Text in Roman characters by Rev. Thomas Jarrett, M.A. Cambridge. 1875.

44. ——————The Sanskrit Text with Translation by Monier Williams, M.A., D.C.L., 2nd Edition. Oxford, 1879

45. ——————Notes by John Peile, M.A. Cambridge, 1881.

46. Nitidaśaprabhandhi—The—Edited by Râdha Krishna Sastri. Puducota, 1894.

47. Nîtiprakâśika—Edited by Gustav Oppert. Madras, 1882.

48. Panchatantram—Edited by G. L. Kosegarten. Bonn, 1845.

49. ——————(Sanskrit Text)—Edited by Pandit Jibânanda Vidyâsâgara, B.A. Calcutta, 1872.

50. ——————Book I—Edited by F. Kielhorn. Bombay, 1873. B. S. S. No. 4.

51. ——————Book I. Edited with notes by F. Kielhorn—5th Edition. Revised (B. S. S. No. IV). Bombay 1885.

52. ——————Books II & III with Notes-By Dr. G. Bühler, C.I.E., Bombay, 1881.

53. ——————German Translation with dissertation by Theodor Benfey, 2 vols. Leipzic, 1859.

54. Sapta Śati or Chandî Pâṭha—Being a portion of the Márkandêya Purâna—English translation with notes—By Cávali Venkata Rámaswámi. Bombay, 1868.

55. Sarala Kâdambarî—Edited by Shyám Charan Kaviratna. Calcutta, 1885.

56. Shatchakra Nirûpaṇam & Gâyatrî Tantram—Edited by Bhuwan Chandra Basak. Calcutta, 1890.

57. Saura Purâṇa—The—By Śrîmat Vyâsa. Edited by Pandit Kâśinâtha Sâstri Lele (A. S. S. No. 18). Poona, 1889.

58. Śeshnâga—Paramârthasâra-Śri-Edited by Śri Bhuvan Chandra Basaka. 1890, Calcutta.

59. Shukrâchârya—Nîtisâra—Edited by Jîbânanda Vidyâsâgara, B.A., Calcutta, 1882.

60. ——————Volume I—Edited by Gustav Oppert. Madras, 1882.

61. Somadêvabhatta—Kathâsaritsâgara—2 vols., Books I to V & IX to XVIII. Edited by Dr. Hermann Brockhaus. Leipzig, 1839 and 1866.

62. ——————Edited by Pandit Durga Prasâda and K. P. Paraba. Bombay, 1889.

63. ——————(English Translation)—By C. H. Tawney, M.A., vols. I and II. (Bib. Ind.), Calcutta, 1884.

64. Subandhu—Vâsavadatta-With the Commentary of Shivarâma—By Pandit Jibânanda Vidyâsâgara. Calcutta, 1874.

65. Śukasaptati—Vier Erzählungen aus der—Edited by Dr. Richard Schmidt Kiel, 1890.

66. SÛTASAMHITA.—Being a portion of the Skanda Purâṇa, with a commentary. Edited by Vâsudêva Sâstri Panasîkara (A. S. S. No. 25. Parts I, II, and III) Poona, 1893.
Schmidt.—Kiel, 1890.

67. Vâlmîki—Râmâyaṇa—Ayodhyâkâṇdam with Râmânuja's Commentary—Edited by Hemachandra Bhatta. Calcutta, 1872.

68. ————Bâlakandam-By Peter Peterson, B A, 1879, Bombay.

69. ————Pûrva Kânda and Uttara Kânda—With the Commentary of Râma—By K. P. Paraba (2 vols.). Bombay, 1888.

70. ————Prose Râmâyana by Krishnâji B. Godbole Kurundawad, 1888.

71. ————(English Translation)—By R. T. H. Griffith, M.A. 5 vols. Benares, 1870.

72. ———— Yoga Vâsishta Maharâmâyana—(English, Translation). Vol. I.—By Vihâri Lâla Mitra. Calcutta, 1891.

73. ————(English Translation)—By Manmatha Nâth Dutt, M.A., Calcutta, 1892. (Vols 1 parts 1—3; Vol. II parts 4—9; Vol. III parts 10—12; Vol. IV parts 13—15; Vol. V parts 16—20; Vol. VI parts 21—30, Vol. VII parts 31 and 32; Vol. VII parts 31—40) complete.

74. Vâyu Purâna—Edited by R. Mitra, Vol. I. Calcutta. 1879.

75. Wealth of India—The—(Translation of Srimad Bhâgavatam and Vishnu Purânam)—By Manmatha Nâth Dutt, M.A., (2 Nos). Calcutta, 1894.

76. YADJNADATTABODHA.—Ou La Mort D'yadjnadatta—Ayodhyâ Kânda of Râmâyana, Edited by A. L. Deslongchamps. Paris, 1829.

IV.—*Poetry, Rhetoric and Drama.*

1. ABHINANDA—Kâdambarî Kathâsâra—Edited by K. P. Paraba and Pandit Durgâ Prasâda. Bombay 1888, (K. M. No. XI).
2. Ananta Bhatta—Champû Bhârata. Bombay, 1864.
3. Appayadîkshita—Kuvalayânanda-With a Commentary—Edited. by Jibânanda Vidyâsâgara. Calcutta, 1874.
4. Arnold, E. M.A.—Indian Poetry in English Verse, 3rd Edition London, 1884 (T. O. S.)
5. Ârya Saptaśati—With the Commentary of Ananta Pandita—Edited by K. P. Paraba and Pandit Durga Prasâda. Bombay, 1886 (K. M. No. I).
6. Bhârâtîya Nâtya Śâstra—Chapters XV & XVI, French Edition —By Paul Regnaud. Paris, 1880.
7. Bhâravi—Kirâtarjunîya—With the Commentary of Mallinâtha—Edited by Durgâprasâda and K. P. Paraba. Bombay, 1889.
8. Bhartrihari—Śatakas—(Nîti and Vairâgya)—Edited with Notes by K. T. Telang, M. A., L. L. B., Bombay, 1874 (B. S. S. No. XI).
9. ————————English Translation—By Rev. B. H. Wortham, B.A. London, 1886. T. O. S).
10. Bhatta Nârâyana—Veṇi Samhâra—Edited by Julius Grill, Leipzig, 1871.
11. ————————With the Commentary of Târânâtha Tarkavâchaspati—Edited by Jibânanda Vidyasâgara. Calcutta, 1875.
12. ————————Edited with English Translation by N. B. Godabole. Poona.
13. Bhatti Kâvyam—2 volumes—With the Commentaries of Jayamangala and Mallinâth—Edited by Jîbânanda Vidyâsâgara. Calcutta, 1876.
14. ————————The first five books with notes and explanations by K. M. Banerjee, D.L., Calcutta, 1876.
15. Bhavabhûti—Mahâvîracharitra—Text only—Edited by F. H.

16. ————————Edited with a full Commentary—By Pandit Jîbânanda Vidyâsâgara, B.A., Calcutta, 1890.

17. ————————Edited by T. R. Ratnam, B.A., and K. P. Paraba. Bombay, 1892.

18. ————————Translated into English Prose by John Pickford, M A., London, 1871.

19. ————Mâlatîmadhava—With the Commentary of Jagaddhara —Edited with notes by R. G. Bhandarkar, M.A., PH.D., Bombay, 1876 (B. S. S. No. 15.)

20. ————————Edited by M. R. Telang with the Commentaries of Tripurâri and Jagaddhara. Bombay, 1892.

21. ————————Edited by Bhuvan Chandra Basak, with Jagaddhara's Commentary. Calcutta.

22. ————————French Translation—By G. Strehly. Paris, 18?5

23. ————Uttara Râmacharitra—Edited by Jîbânanda Vidyâsâgara with notes. Calcutta, 1881.

24. ————————Edited by S. G. Bhânap, 2nd Edition. Bombay, 1893.

25. ————————With Sanskrit Commentary by Pandit Bhatji Sâstri Ghate of Nagpur, together with a close English Translation, Notes and Introduction by Vinâyaka Sadâsiva Patwardhana. Nagpore, 1895.

26. ————————Translated into English Prose—By C. H. Tawney, M.A., (2nd Edition). Calcutta, 1874.

27. Bilhaṇa—Karṇa Sundari—Edited by K. P. Paraba and Pand.. Durgâprâsada. Bombay, 1888 (K. M. No. VII).

28. ————Vikramârkadeva Charitra—Edited by G. Bühler. Bombay, 1875 (B. S. S. No. 14).

29. Chaitanya Chandrodaya—(The Incarnation of Chaitanya.) Edited by Râjendralâl Mitra. Calcutta, 1854.

30. Daṇḍin—Kâvyâdarśa—Edited with a commentary—By Pandit Premachandra Tarkabâgîśa. Calcutta, 1863.

31. ————————Edited by Jîbânanda Vidyâsâgara. Calcutta, 1882.

32. Dhananjaya—Daśarûpa—Edited by Fitz-Edward Hall, D. C. L. with Supplement containing Chapters 18, 19, 20 & 34 of Bhâratîya Nâtyaśâstra. Calcutta, 1861 (Bib. Ind.)

33. Gîtagovindam—(Kâvya Kalâpa)—Edited by Haridâs Hirachand. Bombay, 1865.

34. ——————Edited by Gangâvishnu. Bombay, 1883.

35. Harischandra—Dharma Śarmâbhyudaya—Edited by K. P. Parab and Pandit Durgâ Prasâda. Bombay, 1888 (K. M. No. VIII.)

36. Jagannâtha—Bhâmini-Vilâsa—par Abel Bergaigne. Paris, 1872.

37. ——————Edited with a Commentary by L. R. Vaidya, M.A., Bombay, 1887.

38. ————Rasagangâdhara—Edited by K. P. Paraba and Pandit Durgâprasâda. Bombay, 1888 (K. M. No. XII).

39. Jayadeva—Chandrâloka — Edited Jîbânanda Vidyasâgara. Calcutta, 1874.

40. —————— Edited by Govinda Shâstri Bharadvâja. Benares, 1894.

41. ————Prâsanna Raghava—Edited by S. M. Paranjpe, B.A., and N. S. Panse, B.A. Poona, 1894.

42. Kâlidâsâ—Abhijnâna Śakuntala—Edited by P. A. L. Chézy. Paris, 1830. (rare).

43. ——————Edited by Dr. Otto Böehtlingk. Bonn, 1842. (rare).

44. ——————Sanskrit Text with Notes—Edited by Monier Williams, M.A., D.C.L. (2nd Edition). Oxford 1875.

45. ——————Edited with notes by Îswarachandra Vidyâsâgara; (2nd Edition). Calcutta, 1878.

46. ——————With the Commentary of Râghavabhatta—Edited with English notes by N. B. Godbole, B.A., and K. P. Paraba (2nd Edition). Bombay, 1886.

57. ——————Edited with a close English Translation—By P. N. Patankar, B.A., Poona, 1889.

58. ——————German Translation—By Ludwig Fritze, 1879.

59. ——————German Metrical Translation—By E. Meier. Leipzig.

60. ————Kumâra Sambhava—With notes in English—by K. M. Banerjee. Calcutta, 1872.

61. ——————Cantos. I—VI.—Edited with the commentary of Millinâtha, and an English Translation—By S. G. Deshpânde, B.A. Poona, 1887.

62. ——————The Birth of the War-god. Translated into English Verse—By R. T. H. Griffith, M.A., London, 1879 (T. O. S. V.)

63. ————Mâlavikâgnimitra—Edited by Dr. Otto. Frid. Tullberg. Bonn, 1840.

64. ——————Edited with notes—By Shankar P. Pandit, M.A., B. S. S. No. 6. Bombay, 1869.

65. ————Mâlavikâgnimitra—Edited with notes by S. Pândurang Pandit (B. S. S. No. VI). Second Edition. Bombay, 1889.

66. ——————Literally translated into English Prose—By C. H. Tawney, M.A. Calcutta, 1875.

67. ————Megha Dûta—Sanskrit Text and an English Translation—Edited by H. H. Wilson, M.A., F.R.S. (2nd Edition). London, 1843.

68. ——————With the Commentary of Mallinâtha—Edited by Îswarachandra Vidyâsâgara. Calcutta 1869.

69. ——————With notes and Vocabulary in German—By A. F. Stenzler. Breslau, 1874.

70 ——————With the Commentary of Mallinâtha—Edited with English Notes—By N. B. Godhole, B.A., and K. P. Paraba (3rd Edition). Bombay, 1890.

————Megha Dûta or Megha Sandesa—Transliterated in Telugu characters.

71. ——————Translated into English Prose—By Colonel H. A. Ouvry, C.B. London, 1868.

72. ————————German Translation—By L. Fritze. 1879.

73. ————————English Translation—By T. Clark, M.A., London, 1882.

74. ————Raghuvamśa—(Sanskrit and Latin). Edited by A. F. Stenzler. London, 1832.

75. ————————With extracts from the Commentaries of Hemâdri, Vallabhu and others—Edited with an English Translation by G. R. Nandargikar. Poona, 1885.

76. ————————With a Hindi Translation—By Bajah Lashman Singh. Lucknow, 1889.

77. ————————With English Notes—By K. M. Banerjee (9 cantos). Calcutta.

78. ————————Full explanatory and critical notes—By P. N. Patankar, M.A. Poona, 1896.

79. ————Ritusamhâra—With German Notes and Text in Sanskrit—Edited by P. A. Bohlen. Leipzig, 1840.

80. ————————With the Commentary by Mani Râma—Edited by K. P. Paraba and N. B. Godbole. Bombay, 1885.

81. ————Vikramorvasi—(Urvasia Fabula Kalidasi) Sanskrit Text with Latin Translation and notes—Edited by R. Lenz. Berlin, 1833.

82. ————————By Dr. F. Bollensen (with notes). St. Petersburg, 1846.

83. ————————Edited by Jibânanda Vidyâsâgara. Calcutta, 1873.

84. ————————Edited with English Notes by Shankar P. Pandit, M.A. Bombay, 1879.

85. ————————With the Commentary of Ranganâtha—Edited by K. P. Paraba and M. R. Telang. Bombay, 1888.

86. ————————Translated into English Prose—By Edward Byles Cowell. Hertford, 1851.

87. ——————French Translation—By Ph. Ed. Foucaux, Paris 1879; also Foucaux's French Translation of Mâlavikâgnimitra, Paris 1877 and Abel Bergaigne's French Translation of Nâgânanda, Paris, 1879. (All three in 1 volume).

88. **Karpûra Manjari**—With the Commentary of Vâsudeva—Edited by K. P. Paraba and Pandit Durgâprasâda. Bombay, 1887. (K. M. No. IV).

89. **Kaumudi Sudhâkara**—A Prakarana—By Mahâmahôpâdhyâya Chandrakânta Tarkâlankâra. Calcutta, 1888.

90. **Krishṇadâs, K.**—Draupadîvastraharaṇam—Pândavavanagamana Natakam. Bombay.

91. **Kshemendra**—Samaya Mâtrika—Edited by K. P. Paraba and Pandit Durgâprasâda. Bombay, 1888 (K. M. No. X).

92. **Kuvalayânandakârika**—Bombay, 1886.

93. **Lakshmaṇa**—Champû Râmayaṇa—Edited by Gangâvishṇu—Bombay, 1883.

94. **Mâdhava Bhatta**—Subhadrâharaṇam—Edited by K. P. Paraba and Pandit Dargâprasâda. Bombay, 1888 (K. M. No. IX.)

95. **Mâgha**—Śiśupâlavadha—With the Commentary of Mallinâdha—Edited by Pandit Bhuvan Chandra Basak. Calcutta, 1879.

96. ——————With the Commentary of Mallinâtha—Edited by Pandit Durgâprasâda and Pandit Śivadatta of Jeypore. Bombay, 1888.

97. **Mammata**—Kâvya Prakâśa—Edited with notes by Maheśachandra Nyâyaratna, C.I.E., 2nd Edition. Calcutta, 1886.

98. ——————Edited with a Commentary by Vâmanâchârya Zalakikar. Bombay, 1889.

99. **Murâri**—Anargharâghavam—Edited by Pandit Durgâprasâda and K. P. Paraba. Bombay, 1887 (K. M. No. 5).

100. **Regnaud**—La Rhetorique Sanskrite—With the 6th and 7th Chapters of Bhâratîya Nâtya Śâstra and Chapters 1 to 8 of Rasatarangiṇi. Paris, 1884.

101. Rudrata—Kâvyâlankâra—with the Commentary of Mallinâtha—Edited by Pandit Durgâprasâda and K. P. Paraba. Bombay, 1886 (K. M. No. 2).

102. ————Śringâratilaka and Ruyyaka's Sahridayalîla with notes, Edited by Dr. R. Pischel. Paris, 1886.

103. Sâhitya Darpaṇa—Calcutta Edition.

104. ————————English Translation by Pramadâdâsa Mitra. Calcutta, 1875.

105. ————Sangraha—By Rajanîkânta Gupta. Calcutta, 1881.

106. Sâmba—Sâmbapanchasika—Edited by K. P. Paraba and Pandit Durgâprasâda. Bombay, 1889 (K. M. No. XIII.)

107. Sangíta Ratnâkara—(Parts I & II), Śrí Niśśanka Śârngadeva with its Commentary by Chatura Kallinâth. Edited by Pandit Mangesh Râmkrishṇa Telang A. S. No. 35. Poona, 1897.

108. Sârangadhara—Paddhati—Edited by P. Peterson, M.A., Bombay, 1888. (B. S. S. No. XXXVII).

109. Sati Praṇayam—A poem by Chandra Kânta Tarkâlankâra Deva, 1891.

110. Śesha Krishṇa—Kamsavadha—Edited by K. P. Paraba and Pandit Durgâprasâda. Bombay, 1888. (K. M. No. VI).

111. ————Pârijâtaharaṇachampu—Edited by K. P. Paraba and Pandit Durgâprasâda. Bombay, 1889. (K. M. No. XIV).

112. Śrî Harsha Deva—Nâgânanda—Edited by Bhuvan Chandra Basak. Calcutta, 1886.

113. ————————Edited with Sanskrit and English Notes—By Srînivâs Govind Bhanap—Bombay, 1892.

114. ————————Translated into English Prose—By Palmer Boyd, B.A., London, 1872.

115. ————Priyadarśika—Edited with notes by Vishnu Daji Gadre. Bombay, 1884.

116. ————Ratnâvali—Edited with notes by Jîbânanda Vidyâsâgara. Calcutta, 1876.

117. ———————German Translation—By Ludwig Fritze, 1878.

118. Śrî Kânta Charita—With the Commentary of Jonarâja—Edited by K. P. Paraba and Pandit Durgâprasâda. 1887 (K. M. No. III).

119. Śrî Krishna—Prabodha Chandrodaya—Edited by Rawaji Śrîdhara Gondhalekara. Poona, 1886.

120. Śûdrakà—Mrichhakatika—Edited by A. F. Stenzler. Bonn, 1847. (rare).

121. ———————Edited with Commentary, 8 Acts only. Calcutta.

122. ———————French Translation—By Paul Regnaud. Paris, 1876.

123. ———————German Prose Translation—By Otto Böhtlingk. St. Petersburg, 1877.

124. ———————Metrical German Translation—By Ludwig Fritze.

125. Trivikramabhatta—Nalachampu—With a Commentary edited by Pandits Durgâprasâda and Śivadatta. Bombay, 1885

126. Vallabhadeva—Subhashitâvali—Edited by P. Peterson, B.A., and Pandit Durgâprasâda. Bombay, 1886.

127. Vâmana—Kâvyâlankâra Vritti—Edited by Dr. C. Cappeller. Jena, 1875.

128. Vâmana and Vâgbhatta—Sarasvatî—Edited by Anandorâm Barooah, with a few notes, and extracts from old commentaries. Calcutta, 1883.

129. Vâsantikâsvapnam—(An adaptation of Shakespeare's Mid-Summer Night's Dream in Sanskrit). By R. Krishnamachari, B.A. Kumbakonam, 1892.

130. Viśâkhadatta—Mudrârâkshasa—Calcutta Edition, 1831 (rare).

131. ———————Majumdar's Series. Calcutta, 1870.

132. ———————Edited with Commentary of Dhundhirâja and with introduction and notes by Kâśînâth Triumbak Telang, M.A., L.L.B. Bombay, 1884 (B. S. S. No. 27.)

133. ————————French Translation—By Victor Henry. Paris, 1888.

134. Viddhaśâla Bhanjika—of (Râjaśekhara)—By B. R. Arte, B.A., and Ritusambâra of Kâlidâsa—By Keshava Raoji Godabole. Poona, 1886.

135. Wilson, H. H.—Threatre of the Hindus, Volumes I & II. London, 1871.

V.—*Philology, Grammar, and Elementary Works.*

1. Anubhûtisvarûpa—Sârasvatam Vyâkaraṇam—Edited by Gangâvishṇu. Bombay, 1887.
2. Anandorâm Borooah B.A., Sanskrit Grammar. Calcutta, 1879.
3. ———————A Comprehensive Grammar of the Sanskrit Language (Vol. X, Prosody). Calcutta, 1882.
4. Application of the Roman Alphabet to the languages of India—Edited by Monier Williams, M.A. London, 1859.
5. Âpte, V. S., M.A.,—Guide to Sanskrit Composition. Poona, 1885.
6. ———————Student's Hand-book of Progressive Exercises in English and Sanskrit—4th Edition, Parts I and II. Poona, 1889.
7. Ârya———Grammar of the Sanskrit language (in Sanskrit, Hindi and English). Benares, 1889. Parts I & II.
8. Ashtâdhâyi Sûtrapâṭha—Edited by Târânâtha Tarkavâchaspati. Calcutta, 1875.
9. ———————Bombay, 1885.
10. Ballantyne, J. R.—First Lessons in Sanskrit Grammar, London, 1873 (2nd Edition).
11. Beames J.—A Comparative Grammar of the Modern Âryan Languages of India—3 volumes, London, 1872-79.
12. Benfey—Theodor—Geschichte der Sprachwissenschaftu. Orientalische Philologie in Dentchland. Gottingen, 1869.
13. ———————Sanskrit Grammar—(2nd Edition). London, 1868.
14. Bhandârkar, Dr. R. G.—First Book of Sanskrit. Bombay, 1879.
15. ———————Second Book of Sanskrit—Bombay. Fourth Edition, 1877.
16. Bhattojî Dîkshita—Siddhânta Kaumudî—Edited by Târânâtha Tarkavâchaspati. Calcutta, 1871 (2 vols.)
17. ———————Edited by K. P. Paraba. Bombay, 1865.
18. ———————Siddhânta Kaumudi—Anuvritti Darpanam.

19. Böhtlingk—Otto———Pâṇini's Grammar—Edited by—2 vols. Bonn, 1839-40.

20. ——————Pâṇini's Grammar—Edited with German Translation and Indices by—Leipzig, 1887.

21. ——————Sanskrit Chrestomathie—St. Petersburg, 1845.

22. ——————2nd Edition—St. Petersburg—1877.

23. Bopp. F.—Sanskrit Grammar. Berlin, 1863.

24. ——————Comparative Grammar—Translated from the German by E. B. Eastwick, F.R.S., 3 vols., 4th Edition. London, 1885.

25. Brown, C. P., M. R. A. S.—Sanskrit Prosody. London, 1869.

26. Bühler, Dr. G.—Third book of Sanskrit. Bombay, 1877.

27. Burnell, A. C., PH.D.—On the Aindra School of Sanskrit Grammarians—Mangalore, 1875.

28. Burritt, E.—Sanskrit Hand-book for the Fireside. London, 1876.

29. Colebrook—Grammar of the Sanskrit Language. Calcutta, 1805. (very rare).

30. Delbrück, B.—Introduction to the Study of Language, Leipzig, 1882.

31. Edgren A. H.—On the Verbal roots of the Sanskrit Language (from J. A. O. S.) 1878.

32. Gândhi, D. N.—Dhâturûpakośa—3rd Edition. Ratnagiri, 1878.

33. Gangadâsa—Chhandomanjari and Vrittaratnâkaram—Edited by Târânâtha—Tarkavâchaspati—(3rd Edition). Calcutta, 1876.

34. Goldstücker, Theodor—Pâṇini—His place in Sanskrit Literature. London, 1861.

35. Govind Śankar Śâstri Bâpat—Guide to Sanskrit Verbs, (Parts I and II). Bombay, 1886.

36. Hemachandra—Lingânuśâsanam — By Dr. R. Otto Franke. Göttingen, 1886.

37. Îswarachandra Vidyâsâgara—Discourse on the Sanskrit language and literature (in Bengali), 3rd Edition. Calcutta, 1863.

38. ——————Vyâkaraṇa Kaumudi (Part IV), 5th Edition. Calcutta, 1880.

39. KÂTANTRAM—With the Vritti of Śrî Durgâ Singh—Calcutta edition.

40. KAUMUDÎMAHOTSÂHA—Edited by R. B. Gunjikar and K. P. Paraba, 1877. Bombay, (2 Vols.)

41. Kauṇḍabhatta—Vaiyâkaraṇa Bhûshaṇasâra—Edited by Târânâtha Tarka Vâchaspathi. Calcutta, 1850.

42. Kellner, F. C.—Sâvitrî—Leipzig, 1888.

43. Krishṇa Śâstri Bhátavadekar—Subanta Prakáśa (in Marathi.) Bombay, 1867.

44. Kusumamâla, No. II—with notes by Vâman Sivarâm Âpte, M.A. Poona, 1891.

45. Lanman, C. R.—Sanskrit Reader—with Vocabulary and Notes—Parts I and II. London, 1884.

46. ——————Part III, Notes Boston, 1889.

47. Lassen, C.—Anthologia Sanskritica—Bonn, 1865.

48. Max. Müller, F.—Biographies of Words and the Home of the Âryas. London, 1888.

49. ——————Grammar of the Sanskrit language, 1st Edition. London, 1866.

50. ——————Sanskrit Grammar—(2nd Edition). London, 1870.

51. ——————An abridged edition for beginners—Edited by A. M. Macdonell, M.A. London, 1886.

52. ——————Lectures on the Science of Language—2 vols., London, 1882.

53. ——————Science of Thought. London, 1887.

54. ——————Three Introduotory Lectures on the Science of Thought—Chicago, 1888.

55. MONIER-WILLIAMS, M.—Sanskrit Grammar. (4th Edition. Oxford, 1877.

56. ——————Sanskrit Manual (Parts I and II). London, 1862.

57. ——————With Vocabulary by A. E. Gough. London 1886.

58. ——————Key to.— by A. E. Gough (Part IV). London, 1868.

59. Nâgojibhatta—Bhashyapradîpoddyota on Kaiyyata's Bhashyapradîpa—(in 2 vols.) reproduced by Photolithography under the supervision of Professor T. H. Goldstücker, London, India Museum, 1874. (Presented by the Secretary of State for India).

60. ——————Paribhâshenduśekhara—Edited by F. Kielhorn, PH.D., Part I. (B. S. S. No. 2). Bombay, 1368.

61. ——————Part II, Edited with English Translation and Notes by F. Kielhorn, PH.D., Bombay, 1874.

62. Navînachandra Rai—Laghu Vyâkaraṇa of Sanskrit (in Hindi), Lahore, 1875.

63. Sarala Vyâkaraṇa of Sanskrit (in Hindi). Lahore, 1872.

64. Oppert, Gustav. PH. D.—On the Classification of Languages. Madras, 1879.

65. Pâṇinîyatatvadarpaṇam—An Exposition of the Grammatical Aphorisms of Paṇini—K. C. Banerji and Sûrya Prasâda Miśra. Benares, 1887.

66. Patanjali—Mahâbhâshya—Reported by Photolithography under the supervision of Professor T. H. Goldstücker. In one volume. London, India Museum, 1874. (Presented by the Secretary of State for India.)

67. ——————With Kaiyyata's Bhâshyapradîpa—Reproduced by Photolithography under the supervision of Professor T. H. Goldstücker (3 vols.) London, India Museum, 1874. (Presented by the Secretary of State for India).

68. ——————Edited by F. Keilhorn, PH.D., 3 vols. Bombay, 1880–85.

69. Perry, E. D.—Sanskrit Primer. Boston, 1886.

70. Râmatâraṇa Śiromaṇi—Gaṇadarpaṇa—Edited by——Calcutta, (3rd Edition).

71. Sanskrit Reader—The—vol. I, a monthly magazine of Sanskrit Literature—Bombay, 1884.

72. Sayce, A. H.—Introduction to the Science of language—(2. vols.), 2nd Edition. London, 1883.

73. ————————Principles of Comparative Philology—3rd Edition. London, 1885.

74. Schleicher, A.—Compendium of the Comparative Grammar—Translated from the German Edition by H. Bendall, M.A. Parts I and II. London, 1874-77.

75. Schrumpf, G. A.—First Âryan Reader. London, 1890.

76. Śeshagiri Śastri, M.A.—Notes on Âryan and Dravidian Philology, Vol. I. Madras, 1884.

77. ————————M.—Etymology of Some Mythological Names 1888-89.

78. Śîtala Prasâda Munshi—Vyâkaraṇa Kaumudi—Translated from Bengali into Hindi by——Calcutta, 1868.

79. Speijer, Dr. J. S.—Sanskrit Syntax. Leyden, 1886.

80. Târânâtha Tarkavâchaspati—Âśubodhan Vyâkaraṇam, Calcutta, 1868.

81. ————————Lingânuśâsanam—(Paṇini on Genders). Calcutta, 1872.

82. Ujjvaladatta—Commentary on the Uṇâdi Sûtras—Edited by Theodor, Aufrecht. Bonn, 1859.

83. Varadarâja—Laghu Kaumudi—with an English version—Edited by James R. Ballantyne, L.L.D. (2nd Edition). Benares, 1867.

84. ————————Edited by Pandit Jîbânanda Vidyâsâgara, B.A Calcutta, 1877.

85. Vencatavaradiengar, S. B.A., M.L.,—Guide to Panini (An English Summary of Paṇini's Aphorisms on Sanskrit Grammar). Bengalore, 1884.

86. Viswanâtha Śarma. Pandit,—Madhya Siddhânta Kaumudi—Edited by——Banares, 1884.

87. Vopadeva—Mugdhabodha—Edited by Otto Böhtlingk. St. Petersburg, 1847.

88. Westergaard, N. L.—Radices Linguœ Sanskriti Bonn, 1841.

89. Whitney, W. D.—Sanskrit Grammar—(2nd Edition). Leipzig, 1889.

90. ————————Sanskrit Roots. Leipzig, 1885.

91. Wilson, H. H.—An Introduction to the Grammar of the Sanskrit Language—(2nd Edition). London, 1847.

VI.—*Bibliography and Religion.*

1. Attar Singh, Sardar—Sakhee Book—The Deposition of Guru Govind Singh's religion and doctrines. Benares, 1873.
2. Aufrecht (Theodor)—Catalogus Catalogorum—An Alphabetical Register of Sanskrit Works and Authors. Leipzig, 1891.
3. Barth, A.—The Religions of India—Authorised translation by Rev. J. Wood (T. O. S.) London, 1882.
4. Bhandârkar, R. G.—Report on the Search for Sanskrit MSS. in the Bombay Presidency during the year 1882-83. Bombay, 1884.
5. ——— ——— ——— during the year 1883-84. Bombay, 1887.
6. ——— ——— ——— during the years 1887-88, 1888-99, 1889-90 and 1890-91. Bombay, 1897.
7. ———A Catalogue of the Collection of MSS. deposited in the Deccan College with an index. Bombay, 1888.
8. Bhau Daji, Dr.—The literary remains of—Edited by Râmachandra Ghosha. Calcutta, 1888.
9. Bühler, G.—Catalogue of Sanskrit Manuscripts Fasciculus I. compiled under the superintendence of—By order of Governmant. Bombay, 1871.
10. ———Index to Mr. Muir's Sankrit Texts (Parts I and II) compiled by—London, 1861.
11. Caste—(Its supposed origin, &c.) Madras, 1887.
12. Centenary Review of the Asiatic Society of Bengal from 1784 to 1883, Part I. Cacutta, 1885.
13. Celebrooke, H. T.—Miscellaneous Essays—Edited by E. B. Cowell, 2 vols. London, 1873.
14. Floyer, A. M.—Evolution of Ancient Hinduism. London, 1888.

15. Haug, (Martin)—Essays on the sacred language, writings and religion of the Parsees—(3rd Edition). Edited by E. W. West (T. O. S.). London, 1884.

16. Hindu Mythology popularly treated—Presented as a memento of his visit to India, to H. R. H. The Prince of Wales, K.G., G.C.I.E., by H. H. The Gaekwar of Baroda. Madras, 1875.

17. Hopkins, E. W.—Mutual Relations of the Four Castes. Leipzig, 1881.

18. Lahor, Jean—Histoire de la Litterature Hindoue. Paris, 1888

19. Lyall, Sir. A. C.—Asiatic Studies. London, 1882.

20. Macdonald, Rev. K. S.—The Vedic Religion—Second Edition. London, 1881.

21. Manning, Mrs.—Ancient and Mediæval India—2 vols. London, 1869 (rare).

22. Max Müller, F.—Chips from a German Workshop. 4 vols. London, 1868-1875. Original Edition, (rare).

23. ————History of Ancient Sanskrit Literature. London, 1859. (very rare).

24. ————Hibbert Lectures—Lectures on the origin and growth of religion. London, 1880.

25. ————India, What can it teach us? London, 1883.

26. ————Introduction to the Science of Religion. London, 1882.

27. ————Natural Religion—Gifford Lectures. London, 1889.

28. ————Selected Essays on Language, Mythology and Religion—2 vols. London, 1881. 2

29. ————Theosophy—Gifford Lectures. (Psychological Religion). London, 1893.

30. Milloué, L. de—Precis D' Histoire des Religions. Paris, 1890.

31. Mitra, Râjendralâla—A Catalogue of the Sanskrit Manuscripts in the Library of His Highness the Maharajah of Bikanir, Compiled by—Calcutta, 1880.

32. Monier-Williams, M.—Indian Wisdom—Third Edition. London, 1876.

33. ——— Religious Thought and Life in India, Part I. London, 1883.

34. ———(Brâhmanism and Hinduism)—Third Edition. London, 1887.

35. Muir, J.—Original Sanskrit Texts—Collected and Translated—5 vols. 1872.

36. Olcott, H. S.—The Kinship between Hinduism and Buddhism—Edited by H. Dharmapâla. Calcutta, 1893.

37. Peterson, P.—A fifth report of operation in search of Sanskrit Manuscripts in the Bombay Circle. (April 1892—May 1895). Bombay, 1896.

38. Poor, L. E.—Sanskrit and its Kindred Literatures. London, 1881.

39. Râmachandra, Ghosha.—History of Hindu Civilization. Calcutta, 1889.

40. Reed, E. A.—Hindu Literature—(The ancient books of India). Chicago, 1891.

41. Religious Reform—(Part I. Popular Hinduism). Madras, 1887.

42. Śankar, P. Pandit—A Note on Sâyana's Commentary—on the Kanva Recension of the White Yajur Veda. Poona.

43. Sanskrit College, Calcutta—A descriptive Catalogue of Sanskrit Manuscripts in the Library of—Calcutta, 1892.

44. ——— Calcutta, 1894.

45. Sherring, Rev.—Hindu Tribes and Castes—2 vols. Calcutta, 1872-1879 (very rare).

46. Tassy, M. Garcin de—Histoire de la litterature Hindoui et Hindoustani—2 vols. Paris, 1839.

47. Ward, Rev. W.—View of the History, Literature and Religion of the Hindus—2 vols. in one. London, 1817.

48. Weber, Albrecht—History of Indian Literature. Translated from the Second German Edition by John Mann and T. Zachariae. London, 1878.

49. Whitney, W. D.—Oriental and Linguistic Studies. New York, 1872.

50. Wilson, H. H.—Essays on the Religion of the Hindus—Edited by Dr. Reinhold Rost—2 vols. London, 1861-1862.

——. ——Essays on subjects connected with Sanskrit Literature—Edited by Dr. Reinhold Rost, 3 vols London, 1864-1865.

VII.—*Dharmasútras, Dharmaśástras, and Sciences.*

1. Baudhâyana Dharma Śâstra—Edited by E. Hultzsch. Leipzig, 1884.
2. Chandesvara Vivâda Ratnâkara—Edited by Vidyâlankâra, Pandit, D. Calcutta, 1887.
3. Gautama—Institutes of—Edited by A. F. Stenzler. London, 1876.
4. Jîmûtavâhana—Dâyabhâga—with the Commentary of Krishna Tarkâlankâra. Calcutta, 1829.
5. ———with Commentaries—(in Bengali characters), 1863 (very rare).
6. Law Books—The Minor—Translated by Julius Jolly (S. B. E. vol. XXXIII, Part I). Oxford, 1889.
7. Laws of the Âryas—The Sacred—Translated by G. Bühler (S. B. E. vols. II and XIV, Parts I and II). Oxford, 1879 and 1882.
8. Mânavadharma Mîmâmsa Bhûmika—By Bhîmasena Śarma. Allahabad, 1893.
9. ———Śâstra—Edited by G. C. Haughton. Text and Translation—2 vols. London, 1825. (rare).
10. ———or Lois de Manou—Edited with Notes and Variae Lectiones—by Loiseleur des Long. Paris, 1830. (rare).
11. ———Edited with Six Sanskrit Commentaries by Rao Saheb V. N. Mandlik—3 vols. Bombay, 1886.
12. ———with the Commentary of Govindarâja—Edited by Rao Saheb V. N. Mandlik, 1886.
13. ———(Text only). Edited by J. Jolly. London, 1887.
14. Manu—Translated by G. Bühler (S. B. E. vol. XXV). Oxford, 1886.

15. Medicine—A Manuscript in Sanskrit on—
16. Mîtâkshara—Et le Dattacachandrikâ—Edited by Orianne. Paris, 1845. (rare).
17. ———————Translated by H. T. Colebrooke and P. M. Wynch, Madras. (3rd Edition), 1879.
18. Nârada—Institutes of—Edited by J. Jolly. Calcutta, 1885.
19. Pâlakâpya Muni—The Hastyâyurveda—Edited by Pandit Śivadatta of Jeypore. (A. S. S. No. 26). Poona, 1894.
20. Pratâpa Rudra Dev—Dâyabhâga. London, 1881.
21. Râjanighanta and the Dhanvantrinighanta—(Two Treatises on Medicine). Edited by Vaidya Nârâyaṇa Śâstri Purandare. (A. S. S. No. 33). Poona, 1896.
22. Sarasvatî-Vilâsa—(Hindu Law of Inheritance). Translated from Sanskrit by the Rev. T. Foulkes. London, 1881.
23. Smriti Chandrikâ—By Devanna Bhat, Translated from the original by T. Krishnaswami Iyer. Madras, 1867.
24. Śrîyoga Ratnâkaram—A Treatise on Medicine with a Preface by Anna Moreśwara Kunte. (A. S. S. No. 4). Poona, 1888.
25. Vâchaspati Miśra—Vivâda Chintâmaṇi—Edited by P. C. Tagore Madras, 1865.
26. Vâgbhattâcharya—The Rasaratna Samuchchaya (A treatise on medical preparations containing mercury). Edited by Krishnârao Vinâyaka Bapat. (A. S. S. No. 19). Poona, 1890.
27. Vâsishṭha Dharma Śâstram—Edited by the Rev. A. A. Führer. (B. S. S. No. 23). Bombay, 1883.
28. Vishṇu—Institutes of—Edited by J. Jolly. Calcutta, 1881.
29. ———————Translated by J. Jolly. (S. B. E. vol. VII.) Oxford, 1880.
30. Vrindamâdhava—or Siddhiyoga—with a commentary—Edited by Hanumant Śâstri Pâdhye. (A. S. S. No. 27). Poona, 1894.
31. Vyavahâra Mayûkha—Edited by the Hon'ble V. N. Mandlik—Text and an English Translation. Bombay, 1880.

32. Vyavasthâ Chandrikâ—Edited by Syâmacharaṇa Vidyâbhûshaṇa. Calcutta, 1879.

33. Yâjnyavalkya—Gesetzbuch—Edited by A. F. Stenzler with a German Translation. Berlin, 1849.

34. ———— ———Smriti—Bombay Edition.

VIII.—*Dictionaries.*

1. Amarakośa—Edited by A. Loiseleur Deslongchamps. 2 vols. Paris, 1839-1845.
2. ——— ——— with the commentary of Maheśvara—Edited by Chintâmaṇi Śâstri Thatte. Bombay, 1882.
3. ——— ——— Edited by Jîvânanda Vidyâsâgara—1875.
4. Amarasâra—An abridgement of Amarakośa, being a Sanskrit-English and English-Sanskrit Pocket Dictionary—By Mahâdeva Śivarâm Gole. Bombay, 1888.
5. Âpte, (Vâman Śivarâm)—The Student's English-Sanskrit Dictionary. Poona, 1884.
6. ——— ———The Practical Sanskrit-English Dictionary. Poona, 1890.
7. ——— ———The Student's Sanskrit-English Dictionary. Poona, 1890.
8. Balfour, (Surgeon-General Edward)—The Cyclopædia of India 3 vols. London, 1885.
9. Böhtlingk, Otto—Sanskrit Wörterbuch in Kürzerer Fassung, one large volume St. Petersburg, 1879.
10. ——— and Rudolph Roth—Sanskrit Wörterbuch, 7 vols. in four St. Petersburg, 1858-1875.
11. Capeller, (Carl)—Sanskrit-English Dictionary. London, 1891.
12. ——— Sanskrit Wörterbuch. Strassburg, 1887.
13. Classical Dictionary of India—Illustrative of the Mythology, Philosophy, &c., of the Hindus—Trüber and Co. London, 1879.
14. ———————————Supplement to—Trüber and Co. London, 1879.
15. Grassmann (Hermann)—Wörterbuch Zum Rig Veda. Leipzig, 1873.
16. Halâyudha—Abidhânaratnamâlâ—Edited by T. Aufrecht. London, 1861.
17. Hemachandra—Deśînâmamâlâ—Edited with Notes by Dr. G. Bühler and R. Pischel. Part I, (B. S. S. No. 17). Bombay, 1880.

18. Medinîkośa—Edited by Jîvânanda Vidyaâsâgara. Calcutta, 1872.
19. Williams, Sir, M.—A Sanskrit-English Dictionary. Oxford, 1888.
20. Śabda-Kalpa-Druma—Edited by Râja Râdha Kânta Bahadur. (1 vol and parts). Calcutta, 1885.
21. ——— ——— ——— 2 vols. Calcutta, 1886-1889.
22. Vaidya (Lakshmaṇa Râmachandra)—The Standard Sanskrit-English Dictionary. Bombay, 1889.

B.

Old Persian, Zend, Pehalvi and Pazend.

1. Ardâ-Virâf Namak—The Pahlavi Text with Translation.
2. ———— Vocabulary.
3. Bartholomæ, Chr.—Handbuch der Altiranischen Dialekte. Leipzig, 1883.
4. Benfey, T.—Die Persischen Keilinschriften. Leipzig, 1847.
5. Burnouf, E.—Commentaire Sur le Yaçna—(incomplete copy). Paris, 1835.
6. Darmesteter, J.—Études Iraniennes. Paris, 1883.
7. ———— Haurvatât and Ameretât. Translated by H. P. Wadia (with notes) from the French of— Bombay, 1888.
8. Desatir—The—The sacred writings of the Ancient Persian Prophets—Edited by D. J. Medhora. Bombay, 1888.
9. Dinkard—The—By P. D. B. Sanjana—8 vols. Bombay, 1874-1894.
10. Ganjeshâyagan—Translated by P. D. B. Sanjana. Bombay, 1885.
11. Geiger, W.—Civilization of the Eastern Iranians in ancient times—Translated by D. D. P. Sanjana—2 vols. London, 1885-1886.
12. Gobineau, Count H. De—Method of reading Cuneiform Texts—Translated by M. C. Shapurjee. Bombay, 1865.
13. Harlez, C. de—Manuel de la Langue de L'Avesta. Paris, 1882.
14. Haug, (Dr. Martin)—Die Gâthâs des Zarathustra. Leipzig, 1858.
15. ———— Essays on the Sacred Language, Writings and Religion of the Parsees. Bombay, 1862.
16. Jamaspji, D. H.—An old Zend-Pahlavi Glossary—revised with notes by Haug. Bombay, 1867.
17. Kanga, K. E.—A Practical Grammar of the Avesta Language. Bombay, 1891.

18. Kossowicz, C.—Inscriptiones Palæo-Persicæ. Petropoli, 1872.

19. Mainyo-i-Khard—The book of the—Edited by F. C. Andreas. Kiel, 1882.

20. Nasks—The Contents of the—As stated in the Eighth and Ninth Books of the Dinkard. Translated by E. W. West. (S. B. E. vol. XXXVII, Part I). Oxford, 1892.

21. Nirangistân—Edited by D. D. P. Sanjana.

22. Pahlavi-Pazend Glossary—An old—Edited by D. H. J. Asa—with an Introductory Essay by M. Haug. Bombay, 1870.

23. ——— Texts—Translated by E. D. West. (S. B. E. vols. V, XVIII and XXIV, Parts I, II and III). Oxford, 1880, 1882 and 1885.

24. Patell, D. H.—The Meanings of the Words Avesta and Zend. Bombay, 1877.

25. Pietraszewski, J.—Epitome of Zend Grammar—Translated from the French. By E. Rehastek. Bombay, 1862.

26. Spiegel, Fr.—Die Altpersischen Keilinschriften. Leipzig, 1881.

27. Tolman, H. C.—A Grammar of the Old Persian Language. Boston,1892.

28. Zendavesta—or The Religious Books of the Zoroastrians—Edited and Translated with a Dictionary, Grammar, &c., by N. L. Westergaard. Vol. I. The Zend Texts only. Without the English Introduction. Copenhagen, 1852-1854. (rare).

29. —————Translated by J. Darmesteter. Parts I and II, S. B. E. vol. IV and XXIII and L. H. Mills—Part III. S. B. E. vol. XXXI. Oxford, 1880, 1883, 1887.

C.

Pâli and Singalese Literature, Buddhist-Sanskrit and Works on Buddhism and Jainism.

1. Alabaster, H.—The Wheel of the Law (Buddhism). London, 1877.
2. Anguttara Nikâya—Edited by the Rev. R. Morris, Parts I and II. London, 1885-1888 (P. T. S.)
3. Ârya-Sûra—The Jatakamâlâ or Bodhisattvâvadhânamâla—Edited by Dr. H. Kern. London, 1891.
4. Asvaghosha Bodhisattva—The Fo-Sho-Hing-Tsan-King. A Life of Buddha—Translated from Chinese into English—By S. Beal. (S. B. E. vol. XIX). Oxford, 1883.
5. Âyâramga Sutta—Edited by H. Jacobi. (P. T. S.) London, 1882.
6. Beal, S.—Buddhism in China. London, 1884.
7. ———A Catena of Buddhist Scriptures. London, 1871.
8. Bible Stories—(in Simhalese).
9. Buddha and his Religion—in Simhalese. Colombo, 1891.
10. ———The life of—Translated by W. W. Rockhill. (T. O. S.) London, 1884.
11. ———Sâkya—The romantic legend of—Translated from the Chinese-Sanskrit by S. Beal. London, 1875.
12. ———The imitation of—Quotations from Buddhist Literature for each day in the year—compiled by E. M. Bowden. London, 1893.
13. ———Vamśa and Carîga-patika—Edited by Rev. R. Morris. (P. T. S.). London, 1882.
14. Buddhaghosuppatti—Edited by J. Gray. London, 1892.
15. Buddhist Birth Stories or Jâtaka Tales—Edited by V. Fausböll and Translated by T. W. Rhys Davids. London, 1880.
16. ———Catechism—Compiled by Subhadra Bhikshu. (with notes). London, 1890.

17. ————Mahâyâna Sûtras—The Budhacharita of Asvaghosha—Translated by E. B. Cowell, and edited F. Max Müller and J. Takakusu Part I. (S B. E. vol. XLIX). Oxford, 1894.

18. ————Suttas—Translated from Pâli by T. W. Rhys Davids. (S. B. E. vol. XI). Oxford, 1881.

19. ————Texts from Japan—Edited by F. Max Müller (An. Ox.). Oxford, 1881.

20. Carter, The Rev. C.—An English and Singhalese Lesson Book on Ollendorff's System. Designed to teach Singhalese through the medium of the English Language—Colombo.

21. Carus, P.—The Gospel of Buddha according to old records, told by—London, 1896.

22. Copleston, R. S. Buddhism Primitive and Present in Magadha and Ceylon. London, 1892.

23. Daṭhâvamsa—Translated into English by Mutu Coomaraswamy. London, 1874.

24. Dhammapadam—Edited by V. Fausböll. London, 1855.

25. ————Texts from the Buddhist Cannon. Translated from the Chinese by S. Beal (T. O. S.). London, 1878.

26. ————A book of Buddhist Precepts and Maxims. Translated into English by J. Gray. Second Edition. Calcutta, 1887.

27. ————Translated from Pâli—by F. Max Müller, and the Sutta-Nipâta, translated from Pâli by F. Fausböll. (S. B. E. vol. X). Oxford, 1881.

28. Dhamma Sangani—The—Edited by E. Müller. (P. T. S.). London, 1885.

29. Dharma Sangraha—Edited by F. Max Müller and H. Wenzel (An. Ox.). Oxford, 1885.

30. Dîgha Nikâyâ—Edited by T. W. Rhys Davids and T. E. Carpentar (P. T. S.). London, 1889.

31. Divyâvadâna—A Collection of early Buddhist legends. Edited by E. B. Cowell and R. A. Neil. Cambridge, 1886.
32. English and Simhalese First Book. Colombo, 1895.
33. Famous Children of Long Ago (in Simhalese). Colombo, 1892.
34. Granthasâra or Simhalese Classical Reader. Colombo, 1887.
35. Grünwedel, A.—Rüpasiddhi. Berlin, 1883.
36. Hardy, Dr. E.—Der Buddhismus nach älteren Pâli-Werken. Münster, 1890.
37. ——, S.—Eastern Monachism. An Account of the Origin, Laws, &c., of the order of mendicants founded by Gautama Buddha. London, 1860.
38. ————A Manual of Buddhism in its modern development. Second Edition. London, 1880.
39. Hiuen Tsiang—Buddhist records of the western world—Translated by S. Beal from the Chinese of—2 vols. (T. O. S.). London, 1884.
40. Iti-Vuttaka—Edited by E. Windisch. London, 1890. (P. T. S.)
41. Jaina-Sûtras—Translated from Prakrit by H. Jacobi (S. B. E. vol. XXII). Oxford, 1884.
42. Jâtakas—Ten—With Translation and Notes in English. By V. Fausböll, 1872.
43. ————The—With Commentary Edited by V. Fausböll, vols. I—IV London, 1877-1887.
44. ————The Nine—with Vocabalary. By L. H. Elwell. Boston, 1886.
45. Journal of the Pâli Text Society—Edited by T. W. Rhys Davids. (Number for 1887 wanting). London, 1882-1890.
46. Kachchâyana—Pâli Grammar—By F. Mason. Bib. Ind. Toungoo, 1868.
47. Kalpasûtra and Nava Tatva—Two works illustrative of the Jain Religion and Philosophy. Translated from the Mâgadhî—by the Rev. T. Stevenson. London, 1848.
48. Lalita Vistara—Edited by Dr. S. Lefmann. Berlin, 1874.

49. ————Memoirs of the early life of Sâkya Simha. Edited by R. Mitra. Bib. Ind. Calcutta, 1877.

50. Mahâparinibbânasutta of the Sutta Pitika—The Pâli Text. Edited by R. C. Childers. London, 1878.

51. Mahâwanso—(In Roman Characters). Vol. I containing the first 38 chapters—By the Hon. G. Turnour. Ceylon, 1837. (rare.)

52 Milindapañho—Edited by V. Trenckner. London, 1880.

53. Milinda—The questions of King—Translated from the Pâli by T. W. Rhys Davids—Parts I and II. (S. B. E. vols. XXXV and XXXVI). Oxford, 1890.

54. Müller, E.—Pâli Grammar. London, 1884.

55. Oldenberg, Dr. H.—Buddha—His life, his doctrine, his order. Translated from the German by William. Hœy. London, 1882.

56. Petavatthu—Edited by Prof. Minayeff. (P. T. S.) London, 1889.

57. Pragña Pâramitâ Hridaya Sûtra and the Ushnîshavijaya Dhâranî—Edited by F. Max Müller. (An. Ox) Oxford, 1884.

58. Pragña Pâramitâ—Ashtasâhasrikâ.By Dr. Rajendralâla Mitra. Bib. Ind. Calcutta, 1888.

59. Puggla Paññatti—Edited by the Rev. R. Morris. (P. T. S.). London, 1883.

60. Rhys Davids, J. W.—Buddhism. London.

61. ————The Hibbert Lectures. On the origin and growth of Buddhism. London, 1881.

62. Saddharma Pundarîka—or the Lotus of the True Law-Translated by H. Kern. (S. B. E. vol. XXI). Oxford, 1884.

63. Samyutta Nikâya of the Suttapitaka—Edited by M. Leon. Feer. 4 parts. (P. T. S.). London, 1884-1894.

64. Simhalese First Book—49th Edition. Colombo, 1895.

65. ————Second Reader. Colombo, 1893.

66. ————Third————Colombo, 1893.

67. ————Fourth————6th Edition. Colombo, 1891.

68. ————Fifth————Colombo, 1892.

69. ————Sixth————Colombo, 1883.

70. Sinnet, A. P.—Esoteric Buddhism—(2nd Edition). London, 1883.
71. Sumangala-Vilâsinî—By T. W. Rhys Davids and J. E. Carpenter. (P. T. S.). London, 1886.
72. Sukhâvatîvyûha—Edited by F. Max Müller and B. Nanjio. (An. Ox.). Oxford, 1883.
73. Surasonda Sandeśa—(Simhalese). Edited by the Rev. C. W. De Silva. Colombo, 1892.
74. Sutta Nipâta—Part II Glossary. Edited by V. Fausböll. (P. T. S.). London, 1893.
75. Târanâtha—Geschichte des Buddhismus—By Anton Schiefner. St. Petersburg, 1869.
76. Thera and Therî Gâthâ—By H. Oldenberg and R. Pischel. (P. T. S.). London, 1883.
77. Trenckner, V.—Pâli Miscellany. London, 1879.
78. Udânam—Edited by P. Steinthal. (P. T. S.). London, 1885.
79. Vimâna-Vatthu—Edited by E. R. Gooneratne. (P. T. S.) London, 1886.
80. Vinaya Pitakam—One of the Principal Buddhist Holy Scriptures in the Pâli Language. 5 vols. By H. Oldenberg. London, 1879-1883.
81. Vinaya Texts—Translated from the Pâli—by T. W. Rhys Davids and H. Oldenberg Parts I, II and III. (S. B. E. vols. XIII, XVII and XX). Oxford 1881, 1882 and 1885.
82. Vocabulary of English, Simhalese and Tamil.
83. Williams, Sir M.—Buddhism in its connection with Brâhmanism and Hinduism and in its contrast with Christianity. London, 1889.

Dictionaries.

84. Childers, R. C.—Dictionary of the Pâli Language. London, 1875,

D.

The Prakritas and Vernaculars of India.

Bengali.

1. Abdussubhân, S.—Hindu Mussulman (in Bengali). Calcutta, 1891.
2. Bankim Chandra—Bish Briksho. Romanised, 1881.
3. ———— Devi Chaudhurâni—Calcutta.
4. ————Durgeśa Nandinî. Calcutta, 1881. Romanised.
5. ————(in Bengali). Calcutta, 1888.
6. ————Upakatha. Edited by J. R. Ballantyne. 2nd Edition, 1868.
7. Bengali Reader—The—With a Translation and Vocabulary by D. Forbes. London, 1862.
8. Chattopadhyâya, Nishikânta, Dr.—Yâtras or the popular dramas of Bengal. London, 1882.
9. Forbes, D.—A Grammar of the Bengali Language.
10. Hitopadeśa—In Bengali. 1823.
11. Kâdambari—Translated from the Original Sanskrit into Bengâli by T. Tarkaratna (Seventh Edition). Calcutta, 1861.
12. Tâpasa Mâla—Lives of Mahomedan Saints. Translated into Bengali. Calcutta, 1886.
13. Tatvaratnamâla—in Bengali.
14. Vidyâsâgara, I.—The Story of the Śakuntala of Kalidâsa. Calcutta, 1875.

Dictionaries.

15. Bengali Dictionary—in Bengali. Calcutta.
16. Mitter, G. K.—Bengali and English Dictionary. Calcutta, 1868.
17. Mukerji, J. N.—and two others—Śabdasâra Mohânidhi—A Bengali-English Dictionary, compiled by—Calcutta.
18. Râm Comul Sen—English and Bengali Dictionary—Translated from Todd's Edition of Johnson's English Dictionary. 2 vols. Serampore, 1834. (rare).

Canarese.

19. Æsop's Fables—Translated into Canarese—Madras, 1855.
20. Arokeum Pillay—An Epitome of Hygiene (in Canarese). 2nd Edition. Bangalore, 1883.
21. Cole, Cap. R. A.—An Elementary Grammar of the Coorg Language. Bangalore, 1867.
22. Garrett, J.—The Panchatantra (in Canarese). Second Edition. Bengalore, 1865.
23. Śakuntala—(In Canarese). Translated by R. Churmure. Bombay, 1890.

Gujarâti.

24. Furdoonji, B.—Bejanni Bekasi—Bombay, 1882.
25. Hope, Sir. T. C.—Gujarâti First Book. Bombay, 1887.
26. ———————— Second Book Bombay, 1888.
27. ———————— Third Book. Bombay, 1888.
28. Mahânand Bhatt, P.—A Handbook of Gujarâti Grammar, Bombay, 1889.
29. Modi, J. J.—Meteorology. Colaba, 1883.
30. Patel. N. H.—Lectures on Wealth and the Silver question. (in Gujarâti), with copious notes in English. Bombay, 1880.
31. Ramul Sangraha—in Gujarâti. Ahmedabad, 1891.

Hindi.

32. Âryâ—Hindi Grammar in Hindi and English. Benares, 1888.
33. Baitâl Pachîsî—The 25 tales of a demon. With a Vocabulary by D. Forbes. London.
34. ————————Translated into English by Cap. D. Hollings. Calcutta, 1848.
35. ————————Translated into Hindi by L. Lall. Calcutta, 1877.
36. Ballantyne, J. R.—Elements of Hindi and Braj Bhâkhâ Grammar. Second Edition, 1868.
37. Chand Bardai—Prithiraj Rasâu—An old Hindu Epic. Edited by A. F. Hœrnle. Calcutta, 1886.
38. Lâla Chandrika—In Hindi 2 vols.

Hindi Dictionaries.

39. English-Hindi Dictionary. Benares, 1870.
04. Hindi-English Dictionary. Benares, 1873.

Mahratti.

41. Mâdhava Rao Lele—Suman Vikâs. Mahratti Translation of Sâdî's Bostan. Bombay, 1870.
42. Tikekar, R. V.—The other and true side of the Indore Question. Bombay, 1896.
43. Vâman Śâstri—Brihatkathâ Saritsâgara—in Mahratti. Bombay, 1887.

Panjabi.

44. Âdi Grandh—
45 Punjâbi First Reader.
46. ———Second Reader.

Prakritas.

47. Caldwell, Rev. R.—A Comparative Grammar of the Dravidian Languages. London, 1856.
48. Hemachandra—Grammatik der Prakritsprachen. Edited by R. Pischel. Halle, 1877.
49. Prâkrita Grammar—with English Translation by Pandit Hrishikesh Śâstri. Calcutta, 1883.
50. ———Lakshaṇam—Chandás Grammar. Edited by A. F. R. Hoernle. Calcutta, 1880.
51. Uvâsagadasao—The religious profession of an Uvâsaga. Edited in the original Prâkrita by A. H. R. Hoerule. Calcutta, 1885.
52. ———Vol. II. Translated by A. F. R. Hoernle, 1888.
53. Vâkpati—Gaudavaho—A Historical Poem in Prâkrit. Edited by S. Pandurang Pandit. (B.S.S. No. 34) Bombay, 1887.
54. Vararuchi—Prâkrita Prakâsa—The Prâkrit Grammar of—with the Commentary (Manorama) of Bhamaha, with notes and an English Translation by E. B. Cowell. London, 1868.

Telugu.

55. Arden, A. H.—A Companion Telugu Reader to Arden's Progressive Telugu Grammar. Madras, 1879.
56. Bhâskara, H.—Râmayaṇa. Madras, 1888.
57. ————————(Bâlakânda). Madras, 1880.
58. Brown, C. P.—Telugu Grammar. Madras, 1857.
59. Campbell, A. D.—A Grammar of the Telugu Language. Madras, 1816.
60. ———— Madras, 1849.
61. Chanchîta Kaṭha—Old Telugu Ballad Poetry.
62. Dayâkara Charitra—(Sanford and Merton). Hyderabad, 1889.
63. English-Telugu Dialogues. Madras, 1889.
64. ————First Reader. Madras, 1889.
65. ————Vocabulary—Parts I and II. Madras, 1889-1884.
66. First Book of Lessons. (Telugu). Madras, 1890.
67. Garthwaite—English-Telugu Reader. Madras, 1891.
68. Gopakavi, K.—Bhârata Savitri. A Brief Narrative in Telugu Prose of the Story of Mahâbharata. Madras, 1898.
69. ————Dâśaradhîśatakam. 100 verses in praise of Dâśaradhî or Râma. Madras, 1897.
70. Hamsavimśatikaṭhalu—Stories in Telugu. Madras, 1886.
71. Hanumanta Rao, J.—Suśena Vijayam (in Telugu). An Adaptation of Shakespeare's 'Cymbeline.' Chicacole, 1898.
72. ————Yatiprâsanirnayam—A Discourse in Telugu Prose that Yati and Prâsa or Cæsura and Rhyme are not necessary for good Telugu Poetry. Chicacole, 1897.
73. Hanumatpanchavimśati—Verses in Praise of Hanumân.
74. Jayaramârâma Śatakam—100 Verses in praise of Râma. Madras, 1895.
75. Krishṇakarnâmritam—Śrî—Translated into Telugu from Sanskrit by V. Vengana, verse by verse. Madras, 1898.

76. Lakshmaṇa, P.—Ândhranâmasangraham—A Glossary of pure Telugu words, in verse—Madras, 1899.

77. Lakshmî Nrisimham, M.—Vijayalakshmî Nrisimhaśatakam. 100 verses in praise of Lakshmî Nrisimha. Vijianagram 1887.

78. Morris, H.—A Simplified Grammar of the Telugu Language. London, 1890.

79. Mûrti—Narasabhûpâlîyam. A Work on Telugu Rhetoric. Madras, 1889.

80. Nalopâkhyânam—The Middle School Text Book in Telugu Poetry. Madras, 1890.

81. Nîtichandrika (Telugu), 13th Edition. Madras, 1891.

82. Panchatantram (Telugu), Madras, 1890.

83. Pâparâju, K.—Uttararâmâyaṇam—A Telugu poem in 7 Cantos. Madras, 1894.

84. Peddana, A.—Manucharitra—a romantic poem in Telugu Verse describing the descent and birth of Manu the Legislator, in 6 cantos with meaning. Madras, 1898.

85. Potarâju, B.—Srimad Bhâgavatam in Telugu Verse.

86. Râmarâjabhûshaṇa—Vasucharitram. A Telugu poem in 6 cantos. Madras. 1889.

87. Second Book of Reading—English and Telugu. Madras, 1879.

88. Seshiah, W.—A Rudimentary Grammar of the Telugu Language. Madras, 1861.

89. ——————A Short Telugu Grammar. Madras, 1882.

90. Seshappa—Nrisimhaśatakam—100 verses in praise of Nriśimha. Madras, 1899.

91. Subrahmaṇya Dâsa, P.—Kodandaramaśatakam—100 verses in praise of Kodandarâma. Madras, 1894.

92. Sumatî Śatakam—100 Nîti Verses—Madras, 1899.

93. Telugu Grammar—Elements of. Madras, 1890.

94. ——————Authorised by the Director of Public Instruction. Revised Edition. Madras, 1896.

95. ————Primer—Hyderabad, 1889.

96. ————Second Book, 1879.

97. ————Third Book, 1882.

98. Timmakavi, K—Rasikajana Manobhirâmam—A Romance—in Telugu verse (in 6 cantos). Madras, 1892.

99. Vemana—Nîti verses (in 2 parts). Madras, 1898.

100. Venkatakavi, C—Vijayavilasam. The Marriage of Arjuna and Subhadra. A Telugu poem in 3 cantos. Madras, 1898.

111. Venkayya, T.—Telugu Grammar. Authorised by the Director of Public Instruction. Madras, 1892.

102. Vîreśalingam, K.—Kurangeśvara Charitram. Rajamundry, 1883.

103. ————Râjaśekhara or Moonlight of Instruction. A Telugu Novel. Rajamundry, 1880.

104. ————Sangrahavyâkaraṇam 3rd Edition. Rajamundry. 1887.

105. Vyavahâra Dharma Bôdhini. A farce in 5 acts. Rajamundry, 1891.

Telugu Dictionaries.

106. Brown, C. P.—A Dictionary. Telugu and English, explaining the colloquial style used in business and the poetical dialect with explanations in English and in Telugu. Madras, 1852.

E.

Works on Archæology and Art.

1. Birdwood, Sir G. C. M.—The Industrial Arts of India. London, 1880.

2. Burgess, J.—Notes on the Buddhish Rock-Temples of Ajânta. Bombay, 1879.

3. ————Report on the Antiquities in the Bidar and Aurangabad Districts. London, 1878.

4. ————The Rock Temples of Elura or Verul. Bombay, 1877.

5. Burnell, A. C.—Elements of South Indian Palæography. London, 1878.

6. Catherall, T.—Views in the North Wales District—Published by—

7. Cunningham, A.—The Ancient Geography of India. London, 1871.

8. ————Archæological Survey of India (Reports). Vols. I—XI. Calcutta, 1871-1880.

9. ————The Bhilsa Topes Buddhist Monuments of Central India. London, 1854.

10. ————Corpus Inscriptionum Indicarum. Vol. I. Inscriptions of Asoka. Calcutta, 1879.

11. ————The Stupa of Bharhut. A Buddhist Monument. London, 1879.

12. Daniel—Oriental Scenery.

13. Fergusson, J.—The Rock-cut Temples of India. London, 1864.

14. ————and J. Burgess—The Cave Temples of India. London, 1880.

15. ————A History of Architecture in all Countries. Vols. I and II. Second Edition. London, 1874.

16. ————History of Indian and Eastern Architecture. Forming vol. III of the 'History of Architecture in all Countries.' London, 1876.

17. ——————History of the Modern Styles of Architecture. (Forming vol. IV of the 'History of Architecture in all Countries'). London, 1873.

18. Fleet, F.—Corpus Inscriptionum. Indicarum Vol. III. (Inscriptions of the the early Gupta Kings). Calcutta, 1888.

19. Führer, A.—Monumental Antiquities and Inscriptions in the North Western Provinces and Oudh. Allahabad, 1891.

20. Howson, J. S.—The River Dee—Its Aspect and History. London, 1875.

21. Indraji, Pandit B.—Antiquarian Remains at Sopârâ and Padaṇ Bombay, 1882.

22. Journal of Indian Art—The—Vol. I. (Nos. 1—16.) London, 1886.

23. Lassen, C.—Indische Alterthumskunde—4 vols. Leipzig, 1857-1874.

24. Mitra, R.—Indo-Âryans. 2 vols. Calcutta, 1881.

25. Oppert, G.—On the Ancient Commerce of India. Madras, 1879.

26. ——————Contributions to the History of Southern India. London, 1882.

27. ——————On the original inhabitants of Bhartavarsha. 2 Parts only. Madras, 1888-1889.

28. ——————On the Weapons, Army, Organization and Political Maxims of the Ancient Hindus. Madras, 1880.

29. Princep—Indian Antiquities. Edited by E. Thomas. 2 vols. London, 1858. (very rare.)

30. Senart, E.—Les Inscriptions de Piyâdasi. 2 vols. Paris, 1881-1886.

31. South Indian Inscriptions—Tamil and Sanskrit. Edited and Translated by E. Hultzch. Vols. I and II—(Parts I, II and III). Madras, 1890-1895.

32. Souvenir de Paris et Versailles.

F.

Assyrian, Hebrew and Æthiopic Languages.

1. Arnold, Rev. T. K.—The first Hebrew Book. 5th Edition. London, 1875.
2. ————————————————Key to—Edited by the Rev. H. Browne, 3rd Edition. London, 1874.
3. ————————and the Rev. H. Browne. Second Hebrew Book, containing the book of Genesis. London, 1853.
4. Athanasius—The Festal Letters of—Edited by W. Cureton. London, 1848.
5. Bickell, G. and T. Benfey—Kalilag und Damnag, Ancient Syriac Text with German Translation and Introduction. Leipzig, 1876.
6. Brückner, Dr. G.—Neues Hebräisches Lesebuch. Leipzig, 1844.
7. Davidson, A. B.—An Introductory Hebrew Grammar. Edinburgh, 1887.
8. Delitzsch, F.—Assyrian Grammar. Translated from the German by Archd. R. S. Kennedy. Berlin, 1889. (Porta Linguarum Orientalium).
9. Ethiopic Didascalia—The. With an English translation. Edited and translated by T. Pell Platt. London, 1834.
10. Eusebius—On the Theophania—A Syriac version. By S. Lee. London, 1842.
11. Ewalds—Introductory Hebrew Grammar—Translated from the 3rd German Edition by J. F. Smith. London 1870.
12. Gesenius—Hebrew Grammar. Enlarged by E. Rödiger. Translated by B. Davies. London, 1852.
13. Kirch,—Chrestomathia Syriaca Cum Lexicon. Edited by G. H. Bernstein. Leipzig, 1882.
14. Kossowicz, C.—Canticum Canticorum. Petropoli, 1879.

15. Nestle, E.—A Syriac Grammar. Berlin, 1879. (Porta Linguarum Orientalium).

16. Oppert, M. J.—Elements de la Grammaire Assyrienne. Paris, 1860.

17. Phillips, G.—A Syriac Grammar. London, 1866.

18. Practorius, F.—Æthiopische Grammatik. London, 1886.

19. Roedigero, A.—Chrestomathia Syriaca. Halis Saxonum, 1838.

20. Strack, H. L.—Hebrew Grammar. Leipzig, 1886. (Porta Linguarum Orientalium).

21. Syriac Reading Lessons—Extract from the Peschito version of the Old and New Testaments, and the Crusade of Richard I. London.

22. Tregelles, S. P.—The Hebrew Students' Manual. London.

23. Wolff, J. F.—A Manual of Hebrew Grammar. London.

Dictionaries.

24. Davies, B.—Student's Hebrew Lexicon. A Compendious and Complete Hebrew and Chaldee Lexicon to the Old Testament. Edited by—

25. Gibbs, J. W.—A Manual of Hebrew and English Lexicon. London, 1833.

G.

Greek Language and Literature.

1. Abbott, E. and Mansfield, E. D.—A Primer of Greek Grammar. London, 1883.
2. Æschylus—The seven tragedies of—Oxford, 1844.
3. ———————————————— English Translation and Notes. Oxford, 1829.
4. ————————and Sophocles—(Greek and Latin). Paris, 1846.
5. Arnold, Rev. T. K.—The First Greek Book. 6th Edition. London, 1871.
6. Arundines Cami—Edited by H. Drury, 1860.
7. Bryce, A. H.—First Greek Reader. 3rd Edition. London, 1871.
8. Colson, F. H.—Stories and Legends. A First Greek Reader with notes, vocabulary and exercises. London, 1894.
9. Curtins, Dr. G.—A Smaller Grammar of the Greek Language. 16th Edition. London, 1888.
10. ————————A Grammar of the Greek Language. Edited by Sir W. Smith. 14th Edition. London, 1893.
11. Draper, Rev. W.—A Grammar of the Greek Language, (in Hindi). Amritsar, 1816.
12. Euripidis—Fabulæ. Edited with notes &c., by T. Fix. Paris, 1844.
13. ————————Tragœdiæ Superstites Deperditarum Fragmenta. 2 Vols. Oxford, 1832 and 1833.
14. ————————Hyppolytus—Literally translated. Cambridge.
15. Fergusson, J.—Greek Grammatical Exercises. 4th Edition. Edinburgh.
16. Fowle, Rev. E.—First Easy Greek Reading Book. London, 1875.
17. ———————————————— London, 1876.
18. ————————A Short and Easy Greek Book. 6th Edition. London, 1873.

19. Frost, Rev. P.—Analecta Græca Minora. New Edition. London, 1881.

20. Gladstone, Right Hon. W. E.—Homeric Synchronism. An enquiry into the time and place of Homer. London, 1876.

21. ———————————Homer. (Lit. Pr.). London, 1878.

22. ———————Landmarks of Homeric Study. London, 1890.

23. Græci Poetæ—London, 1863.

24. Greek Anthology—Literally translated chiefly by G. Burgess. London, 1881.

25. Greek Primer—5th Edition. (C. P. S). Oxford, 1876.

26. Green, S. G.—Handbook to the Grammar of the Greek Testament. (R. T. S.). London.

27. Hayes. B. J. and W. F. Masom—Matriculation and Intermediate Greek. (U. C. C. T. S). London.

28. Herodotus—Halicarnassensis. Historia Ex. Editione Jacobi-Gronovii. 9 Vols. Glasguæ, 1761.

29. ———————Edited by G. Long, 1830.

30. ———————Book VIII. Edited by J. Thomson and R. M. Thomas. (U. C. C. T. S.). London.

31. ———————Book VIII. With a Vocabulary and Text papers (U. C. C. T. S). London.

32. ———————Literally translated with a Geographical and General Index by the Rev. H. Cary. London, 1891.

33. ———————Book VIII. Translated by J. Thompson and F. G. Plaistowe. (U. C. C. T. S.). London.

34. Homer—Illiad. With Copious English Notes by the Rev. W. Trollope. London, 1836.

35. ———————Book I. With notes by D. B. Monro (C. P. S.). Oxford, 1878.

36. ———————Literally translated with Explanatory Notes by T. A. Buckley. London, 1890.

37. ——————Odyssey. Greek and Latin. Annotated by S. Clarke. Parts I and II, Sixth Edition. Edinburgh, 1846.

38. ——————Ex. Recognitione Gulielmi Dindorfii. Oxford, 1855.

39. ——————Books I--XII. With Notes by W. W. Merry. Oxford, 1879.

40. ——————Book I. With a Vocabulary, &c., by J. T. White. London, 1880.

41. ——————Edited by J. Bond and A. S. Walpole. London, 1883.

42. ——————Odyssey. With the Hymns, Epigrams and battle of the Frogs and Mice. Translated with notes by T. A. Buckley. London, 1880.

43. ——————Johann Heinrick Vok. (German).

44. Jebb, R. C.--Greek Literature. (Lit. Pr.). London, 1878.

45. —————————— London, 1891.

46. Jelf, W. E.—A Grammar of the Greek Language, 2 vols. 4th Edition. London, 1866.

47. John, St.—Gospel. With a Vocabulary by J. T. White. London, 1874.

48. Larcher, P. H.—Comments on the History of Herodotus. Translated by W. D. Cooley, from the French of. —2 vols. London, 1844.

49. Luke, St.—Gospel—With a Vocabulary by J. T. White. London, 1875.

50. Mahaffy, Rev. J. P.—A History of Classical Greek Literature. London, 1880.

51. ——————Greek Antiquities (His. Pr.). London, 1889.

52. Mark, St.—Gospel—With a Vocabulary by J. T. White. London, 1873.

53. Mayor, Rev. J. B.—Greek for Beginners. New Edition. London, 1878.

54. New Testament—Greek and English by the Rev. Dr. Giles. London, 1870.

55. Novum Testamentum—1862.

56. Paley, F. A.—Greek Wit. 2nd Edition. London, 1888.

57. Papillon, T. L.—A Manual of Comparative Philology (C. P. S). Oxford, 1882.

58. Parry, E. St. J.—An Elementary Greek Grammar. London, 1877

59. Peile, J.—An Introduction to Greek and Latin Etymology. 3rd Edition. London, 1875.

60. Platonis Opera Recensuit Variasque Lectionibus Deligenter-Enotavit I. Bekker. 11 Vols. in Greek and Latin. London, 1826.

61. Smith, W.—A First Greek Course Initia Græca—Parts I and II. 5th Edition. London, 1870.

62. ————Initia Græca. Part III—Sixth Edition. London, 1881.

63. Sophocles—Tragœdiæ Superstites Ex Recensione. G. Dindorfii. Oxford, 1832.

64. ———————————Annotated by G. Linwood. London, 1846.

65. ————Electra—Edited by J. Thompson and B. J. Hayes (U. C. C. T. S.). London.

66 Theatre of the Greeks—The. 3rd Edition. Cambridge, 1830.

67. Theocritus, Bion and Moschus—Rendered into English Prose. By A. Lang. London, 1889.

68. Thucydides—The History of the Peloponnesian War. Edited with Notes, &c., by T. Arnold, 2 vols. 3rd Edition. Oxford, 1847.

69. ——————————————Edited and Translated by Rev. H. Dale., 2 vols. London, 1888.

70. Valpy, A. R.—Delectus Sententiarum Græcarum. London, 1841.

71. Viger—Greek Idioms. Abridged and Translated into English from Prof. Hermann's last edition with original notes. By the Rev. J. Seager. London.

72. Wilkins, H. M.—A Manual of Greek Prose Composition. London, 1878.

73. Xenophon—Opera Quae Extant Interpretatos Est. G. Schneider. 6 Vols. Leipzig, 1815-1859.

74. ————Anabasis. Annotated by J. G. Schneider. Oxford, 1821.

75. ————Historiæ Græcæ Librie Septem. Ex-Editione Ludovici Dindorfii. Oxford, 1831.

76. ————Anabasis. Edited by G. Long. London, 1855.

77. ————————Book II. Edited by J. T. White. London, 1872.

78. ————————Book I. Edited by J. T. White. London, 1873.

79. ————————The First Four Books of—With Notes. Edited by W. W. Goodwin and J. W. White. Boston, 1878.

80. ————————Easy Selections from—By J. S. Phillpotts and J. C. S. Jerram. 3rd Edition. Oxford, 1880.

81. ————————Anabasis. Book I. Edited by A. S. Walpole. London, 1882.

82. ————————Œconomicus of—Edited by J. Thompson and B. J. Hayes (U. C. C. T. S.). London.

83. ————————Minor Works of—Literally translated from the Greek by J. S. Watson. London, 1884.

84. ————————The Memorable Thoughts of Socrates by—Translated by E. Bysshe. London, 1889.

85. ————————Cyropædia or Institution of Cyrus and the Hellenics—Literally translated by the Rev. H. Dale. London, 1891.

86. ————————Anabasis and Memorabilia—Translated by the Rev. J. S. Watson (L. H. B. No. 78). London, 1894.

87. ————————The whole works of—Translated by A. C. S. Smith, Fielding and others. Philadelphia, 1840.

88. ——————Anabasis or the Expedition of Cyrus and the Memorabilia of Socrates. Translated by the Rev. J. S. Watson. London, 1883.

89. ——————Memorabilia of Socrates. The first two books. With a Translation Edited by J. W. Underwood. London.

90. Young, A. W.—The Tutorial Greek Reader or Proœmia Græca (U. C. C. T. S.) London.

Dictionaries.

91. Liddell, H. G. and R. Scott—A Greek English Lexicon. Compiled by—Oxford, 1869.

92. ——————A Lexicon abridged from the Greek-English Lexicon. 12th Edition. Oxford, 1867.

93. Parkhurst, J.—A Greek and English Lexicon to the New Testament. London, 1822.

H.

Latin Language and Literature.

1. Abbott, Rev. E. A.—Latin Prose through English Idiom. London, 1878.
2. Allcroft, A. H. and J. H. Haydon—Latin Composition and Syntax. 3rd Edition. London (U. C. C. T. S.).
3. Arnold, Rev. T. K.—A Practical Introduction to Latin Prose Composition. Part I. London, 1864.
4. ————————The First Verse Book. 11th Edition. London, 1874.
5. Bennett, G. L.—Easy Latin Stories, with Vocabulary and Notes. New Edition. London, 1878.
6. Bland, Rev. R.—Elements of Latin Hexameters and Pentameters. London, 1858.
7. Bradley, W. W.—Lessons in Latin Prose. London, 1870.
8. Bryans, C.—Latin Prose Exercises based upon Cæsar's Gallic War. London, 1884.
9. Cæsar, C. J.—Commentaries on the Gallic War. With English Notes, &c by C. Anthon. London, 1869.
10. ————————————With English Notes by N. C. Brooks. 2nd Edition. Philadelphia, 1873.
11. ————————————Second Book. With a Vocabulary. Edited by J. T. White. London, 1875.
12. ————————————Sixth Book. With a Vocabulary. Edited by J. T. White. London, 1875.
13. ————————————Commentariorum I and II. With English Notes by A. G. Peskett (P. P. S). Cambridge, 1879.
14. ————————————Book I. With English Notes and argument by G. Long and Vocabulary by W. F. R. Shilleto. London, 1889.

15. ——————————The First Six Books with Analytical Interlineal Translation. By J. Hamilton. New Edition. London.

16. Cicero, M. T.—De Oratore Libri Tres, Ex Editione J. Aug. Ernesti Cum Notis Variorum. Edited by J. Greenwood. London, 1824.

17. ——————Select Orations of—With an English Commentary by C. Anthon. London, 1842.

18. ——————Cato Major. With Notes by G. Long. London, 1864.

19. ——————Select Letters. With Notes by C. E. Prichard and E. R. Bernard. Oxford, 1872.

20. ——————————Edited by the Rev. G. E. Jeans. London, 1882.

21. ——————The Letters of to Atticus, Book I. Edited by A. Pretor. Cambridge, 1873.

22. ——————The Orations against Cateline. With Notes by A. S. Wilkins. 3rd Edition. London, 1875.

23. ——————————With short English Notes. Oxford, 1890.

24. ——————The Philippic Orations. With English Notes by the Rev. J. R. King. 2nd Edition. Oxford (C. P. S.), 1878.

25. ——————Second Philippic. Edited by J. E. B. Mayor. 5th Edition. London, 1877.

26. ——————Pro. T. Annio Milone ad indices oratio. Edited by J. S. Reid (P. P. S.). Cambridge, 1894.

27. ——————Cato Major. Edited by G. Ferguson. Edinburgh.

28. ——————Pro Milone. Edited by F. G. Plaistowe and W. F. Masom (U. C. C. T. S.). London.

29. ——————Extracts from—with English Notes by H. Walford Part II. (C. P. S.). Oxford, 1869.

30. ——————Three Books of Offices or Moral Duties. Literally Translated with Notes, &c. by C. R. Edmonds. London, 1850.

31. ——————The four orations against Catiline. Literally translated by R. Mongan, London, 1886.

32. ——————Old Age and Friendship. Essays. Translated by W. Melmoth. London, (C.N.L.) 1889.

33. ——————Oratory and Orator with his Lectures to Quintus and Brutus. Translated and Edited by J. S. Watson. London, 1889.

34. ——————The Orations. Literally Translatad by C. D. Yonge. 4 vols. London, 1891-1894.

35. ——————The Offices. Translated by Cachman, and Cato & Laclius by Molmoh.

36. ——————A Collection of English Exercises translated from the writings of—By W. Ellis. London.

37. Cook. A. M.—Shorter Latin Course, First year. (Macmillan) London, 1989.

38. ——————Latin Course (Macmillan's) Second part London, 1899.

39. Elementary Latin Exercises.—Part I. on accidence. Bombay, 1879.

40. Ellis, A. J.—Quantitative Pronunciatiou of Latin. London, 1874.

41. Eutropius.—Epitome of the History of Rome. The first seven books with English notes and questions by Rev. C. Bradley. New Edition by Rev. J. T. White. London, 1860.

42. ——————Elementary—With notes &c., by W. Welch and C. G. Daffield. London, 1883.

43. ——————An Abridgement of the Roman History with analytical and interlineal Translation. By J. Hamilton. New Edition. London, 1828.

43. Gepp, C. G.—Pogressive Exercises in Latin Eligiac Verse. 4th Edition. London, 1877.

44. ——————Key to Progressive Exercises in Latin Elegiac Verse. London. 1871.

45. Gradatim.—An Easy Latin Translation Book for beginners by, H. R. Heatley and H. N. Kingdon. London, 1894.

46. Hall, T.—Translation at sight or aids to facility in the Translation of Latin. London, 1896.

47. Harkness, A —A Grammar of the Latin language. New York, 1879.

48. Hayes, B. J. and W. F. Masom—The Tutorial Latin Grammar. (U. C. C. T. S.) London.

49. Henry.—First Latin Rook. By the Rev. T. K. Arnold, London, 1886.

50. ————————New Edition. Revised and Edited by C. G. Gepp. London, 1889.

51. Hexameters and Pentameters.—New Edition by the Rev. G. C. Bowden. London, 1858,

52. Horace, Q. F.—The Epistles Book I. with notes by E. S. Shuckburgh. (P. P. S.), Cambridge, 1888.

53. ———Edited with notes by A. S. Wilkins. London, 1889.

54. ———Edited by F. G. Plaistowe and R. P. Shipham. (U.C. C.T.S.) London.

55. ———A Vcoabulary and test papers. (U. C. C. T. S.) London.

56. ————Odes. The first book, with a vocabulary, edited by J. T. White. London, 1871.

57. ————Book I. Edited by T. E. Page, London, 1884.

58. ————Opera Omnia with English Notes by the Rev. A. J. Macleane. London, 1867.

59. ————Poëmata. Edited by C. Anthon. London, 1886.

60. ————The Satires edited with introduction and notes. By F. G. Plaistowe and A. F. Burnet. (U. C. C. T. S.) London.

61. ————The Works. With a commentary by E. C. Wickham 2 vols. 2nd Edition (C. P. S.). Oxford 1877-1891.

62. ———With English notes by J. Currie and a biographical memoir, by the Rev. H. Thomson. London and Glassgow.

63. ———(The Globe Edition) rendered into English Prose by J. Lonsdale and S. Lee. London, 1887.

64. ———Translated literally by C. Smart, with notes by T. A. Buckley. London, 1888.

65. ———The odes and the Carmen Saeculare. Translated by the Rt. Hon. W. E. Gladstone. London, 1894.

66. ———The odes and Epodes. Translated by Lord Lytton (L H. B. No. 67.) London, 1894.

67. ———A translation by W. F. Masom. (U. C. C. T. S.) London.

68. ———Odes and Epodes. Construed literally and word for word. By the Rev. Dr. Giles. Part I. London.

69. ———The Satires, Epistles, &c. Construed with the Text into English word for word by the Rev. Dr. Giles, Part II. London.

70. Ince, J.—The Latin Grammar of Pharmacy. London, 1890.

71. Juvenal and Persius—The Satires. With English Notes, by C. Anthon. New Edition by J. T. Wheeler. London, 1858.

72. ———Edited by G. Long and Rev. A. J. Macleane. With a commentary by the latter. (Bib. Cl.) London, 1867.

73. ———With notes by the Rev. L. Evans. To which is added the metrical version of Juvenal and Persius by the late W. Gifford. London, 1869.

74. ———Thirteen Satires. With a commentary by J. E. B. Mayor. 2 vols. Second Edition. London, 1872-1878.

75. ——————————With notes by G. A. Simcox. Second Edition. London, 1873.

76. ——————————Sixteen. With English Notes by H. Prior. London, 1876.

77. Kennedy, B. H.—Palaestra Stili Latini or Materials for Translation into Latin Prose. New Edition. London, 1872.

78. ——————Curriculum Stili Latini or A Systematic Course of Examples for practice in the style of the best Latin Prose authors. New Edition. London, 1873.

79. ——————Second Latin Reading Book. London, 1850.

80. Latin Reader. Tutorial—A Graduated Series of Extracts for Practice in Translation at sight (U. C. C. T. S). London.

81. Latin Text—Middle School Examination, 1889. With notes, index &c., by G. Maddox. Madras, 1888.

82. Livy, T. P.—Historiarum, ab urbe condita Libri qui supersunt omnes. Ex. recensione Arn. Drakenborchii. Accident Notæ Integræ ExEditionibus. J. B. L. Crevierii Cum. Indice Rerum Locupletissimo. 4 vols.. Oxford, 1825.

83. ——————Books XXI and XXII. Hannibal's First Campaign in Italy. Edited with Notes by W. W. Capes. London, 1879.

84. ——————Book I. Edited with Notes, &c. by Rev. H. M. Stephenson. London, 1883.

85. ——————The Last 2 Kings of Macedon, being Extracts from 4th and 5th Decades of—Selected and Edited by F. H. Rawlins. London, 1886.

86. ——————Book III. Edited by W. F. Masom. (U. C. C. T. S). London, 1895.

87. ——————The first five books. With English Explanatory Notes and Examination Questions by D. B. Hickie.

88. ——————Selections from Books VIII and IX. With Notes and Map by E. Calvert and R. Saward. London, 1874.

89. ——————History of Rome. Literally Translated with Notes, &c., by D. Spillan, C. Edmonds, and W. A. M'Devitte. 4 vols. London, 1868-1888.

90. ——————Books I to V. Tacitus's Germania and Agricola. Literally translated by R. Mongan and W. Lewers (L. H. B. Nos. 83 & 84.) London, 1894.

91. ——————Books I to III. Literally Translated by a Graduate of the University. T. C. D. New Edition. By J. R. Mongan. Dublin.

92. London Undergraduate Unseens—Being all the passages for translation from books not prescribed, set at the Matriculation and Intermediate Arts Examinations of the University of London. Second Edition (U. C. C. T. S.). London.

93. Mackail, J. W.—Latin Literature. London, 1895.

94. Madvig, J. N.—A Latin Grammar. Translated from the Original German of—By the Rev. G. Woods. Oxford, 1878.

95. Nepos, J. C.—With Answered Questions and Imitative Exercises, Part I. By the Rev. T. K. Arnold. 5th Edition. London, 1866.

96. ——————With English Notes. By O. Browning (C. P. S.). Oxford, 1868.

97. ——————Edited by the Rev. C. Bradley. With notes by J. T. White. London, 1884.

98. ——————Published by J. Parker & Co. London.

99. ——————And Eutropius. Literally translated with notes by the Rev. J. S. Watson. London, 1886.

100. Ovid, P. Nasonis—Decerpta ex. Metamorphoseon Libris. With English Notes by G. Ferguson. 15th Edition Edinburgh, 1873.

101. ——————Stories from—With notes by R. D. Taylor. London, 1876.

102. ———A Selection from the Metamorphoses of—Literal and interlineal translation by J. Hamilton. London. 1829.

103. ———The Heroïdes or Epistles of the Heroines. The amours, art of love, remedy of love and minor works. Literally translated into English Prose with notes by H. T. Riley. London, 1869.

104. ———The Metamorphoses. Literally translated into English Prose with notes by H. T. Riley. London, 1870.

105. ———The Fasti, Tristia, Pontic Epistles, Ibis and Halieuticon. Literally translated into English Prose. With notes by H. T. Riley. London, 1872.

106. Papillon, T. L.—A Manual of Comparative Philology as applied to the illustration of Greek and Latin Inflections. 2nd Edition (C. P. S.) Oxford, 1877.

107. Phædrus.—Select Fables from—With English notes by the Rev. C. Bradley. A New Edition by the Rev. J. T. White. London, 1851.

108. ———Fables. Edited by the Rev. G. H. Nall, London, 1895.

109. Plautus—Comedies. Literally Translated into English Prose by H. T. Riley. Vol. I. London.

110. Potts, A. W.—Hints towards Latin Prose Composition. Third Edition. London, 1872.

111. Prendergast, T.—The Mastery Series. Sixth Edition. London, 1888.

112. Preparatory Course in Latin Prose Authors, comprising 4 books of Cæsar's Gallic War, Sallust's Catiline and 8 Orations of Cicero. With notes, illustrations, map of Gaul and a special Dictionary by A. Harkness New York, 1879.

113. Public School Latin Primer. Edited with the sanction of the Headmasters of the Public Schools included in Her Majesty's Commission. London, 1891.

114. Roby, H. J.—A Grammar of the Latin Language. 3rd Edition. Parts I and II. London, 1875-1876.

115 Sallust, C. C.—Opera Edited by C. Anthon. 7th Edition. London, 1836.

116. ———————Catilina et Jugurtha. With notes by G. Long. London, 1860.

117. ———————Catiline War. With a Vocabulary By J. T. White. London, 1875.

118. ———————de Bello Catilinario et jugurthino. London and Edinburgh, 1879.

119. ———————Jugurthine War. Construed with the Text into English, literally word for word, by Rev. Dr. Giles. London.

120. ———————Catilina. Literally translated by H. Owgan, London.

121. ——————— Opera Adapted to the Hamiltonian system by a literal and analytical translation. By J. Hamilton. New Edition. London.

122. Schultz, Dr. F.—Smaller Latin Grammar for High Schools. Bombay, 1882.

123. Simpson, F. P.—Latin Prose, after the best authors. Part I. Cæsarian Prose. London, 1885.

124. Smith, W.—A First Latin Course. Principia Latina. Part I. London, 1891.

125. ———————A First Latin Reading Book, Principia Latina. Part II. London, 1871.

126. ———————An Introduction to Latin Poetry. Principia Latina. Part III. 4th Edition. London, 1888.

127. ———————Short Tales and Ancedotes from Ancient History. For translation into Latin Prose. Principia Latina, Part V. Ninth Edition. London, 1885.

128. ———————and T. D. Hall. A Grammar of the Latin Language. 6th Edition. London, 1873.

129. ———————A Latin English Vocabulary. London, 1892.

130. Tacitus, C.—Historiæ. Opera Francisci Ritteri. London, 1848.

131. ——————Annals. Edited by G. Long. With a Commentary by the Rev. P. Frost. (Bib. Cl.). London, 1872.

132. ——————Über Syntax und Stil des. By Dr. A. Dræger. Leipzig, 1874.

133. ——————A. J. Church and W. J. Brodribb. (Classical Writers). London, 1882.

134. ——————Histories. Books I and II. With Notes by A. D. Godley. (C. S.). London, 1893.

135. —————— Histories. Book I. Edited by F. G. Plaistowe and H. J. Maidment. Text and Notes. (U. C. C. T. S.). London, 1894.

136. ——————Histories. Book I. A Vocabulary and Test Papers. (U. C. C. T. S.). London.

137. ——————Works. The Oxford Translation with Notes. Vol. I. The Annals. London, 1870.

138. ——————The History. Translated into English with Notes and a Map by A. J. Church and W. J. Brodribb. Third Edition. London, 1876.

139. ——————The Annals. Translated into English with Notes and a Map. By A. J. Church and W. J. Brodribb. London, 1879.

140. ——————Histories. Book I. A Close Translation by F. G. Plaistowe and H. J. Maidment. (U. C. C. T. S.). London.

141. Terence, P.—Carthaginiensis Afri Commœdiæ Sex. Edited by J. A. Giles. London, 1837.

142. ——————Comœdiæ Sex. With a Commentary by the Rev. E. St. J. Parry. London, 1857.

143. ——————Afri Andria. Edited by T. L. Papillon. New Edition. London, 1875.

144. ——————Comœdiæ. Edited by G. Wagner. London, 1878.

145. ——————Scenes from the Andria. Edited by F. W. Cornish London, 1883.

146. ———— A Literal Translation of the Andria. London, 1880.

147. ———— Comedies—and the Fables of Phædrus. Literally Translated into English Prose with Notes by H. T. Riley. To which is added a Metrical Translation of Phædrus by C. Smart. London, 1887.

148. ———— Trinummus, T. M. P. With Notes, Critical and Exegetical by W. Wagner. Second Edition. Cambridge, 1875.

149. Tozer, H. F.—Classical Geography. (Lit. Pr.) Edited by J. R. Green. New Edition. London, 1878.

150. Valpy—Latin Delectus. New Edition, with a Copious Vocabulary by A. H. Monteith. London.

151. Virgil, P. M.—Opera. Ex Editione Chr. G. Heyne. Edidit et suas animadversiones adjecit post curas E. C. F. Wunderlichii and F. E. Ruhkopf. 2 vols. London, 1826.

152. ———— Works. Edited by A. H. Bryce and a Biographical Memoir by Rev. H. Thompson. London.

153. ———— The Æneid. With English Notes by E. Anthon. A New Edition. London, 1868.

154. ———— ———— Book II. With a Vocabulary. Edited by J. T. White. London, 1871.

155. ———— ———— Book VI. With a Vocabulary. Edited by J. T. White. London, 1873.

156. ———— ———— Book IV. With a Vocabulary. Edited by J. T. White. London, 1875.

157. ———— Opera. With Notes by S. L. Papillon. 2 vols. (C. P. S.). Oxford, 1882. Large Paper Edition.

158. ———— Æneid. Book I. Edited by A. S. Walpole. London, 1882.

159. ———— ———— Book I. With English Notes and Argument by the Rev. J. G. Sheppard. With Vocabulary by W. F. R. Shilleto. London, 1889.

160. ——————Georgics. Books I and II. Edited by A. W. Young and W. F. Masom (U. C. C. T. S.), London.

161. ——————Abridged Ænied. Edited by Conington. Books V to XII.

162. ——————Ænied. Book VI. Edited with Introduction and Notes by A. H. Allcroft, and B. J. Hayes. (U. C. C. T. S.). London.

163. ——————Ænied. Book VII. Edited with Introduction Notes &c., by A. H. Allcroft and T. M. Neatby (U. C. C. T. S.). London.

164. ——————Works. Translated into English Prose with Explanatory Notes. Vol. II. Oxford, 1826.

165. ————————————Rendered into English Prose by J. Lonsdale and S. Lee. The Globe Edition. London, 1887.

166. ——————Ænied. Translated by J. Dryden (L. H. B. No. 13). London, 1891.

167. ——————The whole works. Construed literally and word for word. Vol. III. Ænied, Books V—VIII. By the Rev. Dr. Giles. London.

168. ——————Bucolics and Georgics. Construed with the Text into English, literally and word for word. By the Rev. Dr. Giles. London.

169. Welch, W. and C. G. Duffield—Exercises in Unseen Translation in Latin. London, 1893.

170. Wilkins, A. S.—Roman Antiquities. (His. Pr). London, 1891.

171. ——————Roman Literature (Lit. Pr.) London, 1891.

172. ————H. M.—Easy Latin Prose Exercises Sixth Edition. London, 1872.

173. ——————Key to the Latin Prose Exercises. London, 1877.

174. Zumpt, C. G.—A Grammar of the Latin Language. Translated by L. Schmitz. London, 1845.

Dictionaries.

175. Boetticher, G.—Lexicon Taciteum. Berlin, 1830.

176. Cassell's Latin Dictionary—Latin-English and English-Latin. Revised by J. R. V. Marchant and J. F. Charles London, 1893.

177. Dictionary of Quotations—From the Greek, Latin and Modern Languages. Translated into English. London, 1861.

178. Entick.—English-Latin Dictionary. To which is added a Latin-English Dictionary. To which has been annexed an Etymological Paradigm by D. Crakelt. Revised by the Rev. M. G. Sarjant. New Edition. By J. Carey. London, 1836.

179. Henderson, A.—Latin Proverbs and Quotations, with translations, parallel passages and a copious English Index. London, 1869.

180. King, W. F. H.—Classical and Foreign Quotations. London, 1889.

181. Krebs, Dr. J. Ph.—Anti Barbarus der Lateinischen Sprache. Frankfurt, 1866.

182. Lempriere.—Classsical Dictionary of Proper Names. Corrected and enlarged. By Prof. Anthon and E. H. Barker. London.

183. Ramage, C. T.—Beautiful Thoughts from Latin authors with English translations. London, 1884.

184. Riley, H. T.—Dictionary of Latin Quotations, Proverbs. Maxims and Mottos, classical and mediaeval, including law terms and phrases, with a selection of Greek quotations. Edited by———. London, 1860.

185. Smith, W.—A Smaller Latin-English Dictionary. London, 1872.

186. —————A Smaller English-Latin. Dictionary Twelfth Edition. London, 1886

I.

Italian and Spanish Languages and Literature.

1. Alfieri, Vittorio.—Oreste. Tragedia in Cinque Atti. With Notes and a Vocabulary. By Rev. A. C. Clapin. (Bib. It. No. I.) London, 1890.
2. Alighieri Dante.—Tutte Le Opere. Nuovamente Rivedute Nel Testo Da. Dr. E. Moore. Oxford, 1894.
3. Amicis, Edmondo de.—Gli Amici di Collegio. Una Medaglia. Due Novelle. With Notes and a Vocabulary, by Rev. A. C. Clapin. (Bib. It. No. IX.) London.
4. Carcano, Giulio.—La Madre E Il Figlio. Novelle. With Notes and a Vocabulary. By Rev. A. C. Clapin. (Bib. It. No. II.) London.
5. ——————Memorie D'un Fanciullo. Il Cappellano Della Rovella. Novelle. With Notes and a Vocabulary by Rev. A. C. Clapin. (Bib. It. No. III.) London.
6. Castelnuovo, Enrico.—Novelle. With Notes and a Vocabulary by Rev. A. C. Clapin. (Bib. It. No. VIII.) London.
7. Cervantes, Miguel de-Saavedra.—El Ingenioso Hidalgo Don Quixote de la Mancha. A New Edition. London, 1876.
8. Filippi, P. A. de.—First Italian Course. A new practical and easy method of learning the Italian Language after the system of F. Ahn. Adopted from the Text of. By A. H. Monteith and revised by N. Bottone. London, 1887.
9. Goldoni, Carlo.—Il Burbero Benefico. Commedia. With Notes and a Vocabulary by Rev. A. C. Clapin. (Bib. It. No. IV.) London.
10. ——————Un Curioso accidente. Commedia in Tre Atti. With Notes and a Vocabulary by Rev. A. C. Clapin. (Bib. It. No. V.) London, 1890.

11. ——————Il Vero Amico. Commedia Tre Atti in Prosa. With Notes and a Vocabulary by Rev. A. C. Clapin. (Bib. It. No. VI.) London, 1890.

12. Guastavino, Pietro.—Verse Roma. Genova, 1893.

13. Gurrin, T. E.—Spanish Grammar. Hossfeld's New Practical Method for Learning the Spanish Language. 3rd Edition. London, 1896.

14. ——————Key to above. 3rd and Revised Edition. London, 1892.

15. Hossfeld—New Spanish Reader. With explanatory footnotes by T. E. Gurrin. London.

16. Italian Principia. Parts I and II on the plan of Dr. William Smith's Principia Latina. 4th Edition. London, 1883-1890.

17. Lemmi, E—A Theoretical and Practical Italian Grammar. 11th Edition. Edinburgh, 1874.

18. ————Key to Italian Grammar. New Edition. Edinburgh.

19. Lesage—Historia De Gil Blas, De Santillana, Traducida Al Castellano, por El Padre Isla. London.

20. Machiavelli, Niccolo.—Opere. Cittadino E Segretario Florentino. 10 vols. Italia, 1826.

21. Maffei, Scipione—Merope. Tragedia. With Notes and a Vocabulary by Rev. A. C. Clapin. (Bib. It. No. VII). London, 1890.

22. Manzoni, Alessandro.—I promessi Sposi. Firenze, 1845.

23. —————— ——————Adapted by Rev. A. C. Clapin. London, 1892.

24. Motti, Peitro—Elementary Italian Grammar for Beginners. London, 1894.

25. Ollendorff, H. G.—A Key to the Exercises in the New Method of Learning to read, write and speak a Language in six months. Adapted to the Italian. London, 1861.

26. Parato, Antonino.—Il Libro Dei Fancinlli Proposto Alle Scoule Primarie D' Italia. Rome, 1885.

27. ——————Il Primo Libro Dei Fanciulletti Ossia Prime Letture. Rome, 1886.

28. Parini, Giuseppe.—Opera. Published by F. Reina. 6 vols. Milano, 1801-1804.

29. Pellico, Silvio—Le Mie Prigioni Memorii. London, 1887.

30. —————— ——————with notes by Rev. A. C. Clapin. New Edition. London.

31. ——————My ten years' imprisonment. Translated from the Italian by Thomas Roscoe. London, 1886.

32. ——————Spanish Conversation Grammar. 3rd Edition.

33. Prendergast, Thomas. The Mastery Series (Spanish). 7th Edition. London, 1882.

34. Rota, A.—Italian Grammar. Hossfeld's New Method for Learning the Italian Language. London.

35. Sanderson, E.—L' Italien Sans Professeur en 50 lessons. Paris.

36. Sauer, Charles Marguard.—Italian Conversation Grammar. 4th Edition. Heidelberg, 1879.

37. ——————Key to above. 4th Edition. London, 1887.

38. ——————and G. C. Kordgien. Portugiesische Konversations-Grammatik. Heidelberg, 1887.

39. ——————and G. C. Cordjan. Schlüssel Zur Portugiesischen Konversations.—Grammatik. Heidelberg, 1887.

40. ——————Spanish Conversation Grammar. 3rd Edition. Heidelberg, 1880.

41. ——————Key to the above 2nd Edition. Heidelberg, 1880.

42. Scavia, Giovanni.—Italian Grammar. Nozioni di Grammatica Italiana. Torino.

43. Tornes, Alberto de.—The Combined Spanish Method. A New Practical and Theoretical System of Learning the Castilian Language. With a Vocabulary. New York, 1876.

Dictionaries.

44. Falzon, G. Battista.—Dizionario Maltese, Italiano, Inglese. 1845.

45. Meadows, F. C.—New Italian and English Dictionary. 5th Edition. London, 1840.

46. Melzi, B.—A New English-Italian and Italian-English Dictionary, 2 parts. London, 1895.

47. Mungica, P. de.—Spanish Pocket Vocabulary. Compiled by—Berlin, 1896.

48. Nuova Guida alla Conversazione Italiana, Inglese, Maltese, ad uso Delle Scuole. 2nd Part. Malta, 1879.

49. Vecchio, di Bologne, D. F. de—Italian Pocket Vocabulary, Compiled by—Berlin, 1890.

50. Velazquez de la Cadena, M.—A Dictionary of the Spanish and English Languages. 2 parts. Spanish-English and English-Spanish. London.

J.

Russian Language and Literature.

1. Alexandrow, F.—Russian Grammar. London, 1884.
2. Freeth, F.—A Condensed Russian Grammar. London, 1886.
3. Fuchs, P.—Methode Ollendorff Grammaire Russe. Second Edition. Francfort, 1874.
4. ————Methode Ollendorff. de la Grammaire Russe. Second Edition. 1874.
5. Ivánoff, A.—Russian Grammar. Translated by W. E. Gowan. London, 1882.
6. Jaffer, Mirza G.—Russian and Persian Idioms. 1883.
7. Kinlock, A.—Russian Conversation Grammar. With Vocabulary. London, 1890.
8. Motti, Proff. P.—The Russian Conversation Grammar. London, 1890.
9. ————Key to the above. London, 1890.
10. Manassowitsch, B and Dr. D. Fischer—Russische National Bibliothek. Leipzig, 1881.
11. New Testament in the Russian Language. 1869.
12. Reiff, Ch. Ph.—English-Russian Grammar. London, 1883.
13. Riola, H.—Graduated Russian Reader. With a Vocabulary London, 1879.
14. Russian Chrestomathie.
15. Russian Reader. Prag, 1874.
16. School History of Russia—St. Petersburg, 1877.
17. Tseytline, B.—Le Progress et L'Instruction Publique En Russi. Paris, 1890 (in French).

Dictionaries.

18. Alexandrow—English-Russian and Russian-English Dictionary. 2 vols. 1879 and 1885.
19. English and Russian Languages—A New Pocket Dictionary. Leipzig, 1884.
20. Tauchnitz, K.—English and Russian Dictionary. Leipsig, 1884.

K.

German Language and Literature.

1. Ahn, F.—A new practical and easy method of learning the German Language. Third Course.; Third Edition. Leipzig, 1861.
2. Allgemeine Berggesetz, Das—Berlin, 1866.
3. Arabian Nights Entertainments in the German Language—By Boffman. Stuttgart, 1862.
4. Aue, Carl Edward.—Elementary German Grammar. London, 1877.
5. ——————Grammar of the German Language with Exercises. London, 1878.
6. Baumgart, Dr. Max—Grundsätze und Bedingungen-der Ertbeilung der Doctorwürde. Berlin, 1885.
7. Bodenstedt, Frederich—Die Lieder Des Mirza Schaffy. Berlin, 1890.
8. Bologna Dr. F. del Vecchio Di—Kleines Vokabelbuch. Berlin, 1890.
9. Bopfen, B.—Der Genius und sein Erbe. Stuttgart, 1887.
10. Bremer, Frederiche.—Das Hans. Leipzig, 1864.
11. Bülow, F. F.—Am andern Ende der Welt. Berlin.
12. Bunkin Chandra—Kopal. Kundala Deutsch. Von Carl Klemm. Leipzig, 1886.
13. Caffian, Dr. H.—Handbuch der Allgemeinen Weltgeschichte. Frankfurt am Main, 1866.
14. Camer, Armin—Vor fünf Generationen. Berlin, 1890.
15. Chamisso. Peter Schlemihls Wundersame Geschichte—Edited by Emma. S. Buchheim. Oxford, 1889.
16. Daudet, Alphonse.—Der Alte Zuave. Berlin.
17. Deutsche Lyrik—Selected and Arranged with Notes and a literary introduction by C. A. Buchheim. Third Revised Edition. London, 1881.
18. Ebers, George.—Die Frau Burgemeisterin. Leipzig, 1882.

19. Engelhorn—Allgemeine Roman-Bibliothek. Das Tagebuch-Einer Frau. Stuttgart, 1887.

20. Fasnacht, Eugene.—Macmillan's Course of German Composition. First Course. London, 1893.

21. Firdosi—Königsbuch (Schah name). Ubersetzt von. F. Rückert. Berlin, 1890.

22. Fischer-Fixbrat, Charles—A German class book for beginners, being a series of German stories. Edinburgh, 1872.

23. Fouqué, Baron de-la Motte—The German Prose Reader. A Tale No. 1. Undine. With a Translation of all difficult words and phrases. By D. K. Klattowsky. London, 1834.

24. Freunden, Seinen—Festgrüss an Otto von Böhtlingk. Zum Doctor Jubiläum. Stutttgart, 1888.

25. Geibel, Emanuel—Gedichte. Stuttgart, 1867.

26. Geiger, Ibraham—Divan des Castiliers Abdul Hussan Indaba Levi. Breslau, 1851.

27. German Classics—Vol. I. Goethe's Egmont. A Tragedy. By C. A. Buchheim (C. P. S.) Oxford, 1869.

28. ——————Vol. III. Lessing's Minna von Barnhelm. A Comedy. Edited with Notes by C. A. Buchheim. (C. P. S). Oxford, 1873.

29. ——————Vol IV. Historiche Skizzen Egmont's leben undtod. Belagerung von Antwerpen. von Schiller. Edited with Notes &c., by C. A. Buchheim. (C. P. S.) Oxford, 1891.

30. ——————Edited with Notes &c., by C. A. Buchheim. Vol. IX. Becker's Friedrich der Grosse—(C. P. S.) Oxford, 1888.

31. ——————Lessing's Laokoon. Edited with Notes, &c. by A. Hamann. (C. P. S.) Oxford, 1878.

32. ——————Schiller's Wilhelm Tell. By C. A. Buchheim. 2 vols. Oxford, 1877.

33. ———Historical Anthology, being a sequel to the German Reader. Edited by A. Bernays. 2nd Edition Revised. London, 1846.

34. ——Plays—Modern. Edited with Notes and Vocabulary by Dr. A. Buchheim. Part I. Fourth Edition. London, 1871.

35. ——Poetry—A Thesaurus of—Consisting of 450 select pieces by the most celebrated authors. By C. Graeser. London, 1860.

36. ————Translated into English Verse. By Dr. A. Baskerville. Fourth Edition. Hamburg, 1876.

37. ——Prose Composition—Materials for—or Selections from Modern English writers with notes, &c. By C. A. Buchheim. Fifth Edition Revised. London, 1878.

38. ————Writers—A Selection from.—With a double translation for the use of students on the Hamiltonian System. London, 1828.

39. ——Reading Book. Selections in prose and poetry from best authors.

40. ——————A First. German Principia. Part II, on the plan of Dr. W. Smith's 'Principia Latina.' Third Edition. London, 1884.

41. ——Reader—The Modern. A graduated collection of extracts in Prose and Poetry from Modern German writers. Edited by C. A. Buchheim. Part II. (C. P. S.) Oxford, 1885.

42. ——Songs—The Book of. Translated and Edited by H. D. Dulcken. London, 1856.

43. ————and Ballads—Diprose's Selection. Translated from the best authors. London.

44. ——Writers—Easy Selections from. Hanover, 1854.

45. Gilmar, A. and Richter A—Two German Epic tales in prose. Edited with introduction and notes by C. Neuhaus. London, 1888.

46. Goethe, T. W—Aus Meinem Leben. 2 vols. Stuttgart, 1853.

47. ————Boyhood. 1749-1759. Being the 1st 3 books of his autobiography arranged and annotated by W. Wagner (P. P. S.) Cambridge, 1880.

48. ——————The boyhood and youth, being books I to XI of the Autobiography. Translated from the German by John Oxenford. 2 vols. New York.

49. ——————Faust, First part. Translated by J. Anster. The Henry Irving Edition. London, 1887.

50. ——————The Spirit of—By W. C. Coupland. London, 1885.

51. ——————Gedichte. Berlin, 1875.

52. ——————Hermann and Dorothia. Berlin, 1868.

53. ——————Italianische Reise. 2 vols. Stuttgart, 1862.

54. —————— ——————With notes and Vocabulary by Dr. A. Buchheim. London, 1876.

55. ——————Leiden Des Jungen Werthers. Berlin, 1873.

56. —————— —————— Stuttgart, 1874.

57. —————— —————— Leipsig.

58. ——————Die Mitschuldigen. Leipsig, 1787.

59. ——————Reineke Fuchs. Berlin, 1870.

60. ——————The Poems. Translated into the Original Metres. By E. A. Bowring. Second Edition Revised. London, 1881.

61. ——————The Sorrows of Werther. Edited by Prof. H. Morley. (C. N. L.) London, 1886.

62. Goldsmith, Oliver.—Der Landprediger von Wakefield. Leipsig.

63. Gostwick, J. and R. Harrison—Outlines of German Literature. London, 1873.

64. Gribble, J. D. B—Borrowed Plumes. Translations from German Poets. London, 1887.

65. Gutzkow, Karl.—Zopf and Schwert. Lustspiel in Fünf Aufzügen. With a Biographical and Historical Introdution. By H. J. Wolstenholme. (P. P. S.) Cambridge. 1887.

66. Hauff, W—Das Wirthshaus im Spessart. Edited with notes by A. Schlottman (P. P. S.) Cambridge, 1895.

67. Heimann, A—Materials for translating from English into German. Fourth Edition. London, 1871.

68 Heine, Heinrich.—Buch Der Lieder. Hamburg, 1885.

69. ——————— Werke. 6 vols. Illustrated Edition. Paris and Hamburg, 1844—1853.

70. ———————The Works of Florentine Nights and Shakespeare's Maidens and Women. Translated from the German. By C. G. Leland. Vol. I. London, 1891.

71. Hense, Dr. T. S. M—Lietfaden zum gründlichen Unterricht in der Deutschen Sprache. Hanover, 1863.

72. Horn, Karl.—Die Sozialisten. The Bread Winners. Stuttgart, 1885.

73. Hossmann, S. Z. M—Meister Martin. Leipzig.

74. Hulfe in der Noth, oder der ostindienfahrer.

75. Kotzebue, A—Pagenstreiche. Leipsig.

76. Körner, Theodor—Sämmtliche Werke. Berlin, 1869.

77. Kortum, Dr. Carl Ænold—Die Jobsiade komisches Heldengedicht. Leipzig, 1868.

78. Krasjemski, J. J.—Ein Heroisches Weib. Stuttgart, 1885.

79. Kummel, M.—Die Eroberung Constantinoples durch die Türken.

80. Lange, H.—The Germans at Home. Third Edition. (C. P. S). 1887.

81. —————The German Composition. (C. P. S.). Third Edition. Oxford, 1891.

82. —————The German Grammar. (C. P. S.). Oxford, 1876.

83. —————The German Manual. (C. P. S.). Oxford, 1884.

84. Lennis, Johannes —Schul-Naturgeschichte. Hanover, 1856.

85. Le Sage—Geschichte des Gil Blas. Leipzig.

86. Lessing und Gellert—Fabeln und Erzählungen. With an Introduction, English Notes, &c. By Karl Breul. (P. P. S.). Cambridge, 1887.

87. —————Nathan the Wise—Translated into English Verse. by E. K. Corbett. London, 1883.

88. ——————————Translated by W. Taylor. (C. N. L.). London, 1886.

89. —————Plays. Nathan the Wise and Minna von Barnheln. Translated into English, by E. Bell. London, 1888.

90. Lester, Rev. J. D.—German Accidence.
91. Lewald, Fanny.—Adele. Berlin, 1864.
92. Licht and Schatten—Halle. 1858.
93. Meissner, A. L.—The Children's Own German Book. London, 1876.
94. Mendelssohn Bartholdy, F.—Briefe. Selected and Edited with Introduction and Notes by J. Sime. (P. P. S.). Cambridge, 1887.
95. Mugica, Lic, P. de—Kleines Vokabelbuch. Berlin, 1890.
96. Müller—Kleiner Briefftteller. By M. Mechs. Regensberg, 1872.
97. Niebuhr—Heroen Geschichten. With Notes, Vocabulary, &c. by Dr. A. Buchheim. London, 1877.
98. Otto, Dr. Emil—The German Conversation Grammar. Heidelberg, 1877.
99. ——————Key to the above. 7th Edition. London, 1866.
100. ——————The German Reader. Part I. 3rd Edition. Heidelberg, 1876.
101. —————— Materials for Translating English into German. Heidelberg, 1874.
102. Peterson—Prinzessin Ilse von Marie. Leipzig.
103. Petraris, K.—Neugriechische Konversations-Grammatik. Heidelberg, 1895.
104. ——————Schlüssel. Konversations. Grammatik. Heidelberg, 1896.
105. Riehl, W. H.—Culturgeschichtliche Novellen. With Notes, &c. by H. J. Wolstenholme. Cambridge, 1884.
106. Schiller,——Marie Stuart. Leipzig.
107. ——————Der Neffe als Onkel. ("The Nephew his own Uncle"). Annotated by L. Dyer. London, 1895.
108. ——————Prose, consisting of Selections from Schiller's Prose Works. With an Introduction and English Notes by C. A. Buchheim. London, 1875.
109. ——————Wallenstein. Stuttgart, 1874.
110. ——————Werke. Von T. C. Fischer. 4 vols. Illustrated Edition. Stuttgart, 1877.

111. ———— Wilhelm Tell. Edited By C. A. Buchheim. Oxford, 1884.

112. ———— ————von H. Dünker. Leipzig, 1887.

113. ———— ————Leipzig.

114. ————and Horace—Translated by the Rt. Hon. Lord Lytton. The Knebworth Edition. London, 1875.

115. ————Poems and Ballads Translated by Edward Lord Lytton. With Introduction by H. Morley. London, 1887.

116. Schmid, Ch.—Heinrich Von Eichenfels. With Notes, Vocabulary, &c., by G. E. Fasnacht. London, 1889.

117. ————Tales. The Dove and Henry of Eichenfels. With English Vocabulary by T. Matthay. London, 1864.

118. ————one Hundred German Tales. By H. Mathias. Seventh Edition. London, 1874.

119. Schopenhauer, A.—The Art of Literature. A Series of Essays. Selected and Translated by T. Bailey Saunders. London, 1897.

120. ————Counsels and Maxims. Translated by T. Bailey Saunders. London, 1897.

121. ————Religion. A Dialogue and other Essays. Selected and Translated by T. Bailey Saunders. London, 1893.

122. ————Studies in Pessimism. A Series of Essays. Selected and Translated by T. Bailey Saunders. London, 1-98.

123. ————The Wisdom of Life. Translated with a preface. By T. Bailey Saunders. London, 1897.

124. ————Works (complete) 12 volumes. With Introduction by Dr. Rudolf Steiner. Stuttgart.

125. Song of the Bell and other translations from Schiller, Goethe, Uhland and others—By Sir. Th. Martin. London, 1889.

126. Swan, H.—Traveller's Colloquial German. London, 1891.

127. Stacke, Dr. Ludwig—Erzählungen aus der Gefehichte des Mittelalters. Oldenburg, 1872.

128. Uhland—Ballad and Romances, Selections from. With notes &c. by G. E. Fasnacht. London, 1882.

129. Viehoff—Handbuch der Deutschen National Literatur. Braunschweig, 1877.

130. Vilmar, A. E.—Literatur Geschichte. 2 parts. Marburg, 1857.

131. Virchow, R.—Die Freiheit der Wissenschaft im Modernen Staat Rede. Berlin, 1877.

132. Weigand, Wilhelm—Im Exil. Leipzig, 1890.

133. Weikenfels, S.—Captain Bonaparte. Berlin, 1869.

134. Weisse, Heinrich—Complete Practical Grammar of the German Language. London, 1872.

135. Wirth, L. E.—The German Chit Chat. London, 1873.

Dictionaries.

136. Brochhaus—Conversations Lexicon Allgemeine Deutche Real Encyklopädie. 16 vols. and a supplement in 1 vol. Leipzig, 1882-87.

137. Flugel, Schmidt. Tanger—German-English and English-German Dictionary. 2 vols. Brunswick, 1896.

138. Grieb, Chr. Fr.—Dictionary of the English and German Languages. Vols. 2, English and German and German and English. 7th Edition. Stuttgart, 1873.

139. Kaltschmidt, Dr. J. H. Fremdwörterbuch. French and German. Leipsig, 1876.

140. Weir. Elizabeth.—Cassell's New German Dictionary. 2 parts. German-English and English-German. London, 1889.

141. Whitney—German Dictionary.

142. Williams, Frank—German Dictionary. 2 parts. English-German and German-English. London.

L.

French Language and Literature.

1. About, Edmond—French Reader Vol. I. Hachette's series. Edited by P. H. E. Brette and G. Masson. Second Edition. Paris, 1874.

2. Achard, Amédée—Récits d'Un Soldat. Paris, 1871.

3. Augier, Emile—La Ciguë. Edited by A. W. Kastan. (Th. Fr. No. 91). Berlin, 1879.

4. ——————Gabrielle. Edited by A. W. Kastan. Second Edition (Th. Fr. No. 100). Berlin, 1884.

5. ——————and J. Sandeau—Le Gendre de M. Poirier. Edited by Henri Guerrin. 5th Edition (Th. Fr. No. 58). Berlin, 1888.

6-7. ——————La Pierre De Touche. Edited by A. W. Kastan. 2nd Edition (Th. Fr. No. 72.) Berlin, 1884.

8. Banville, Th. De—Gringoire. Edited by A. W. Kastan (Th. Fr. No. 68). Berlin, 1879.

9. Bardoux, A.—Guizot—(L. G. E. F.) Paris, 1894.

10. Barine, Arvéde—Alfred de Musset. (L. G. E. F.) Paris, 1893.

11. ——————Bernardin de Saint-Pierre. (L. G. E. F.) Paris, 1891.

12. Bayard—La Reine de Seize Ans. Edited by Dr. E. Kurtz. (Th. Fr. No. 31). Berlin, 1889.

13. ——————And De Vailly—Le Mari Laà. Campagne. Edited by G. V. Muyden. (Th. Fr. No. 35.) Berlin, 1878.

14. ——————And Sauvage. Le Gant et L'Eventail. Edited by A. W. Kastan. (Th. Fr. No. 113). Berlin, 1883.

15. ——————And Vanderburgh. Le Gamin de Paris. Edited by G. V. Muyden. (Th. Fr. No. 47). Berlin, 1680.

16. ——————————Un Premier Amour. Edited by A. W. Kastan. (Th. Fr. No. 76). Berlin, 1879.

17. Beaumarchais—Le Barbier De Séville. Edited by A. W. Kastan. (Th. Fr. No. 36). Berlin, 1883.

18. —————— ——————Edited by Austin Dobson. (C. P. S.) Oxford, 1884.

19. ——————Le Mariage De Figaro. Edited by A. W. Kastan. (Th. Fr. No. 106). Berlin, 1884.

20. Belfond, J.—Histories Choisies. Extraitos De Nos Meilleurs Ecrivans Contemporains. First and Second Series, 2 vols. Second Edition. London, 1891-1892.

21. Bell, Mrs. Hugh—Théatre de la Jeunesse or 12 little French Plays. London, 18·9.

22. Belot, A and E. Villetard—Le Testament de César Girodot. Edited by A. W. Kastan. (Th. Fr. No. 59). Berlin, 1878.

23. Bertrand, Joseph—D' Alembert, (L. G. E. F.) Paris, 1889.

24. Betis, Victor and H. Swan—Psychological method of teaching and studying languages. Class room conversation in French. London, 1896.

25. Blum, Carl—Theatre. Berlin, 1839.

26. Boccace—Contes de—par A Sulatier de Castres. New Edition, Paris.

27. Boissier, Gaston—Madame de Sévigné. (L G. E. F.) Paris, 1887.

28. ——————Saint-Simon. (L. G. E. F.) Paris, 1892.

29. Boucicaut, Aristide—Souvenir of the Bon Marché. Founded by—Plan of Paris and the Exhibition of 1889.

30. Bougeault, A.—Précis Historique et Chronologique de la Litterature Française. Paris, 1886.

31. Bouilly, M. J. N.—L' Abbé De L'épée. Edited by H. Guerin. (Th. Fr. No. 6.) Berlin. 1885.

33. Brachet, A.—Historical Grammar of the French Language. Translated by G. W. Kitchin. (C. P. S.) Fourth Edition. Oxford, 1877.

34. Brette and Masson—The Public School French Grammar. Part I. London, 1890.

35. Breymann, Hermann—French Grammar based on Philological Principles. Second Edition. London, 1874.

36. Broglie, Le Duc De—Malherbe. (L. G. E. F). Paris, 1897.

37. Bue, Henri—The First Steps in French Idioms. Second Edition Revised. London, 1882.

38. ——, Jules—Exercises Sur les formes idiomatiques comparees. 9th Edition. Boston, 1894.

39. Camp, Maxime du—Théophile Gautier. (L. G. E. F.). Paris, 1890.

40. Caro, E.—George Sand. (L. G. E. F). Paris, 1887.

41. Cassal, Ch. and K. Karcher—The Graduated Course of Translation from English into French. The Junior Course. Edited hy—London, 1877.

42. César, J.—Commentires de La Guerre Des Gaules. (Bib. na). Paris.

43. ——————Histoire des Paris, 1865.

44. Charente, A. A. De—Course of Studies of the French Language. 3 vols. London, 1866-1868.

45. Charnace, Guy de—Vaincu. Paris, 1887.

46. Chateaubriand, De—Atala René Les Abencerages. Paris, 1867.

47. Chuquet, Arthur—J. J. Rousseau. (L. G. E. F.). Paris, 1893.

48. Clédat, Léon. Rutebeuf (L. G. E. F.). Paris, 1891.

49. Colomb, L. C.—Le Caniche Blanc. (H. I. F. P. R.). London.

50. ————Mme.—Les Aventures de Trottino, Edited by L. Gaborit. (H. I. F. P. R.). London.

51. ————J.—Entre Oiseaux. Edited by H. A. De Joauries. (H. I. F, P. R.). London.

52. Condorcet—Vie de Voltaire Paris, 1875.

53. Corneille, P.—Cinna. Edited by G. V. Muyden, (Th. Fr. No. 65). Berlin, 1879.

54. ———————Horace. Edited by Dr. E. Kurtz. (Th. Fr. No. 16). Berlin, 1890.

55. ———————Le Cid. Edited by Dr. E. Kurtz. (Th. Fr. No. 25). Berlin, 1889.

56. ———————Le Menteur. Edited by G. V. Muyden. (Th. Fr. No. 73). Berlin, 1879.

57. ———————Polyeucte. Edited by G. V. Muyden. (Th. Fr. No. 67). Berlin, 1885.

58. ———————Rodogune. Edited by A. W. Kastan. (Th. Fr. No. 92). Berlin, 1879.

59. ———————Theatre de Pierre et de Thomas. 2 vols. Paris, 1850.

60. Couvray, Louvet De—Les Amours du Chevalier de Faublas. New Edition. 2 Vols. Paris.

61. Croix, Petis, De la—Les Mille et Un Jours. New Edition. Paris.

62. Darmesteter, James—Lettres Sur L'Inde. A la Frontiere Afghane. Paris, 1888.

63. ———————Nouvelles Etudes Anglaises. Paris, 1896.

64. ———————, Mary—Foissart. (L. G. E. F.). Paris, 1894.

65. Daru, M.—Par M. C. A. Sainte-Beuve, with Notes by G. Masson, Cambridge, 1878.

66. Daudet, Alphonse—Les Femmes D'Artistes. Paris, 1896.

67. Delavigne, Casimir—L'Ecole des Vieillards—Edited by C. Ansore. (Th. Fr. No. 13). Berlin, 1878.

68. ———————Les Enfants D'Edouard Edited by C. Ansore. (Th. Fr. No. 20). Berlin, 1885.

69. ———————Louis XI. Edited by Dr. E. Kurtz. (Th. Fr. No. 34). Berlin, 1889.

70. Delille, J.—Les Jardins Poëme. Paris, 1822.

71. Descartes, R.—Discourse De La Méthode. Paris, 1877.

72. ——————— ———————With Introduction and Notes by T. V. Charpentier. (L. H. B. No. 82.) London, 1894.

73. Deschamps, Gaston—Marivaux. (L. G. E. F.). Paris, 1897.

~~92. Bourdeau, J. La Rochefoucauld. (L. G. E. F.) Paris, 1895.~~

74. Dumas, A.—Halifax. Edited by A. W. Kastan. (Th. Fr. No. 98). Berlin, 1880.

75. ————Swiss Travel. Passages from———Impressions De Voyage. Edited by C. H. Parry. London, 1890.

76. Etienne, C. G.—La Jeune Femme Colère. Edited by G. V. Muyden. Berlin, 1882.

77. Eugéne, G.—Comparative French English Studies. Grammatical and Idiomatic. London, 1876.

78. Eugéne-Fasnacht—Macmillan's Course of French Composition. First Course. London, 1888.

79. ————Macmillan's Progressive French Course. II. Second year. Containing an Elementary Grammar, &c. London, 1889.

80. Faguet, Emile—Flaubert. (L. G. E. F.). Pȧris, 1899.

81. Fasquelle, Louis—Lessons in French. Enlarged by Pro. E. Roubaud. Part II. London.

82. Feuillet, O.—Le Roman D'Un Jeune Homme Pauvre. Edited by A. W. Kaston. (Th. Fr. No. 115). Berlin. 1889.

83. ————Le Village. Edited by A. W. Kastan. (Th. Fr. No. 101). Berlin, 1886.

84. Fénélon, M.—Les Aventures De Télémaque. Edited by M. V, Wanostrocht. London.

85. ————Lettre a l'Academie Francaise. Edited by M. L. Feugere. Paris.

86. Filon, Augustin—Merimée. (L. G. E. F.). Paris.

87. Fouillée, Alfred—Descartes. (L. G. E. F.). Paris, 1893.

88. French Principia—Part I. A First French Course. Containing Grammar, Delectus and Exercise Book, with Vocabulary and Materials for French conversation on the plan of Dr. W. Smith's 'Principia Latina.' 15th Edition. London, 1892.

89. ————————Part II. A First French Reading Book, containing fables, &c. With Grammatical Questions and Notes and a Copious Etymological Dictionary on the plan of Dr. W. Smith's 'Principia Latina.' 6th Edition. London, 1891.

90. ————————Part III. An Introduction to French Composition, containing Hints on Translation, &c. By P. H. E. Brette on the plan of Dr. W. Smith's 'Principia Latina.' London, 1886.

91. Gaboriau, Emile—La Dégringolade. Paris, 1873.

92. Gabourd, Amédée—Histoire De Louis XIV. Tours, 1852.

93. Galerie La Comique—Du Dix-Neuvieme Sciécle. Caricaturistes Contemporarins. Paris.

94. Geruzez, Eugéne—Essais D'Histoire Litteraire. Second Edition. Paris, 1853.

95. Girardin, J.—Mon Oncle et Moi. Edited by D. Devaux. (H. I. F. P. R.) London.

96. ————————Mme Emile de—Lady Tartuffe. Edited by Dr E. Kurtz. (Th. Fr. No. 21). Berlin, 1882.

97. ————————————La Joice Fait Peur. Edited by G. Hessel. (Th. Fr. No. 27). Berlin, 1889.

98. Gogorden, G.—Joseph de Maistre. (L. G. E. F.) Paris, 1893.

99. Hachette—First French Reader Containing a selection from the best French authors, in prose and poetry. Edited by the Rev. P. H. E. Brette and G. Masson. London.

100. ————————French Reader. Edited by Rev. P. H. E. Brette, 1874.

101. Hallays, Andre—Le Grands Beaumarchais. (L. G. E. F.) Paris, 1897.

102. Haussonville, Comte De—Lacordaire. (L. G. E. F.) Paris, 1895.

103. ————————————Madame de La Fayette. (L. G. E. F). Paris, 1891.

104. Hávet, A. G.—French Composition Comprehending English Prose specimens to be translated into French London, 1874.

105. ——————French Studies, Comprehending Graduated coversations and select extracts from standard writers and a dictionary of 10,000 words and numerous idioms. Fifth Edition, London.

106. Hodgson, R. F.—Selections from French Poets. Calcutta, 1850.

107. Hossfeld—French conversation, consisting of Dialogues and selected literary productions from the best modern authors. London.

108. Hugo, Victor—Hernani ou L'Houneur Castillan. Edited by G. V. Muyden. (Th. Fr. No. 52). Berlin 1889.

109. ——————Lucréce Borgia. Edited by A. W. Kastan. (Th. Fr. No. 107). Berlin, 1887.

110. ——————Les Miserables. English Translation. 2nd Edition. 3 vols. London, 1862.

111. ——————Les Travailleurs De La Mer. By Chifflast. Paris, 1869.

112. Janet, Paul—Fénélon. (L. G. E. F.) Paris, 1892.

113. Karcher, T.—Les Ecrivains Militaires de la France. London, 1866.

114. Lacombe, Paul—French Reader. With notes, &c. By Jules Bue. Third Edition. Paris.

115. Lafenestre—La Fontaine. (L. G. E. F). Paris, 1895.

116. La Fontaine—De Fables. With notes, &c., by F. Tarver. (H. F. C.) New Edition. Paris, 1876.

117. ——————Edition Classique. Edited by L. Feugere. Paris.

118. Lamartine, Alphonse de—Histoire des Girondins. 8 vols. Paris, 1848.

119. ——————Graziella. Paris, 1876.

120. ——————Jeanne D'Arc. Edited by the Rev. A. C. Clapin. (C. P. S.) Cambridge, 1886.

121. ——————Toussaint Louverture. Edited by A. W. Kastan. (Th. Fr. No. 87.) Berlin, 1889.

122. ————————Oeuvres Complétes De M. De—Voyage En Orient. 3 vols. with steel-plates. Paris, 1852.

123. ————————Voyage en Orient. London, 1857.

124. Lanson, Gustave—Boileau. (L. G. E. F.) Paris, 1892.

125. ————————Corneille. (L. G. E. F) Paris, 1898.

126. Larouse, P.—Troisieme Année. Grammaire Superieure. New Edition. Paris.

127. Larroumet, Gustave—Racine. (L. G. E. F.) Paris, 1898.

128. Laun, Henri Van—History of French Literature. 3 vols. London, 1883.

129. Lépage, Auguste—Le Roman D'un Gentilhomme. Paris, 1880.

130. Lesage—Histoire de Gil Blas de Santillane. Vignettes Par Jean Gigoux. Paris, 1835. (rare).

131. Lescure, M. de.—Chateaubriand. (L. G. E. F.) Paris, 1892.

132. Liancourt, C. A. G. de—Political Aphorisms, moral and Philosophical thoughts of the Emperor Napolean. collected from upwards of 80 original works. Edited by J. A. Manning. London, 1848.

133. Lintilhac, Eugine—Lesage. (L. G. E. F.) Paris, 1893.

134. Lolme, De—The French Reader containing extracts from the best authors. London.

135. Loti, Pierre—Jerusalem (Bib. Con.). 7th Edition. Paris, 1895.

136. Lutrin, Le Boileau-Despréaux. Edition Classique. Edited by N. A. Dubois. Paris.

137. Mabilleau, Leopold—Victor Hugo. (L. G. E. F.). Paris, 1893.

138. Malherbe-Oeuvres de J. B. Rousseau and E. Lebrun. Paris, 1852.

139. Mariette, A.—Half hours of French Translation, or extracts from the best English Authors to be rendered into French. 6th Edition. London, 1872.

140. ————Key to above New Edition. London, 1874.

141. Masson, Gustave—French Classics. Edited with Notes Vol. I. (1) Cinna, a tragedy. By P. Corneille (2) Les Femmes Savantes, a Comedy—by Moliere. Oxford, 1862 (C. P. S.).

142. ——— ——— Vol. II—(1) Andromaque, a tragedy by Racine. (2) Le Menteur, a Comedy by Corneille. (C. P. S.). Oxford, 1869.

143. ——— ——— Vol. III. Oxford, 1868 (C. P. S.).

144. ——— ——— Vol. IV. A Selection from the Letters of Madame de Sévigné. (C. P. S). Oxford, 1868.

145. ——— ——— Vol. V. A Selection of Tales of Modern Writers. Second Edition. (C. P. S.). Oxford, 1876.

146. ——— ——— Vol. VI. (1) Le Joueur, a Comedy by Regnard. (2) Le Grondeur, a Comedy by Brueys and Palaprat. (C. P. S.). Oxford, 1875.

147. ———La Lyre Française. Edited by—London, 1881.

148. ———Jules—Aventures de L'Anon Baudinet. (H. I. F. P. R.). London.

149. ———Le Rêve de Noël. Edited by G. J. Brocher. (H. I. F. P. R.). London.

150. ———Une Vengeance de Jeannot Lapin. Trottinette. Edited by Madame C. Da Costa Tallon. (H. I. F. P. R.). London.

151. Maurel, André—Les Trois Dumas. Paris.

152. Melesville, M.—Elle Est Folle. Edited by A. W. Kastan. (Th. Fr. No. 108). Berlin, 1881.

153. ———and Duveyrier—Michel Perrin. Edited by C. Ansorg. (Th. Fr. No. 15). Berlin, 1888.

154. ———and Hestienne—La Berline De L'Emigré. Edited by A. W Kastan. (Th Fr. No. 32). Berlin, 1880.

155. ————, Merle and Boirie—Le Bourgmestre De Sardam. Edited by G. V. Muyden. Berlin, 1878 (Th. Fr. No. 49).

156. Merville, M.—La Première Affaire. Edited by A. W. Kastan. (Th. Fr. No. 86). Berlin, 1879.

157. Millet, René—Rabelais. (L. G. E. F.). Paris, 1892.

158. Molière, J. B. P. De—Le Bourgeois Gentilhomme. Edited by A. C. Clapin. New Edition. (P. P. S.). London, 1888.

159. ————————————Edited by A. W. Kastan. (Th. Fr. No. 39). Berlin, 1890.

160. ————L'école des Femmes. Edited by A. W. Kastan. (Th. Fr. No. 74). Berlin, 1885.

161. ———— ————Comédie. Edited with Introduction and Notes by G. Saintsbury. (P. P. S.). Cambridge, 1888.

162. ————L'Ecole des Maris. Edited by A. W. Kastan. (Th. Fr. No. 99). Berlin, 1880.

163. ————Les Femmes Savantes. Edited by G. V. Muyden. (Th. Fr. No. 38). Berlin, 1889.

164. ————Les Fourberies de Scapin. Edited by G. V. Muyden. (Th. Fr. No. 56). Berlin, 1880.

165. ————Le Malade Imaginaire. Edited by E. Kurtz. (Th. Fr. No. 23). Berlin, 1888.

166. ————Le Médicin Malgré Lui. Edited by G. Hessel (Th. Fr. No. 28). Berlin, 1888.

167. ————Le Misanthrope. With Notes by Rev. P. H. E. Brette. (H. F. C.). London, 1879.

168. ———— ————Edited by A. W. Kastan. (Th. Fr. No. 37). Berlin, 1889.

169. ———— ————with Introduction and Notes by E. G. W. Braunholtz. (P. P. S.). Cambridge, 1894.

170. ————Oeuvres de. Avec des Notes de Tous Les Commentateurs 2 vols. Paris, 1843.

171. ————————Les Oeuvres de. Edited by Sainte. Beuve. (L. H. B. No. 80). London, 1894.

172. ————————Plays. By English Dramatists. With an Introduction by Henry Morley. (L. H. B. No. 61.) London, 1893.

173. ————————Les Precieuses Ridicules. Edited by A. W. Kastan. (Th. Fr. No. 90). Berlin, 1889.

174. ————————Les Precieuses Ridicules. With Introduction and Notes by G. W. Braunholtz. (P. P. S.). Cambridge, 1891.

175. ————————Recueil des Plus Belles Scenes de—Edited by W. Durerger. 5th Edition. London, 1841.

176. ————————Le Tartuffe. Edited by Dr. E. Kurtz. (Th. Fr. No. 2). Berlin, 1888.

177. ———————— Dramatic Works. Translated into English Prose with Introduction and Notes by Charles Herson Wall. 3 vols. London, 1876, 1878, 1879.

178. Montesquieu—Des Romains. Lettres Persanes et Temple de Guide. Paris, 1864.

179. Musset, Alfred De)—On Ne Badine Pas avec L'Amour, and Fantasio. Edited with Introduction and Notes by W. H. Pollock (C. P. S.). Oxford, 1884.

180. ————————Un Caprice. Edited by A. W. Kastan. (Th. Fr. No. 96). Berlin, 1884.

181. ————————Il Faut Qu'une Porte Soit Ouverte on Fermée. Edited by A. W. Kastan. (Th. Fr. No. 102). Berlin, 1886.

182. Mutuelle, L'Ecole—Grammaire Française. Paris, 1877.

183. Noël, M. and M. Chapsal—Abrégé de la Grammaire Française on Extrait de la Nouvelle Grammaire Francaise. Paris, 1875.

184. ————————Nouvelle Grammaire. London, 1876.

185. Nyon, Eugéne.—Les Indiscretions D'une Jeune Mouche. Paris.

186. Oger, Victor.—The Oxford Local French Examiner, containing a Series of Papers on Bertrand and Raton. London, 1876.

187. Paerio, Joseph—La France Litteraire. 1882.
188. Paléologne, Maurice—Alfred De Vigny. (L. G. E. F.). Paris, 1891.
189. ——————Vauvenargues. (L. G. E. F.). Paris, 1890.
190. Patria—La France Ancienne et Moderne.
191. Payen-Payne, De V.—French Idioms and Proverbs, a Companion to Deshumbert's "Dictionary of Difficulties." London, 1893.
192. Pellissier, Eugéne.—Junior French Exercises with complete Vocabulary (Junior Course). London, 1891.
193. ——————French and English Passages for unseen translation and composition with examination papers in Grammar (Junior Course). Edited by —London, 1891.
194. ——————French and English Passages. (Middle Course). London, 1891.
195. ——————————(Senior Course) London, 1892.
196. Picard, L. B.—Les Deux Philibert. Edited by G. V. Muyden. (Th. Fr. No. 54). Berlin, 1878.
197. ——————And Mazères. Les Trois Quartiers. Edited by A. W. Kastan. (Th. Fr. No. 57). Berlin, 1878.
198. Poëy, Andre.—Le Positivisme. (Bib. Pos.) Paris, 1876.
199. Ponsard, F.—L' Honneur et L'Argent. Edited by A. W. Kastan. (Th. Fr. No. 43.). Berlin, 1886.
200. ——————M.—Lucréce. Edited by A. W. Kastan. (Th. Fr. No. 50). Berlin, 1878.
201. Pougy, Diane de.—L. Insassissable.
202. Quinet, Edgar.—Letters a sa Mère. Selected and Edited by G. Saintsbury. (C. P. S.). Oxford, 1885.
203. Rabelais, F.—Oeuvres. Paris, 1835.
204. ——————Works. Edited By Gustave Dore, London.
205. Rachilde—Les hors Nature. Paris, 1897.

206. Racine, J.—Andromaque—Edited by G. V. Muyden. (Th. Fr. No. 71). Berlin, 1885.

207. ————Athalie—Edited by H. Guerin. (Th. Fr. No. 4). Berlin, 1889.

208. ————Britannicus. Edited by G. V. Muyden. (Th. Fr. No. 63). Berlin, 1887.

209. ————Esther. Edited by H. Guerin. (Th. Fr. No. 24.) Berlin, 1890.

210. ————Iphigénie—Edited by C. Ansorg. (Th. Fr. No. 12). Berlin, 1889.

211. ————Mithridate—Edited by A. W. Kastán. (Th. Fr. No. 104). Berlin, 1883.

212. ————Phédre—Edited by C. Ansorg (Th. Fr. No. 9.) Berlin, 1885.

213. ————Les Plaideurs—Edited by G. V. Muyden. (Th. Fr. No. 76). Berlin, 1880.

214. Rébelliau, Alfred.—Bossuet. (L. G. E. F.). Paris, 1900.

215. Reinach, Joseph.—Diderot. (L. G. E. F.). Paris, 1894.

216. Rémusat, Madame La Comtesse De.—Essai Sur L' Education Des Femmes. Paris, 1842.

217. ————Thiers. (L. G. E. F.). Paris, 1889.

218. Renan, Ernest—Lettres Intimes 1842-1845. précedeés de ma Soeur Henriette—Paris, 1896.

219. Revoil, B. H.—Chasses Dans L'Amerique du Nord. New Edition. Tours, 1869.

220. Roche, Antonin.—Les Pöetes Français. London, 1853.

221. Rod, E.—Stendhal.(L. G. E. F.). Paris, 1892.

222. Roget, F. F.—First Steps in French History, Literature and Philology. London, 1896.

223. ————Introduction to Old French. 3rd Edition. London, 1996.

224. Roulier, A.—Charterhouse first book of French Composition. London, 1875.

225. Rousse, E.—Mirabeau. (L. G. E. F. Paris, 1891.

226. Rousseau, J. B.—Oeuvres Lyriques De—Edition Classique. Edited by E. Pessonneaux. Paris, 1860.

227. Saintsbury, George.—French Lyrics. Selected and Annotated. London, 1882.

228. ——————L'école des Femmes. Cambridge, 1888.

229. ——————A ShortHistory of French Literature. New Edition. (C. P. S.). Oxford, 1884.

230. Sand, George.—Le Beau Laurence. Paris, 1870.

231. ——————Le Champi—Edited by A. W. Kastan. (Th. Fr. No. 82.). Berlin, 1879.

232. ——————Maitre Favilla. Edited by A. W. Kastan. (Th. Fr. No. 103). Berlin, 1881.

233. ——————Molière—Edited by M. Strack. (Th. Fr. No. 81). Berlin, 1885.

234. ——————Pierre qui Roule. Paris, 1870.

235. Sandeau, Jules.—Mademoiselle De la Seigliere. Edited by C. Ansorg. (Th. Fr. No. 14.). Berlin, 1889.

236. Say, Leon.—Turgot. (L. G. E. F.). Paris, 1887.

237. Scribe, E.—L'Ambitieux. Edited by A. W. Kastan. (Th. Fr. No, 44). Berlin, 1882.

238. ——————Bertrand et Ratonou ou L'Art De Conspirer. Edited by C. Ansorg. (Th. Fr. No. 7). Berlin, 1886.

239. ——————La Calomnie—Edited by C. Ansorg. (Th. Fr. No. 22). Berlin, 1886.

240. ——————La Camaraderie. Edited by G. Hessel. (Th. Fr. No. 29). Berlin, 1886.

241. ——————Une Chaine. Edited by A. W. Kastan. (Th. Fr. No. 46). Berlin, 1881.

242. ——————Une Faute. Edited by A. W. Kastan. (Th. Fr. (No. 70). Berlin, 1879.

243. ——————Le Fils De Cromwell. Edited by A. W. Kastan. (Th. Fr. No. 78). Berlin, 1879.

244. ——————Les Independants. Edited by G. V. Muyden (Th. Fr. No. 41). Berlin, 1886.

245. ——————Le Lorgnon. Edited by A. W. Kastan. (Th. Fr. No. 80). Berlin, 1879

246. ———Malvina. Edited by G. V. Muyden. (Th. Fr. No. 40). Berlin, 1878.

247. ———Le Mariage D'Argent—Edited by G. Hessel. (Th. Fr. No. 30). Berlin, 1880.

248. ———Mon Etoile—Edited by Dr. G. Hessel. (Th. Fr. No. 26). Berlin, 1889.

249. ———La Passion Secréte. Edited by A. W. Kastan. (Th. Fr. No. 53). Berlin, 1885.

250. ———Le Verre d'eau ou les effets et les causes—Edited by C. Ansorg. (Th. Fr. No. 1). Berlin, 1890.

251. ———And Delavigne—Le Diplomate. Edited by C. Ansorg. (Th. Fr. No. 18). Berlin, 1885.

252. ————Devilleneuve and Desvergers. Yelva, ou L'Orpheline Russe. Edited by G. V. Muyden. (Th. Fr. No. 48.) Berlin, 1880.

253. ————And Dupin—Michel et Christine. Edited by G. V. Muyden. (Th. Fr. No. 69). Berlin, 1878.

254. ————And Duveyrier—Oscar. Edited by A. W. Kastan. (Th. Fr. No. 64). Berlin, 1879.

255. ————And Legouvé—Adrienne Lecouvreur. Edited by G. Hessel. (Th. Fr. No. 33). Berlin, 1889.

256. ——————Bataille de Dames ou un duel en amour. Edited by C. Ansorg (Th. Fr. No. 11.) Berlin, 1889.

257. ——————Les Contes De La Reine De Navarre ou La Revanche De Pavie. Edited by H. Guerin. (Th. Fr. No. 5.) Berlin, 1889.

258. ——————Les Doigts De Fée.—Edited by C. Ansorg. (Th. Fr. No. 19.) Berlin, 1890.

259. ————And Lemoine—Une Femme Qui Se Jette par la Fenêtre. Edited by G. V. Muydon. (Th. Fr. No. 51) Berlin, 1880.

260. ————and Melesville—La Demoiselle a marier. Edited by A. W. Kastan. (Th. Fr. No. 55). Berlin, 1880.

261. ——————————Valerie. Edited by A. W. Kastan. (Th. Fr. No. 95). Berlin, 1888.

262. ——————————and de Rougemont—Avant Pendant et. Après. Edited by C. Ansorg. (Th. Fr. No. 8.) Berlin, 1882.

263. ——————————et. Varner—Le Mariage de Raison. Edited by A. W. Kastan. (Th. Fr. No. 66.) Berlin, 1879.

264. ——————————Toujours. Edited by A. W. Kastan. (Th. Fr. No. 62.) Berlin, 1879.

265. Ségur, Mme. La Comtesse de.—Aprés La Pluie Le Beau Temps. Paris, 1871.

266. Simon, Jules.—Victor Cousin. (L. G. E. F.) Paris, 1887.

267. ——————————Dieu, Patrie, Liberté. Paris, 1883.

268. Sörel, Albert.—Madame De Staël. (L. G. E. F.) Paris, 1890.

269. ——————————Montesquieu—(L. G. E. F.) Paris, 1887.

270. Souriau, Paul.—Le Mouche. L'oiseau Bleu. Edited by J. Leriche. (H. I. F. P. R.) London.

271. Sourjan, P.—Les Deux Brigands. Edited by L. Gaborit. (H. I. F. P. R.) London.

272. Souvestre, Emile.—Henri Hamelin. Edited by A. W. Kastan. (Th. Fr. No. 84). Berlin, 1879.

273. ——————————Un Philosophe Sous les Toits. With notes by J. Bue. New Edition, London, 1889.

274. ——————————Le Serf—Edited by A. R. Ropes. (C. P. S.) Cambridge, 1895.

275. Spuller, E.—Royer-Collard. (L. G. E. F.) Paris, 1895.

276. Staël, Madame De.—De L' Allemagne. New Edition. Paris, 1876.

277. Staël-Holstein, Madame La B. De—Le Directoire with notes by G. Masson. (C. P. S.) Cambridge, 1877.

278. Stapfer, Paul.—Montaigne. (L. G. E. F.) Paris, 1895.

279. Storm, J.—The French Dialogues. A Systematic Introduction to the Grammar and Idiom of the Spoken French. Intermediate Course. Edited by G. Macdonald. London, 1892.

280. Tarver, J. C.—Choix En Prose et En Vers. New Edition. London, 1851.

281. Tassy, Garcin de.—Bag O Bahar. Le Jardin et Le Printemps Poëme Hindoustani. Paris, 1878.

282. Theuriet, André.—Tentation. Paris, 1894.

283. Tolstoi, Comte Leon.—Le Progrés et l' Instruction Publique en Russe. Edited by B. T. E. Jaubert. Paris, 1890.

284. Vigny, Alfred de.—Chatterton. Edited by A. W. Kastan. (Th. Fr. No. 79.) Berlin, 1879.

285. Villemain, A. F.—Lascaris. Où les Grecs Du XVe. Sciécle. With notes by G. Masson, (P. P. S.), Cambridge, 1875.

286. Voltaire—Mahomet. Edited by H. Guerin. (Th. Fr. No. 93.) Berlin, 1879.

287. ————————Mérope. Edited by A. W. Kastan. (Th. Fr. No. 83.) Berlin, 1882.

288. ————————————Edited with introduction and notes by G. Saintsbury. (C. P. S.) Oxford, 1885.

289. ————————Zadig et Micromégas. (L. H. B. No. 79). London, 1894.

290. Wafflard and Fulgeneé—Le Voyage à Dieppe. Edited by C. Ansorg. (Th. Fr. No. 10). Berlin, 1877.

291. Wall, C. H.—A Smaller Grammar of the French Language. 2nd Edition. London, 1889.

292. ————The Student's French Grammar. London, 1878.

293. Xavier.—Count de Maistre. La Jeune Siberienne. Le Lepreux De La Cité D' Aoste Tales.

294. Zola, Emile.—La d'Ebacle. Paris, 1892.

295. ————Rome—Les Trois Villes. Paris, 1896.

Dictionaries.

296. Barrére, Albert.—Argot and Slang. A new French and English Dictionary of the cant words, quaint expressions, slang terms and Flash Phrases. London, 1889.

297. Belot, P. J. B.—Dictionaire Française Arabe 2 vols. Beyrouth, 1890.

298. Boileau, D and A. Picquot—A New Dictionary in French and English and English and French. London, 1831.

299. Clifton, E. C. and Grimaux—A New Dictionary of the French and English Languages. Paris, 1881.

300. Contanseau, Leon.—A Pocket Dictionary of the French and English Languages, new Edition. London.

301. Eid, Michel, J.—Le Manuel Indispensable. Franco-Arabe. Alexandria, 1894.

302. Meadows, F. C.—French-English and English-French Dictionary, London, 1884.

303. Ragonot, L. C.—A Symbolic French and English Vocabulary. Eleventh Edition Revised. London, 1883.

304. Roubaud, E.—Cassell's French and English and English and French Dictionary. London.

305. Spiers, A.—Nouveau Dictionaire General Anglais Français. London, 1885.

306. ————————A New French-English General Dictionary. London, 1885

307. Tarver, J. C.—The Royal Phraseological English-French and French-English Dictionary. (French and English part)—. 5th Edition London, 1879.

317 ———— Germinal —— Paris - 189[illegible]

318 ———— Lourdes —— Paris - 1896

319 Bourget. Paul - Cosmopolis — Paris

320 France - Anatole - Le Livre de Mon Ami - Paris

321 ———— Le Lys Rouge —— Paris

322 ———— Le Crime de Sylvestre Bonnard. Pa

323 Scribe et Potron - Feu Lionel ou qui Vivra

(Th. Fr ho[illegible]

M.

English Language and Literature.

1. Abbott, E. A.—Shakespearean Grammar. London, 1878.
2. Acworth, H. A.—Ballads of the Mahrattas rendered into English Verse from the Mahratti originals. London, 1894.
3. Adams, W. H. D.—A Concordance to the Plays of Shakespeare. London, 1886.
4. ——————The secret of success or how to get on in the world. London.
5. Addison, Joseph.—Essays from the Spectator, with notes. (L. H. B. No. 73). London, 1894.
6. Aeschylus.—By R. S. Copleston, and Sophocles by C. W. Collins. Edited by Rev. W. L. Collins. (A. C. E. R). Edinburgh, 1870 and 1871.
7. ——————Plays—Translated into English by R. Potter. With introduction and notes by H. Morley. (L. H. B. No. 30). London, 1892.
8. Æsop—Fables. Translated by S. Croxall and Sir R. L. Estrange. (Ch. Cl.) London.
9. Ali Khan, Hamid.—A Farewell to London, The story of the slave and the nose ring. Second Edition. London, 1885.
10. Anderson, H.—Fairy Tales. Translated by Mrs. H. B. Paull. (Ch. Cl.) London, 1892.
11. Arabian Nights' Entertainments or The Thousand and one Nights' Entertainments. Translated by E. W. Lane. Edited by E. S. Poole. 3 vols. New Edition. London, 1865.
12. ——————————————————————————————and the supplemental nights. Translated from the Arabic by Cap. Sir. R. F. Burton. Reprinted from the original Edition vol. II. Parts 6, 7, 8, 9, and 10.

13. ———————
Revised with notes by G. F. Townsend. New Edition. (Ch. Cl.) London.

14. ———————
(L. H. B. No. 57). London, 1893.

15. Arabian Poetry—Translations of ancient—By Charles James Lyall. London, 1885.

16. Aristophanes, Sophocles and Euripides.—Plays. Translated by J. H. Frere, T. Franklin and M. Noodhull. (L. H. B. No. 69). London, 1894.

17. Arnold, Edwin.—Death and Afterwards. London, 1887.

18. ————The Light of the World or the Great Consummation. London, 1891.

19. ————Lotus and Jewel. London, 1887.

20. ————Potiphar's Wife and other poems. London, 1892.

21. ————The Secret of Death. London, 1885.

22. ————Mathew.—Essays in Criticism. Second Series. (M. C. L. S.) London, 1888.

23. Arthur, T. C.—Reminiscences of an Indian Police Official. London, 1874.

24. Bacon, Francis.—Advancement of Learning. Edited by W. A. Wright, 2nd Edition (C. P. S.) Oxford, 1876.

25. ————Essays—Civil and Moral, Advancement of learning, Novum Organum, &c. Edited by G. T. Bettany. (M. L. F. B.) London, 1892.

26. ————Including Moral and Historical Works (Ch. Cl.) London.

27. ————or Counsels Civil and Moral. (L. H. B. No. 5.) London, 1895.

28. ————The Wisdom of the Ancients and new Atlantis. (C. N. L). London, 1886.

29. Bailey, James.—Oral Teaching in Infant Schools. Second Edition. London.

30. Bain, Alexander.—English Composition and Rhetoric—A Manual. 4th Edition. London, 1877.

31. ——————Practical Essays. London, 1884.
32. Ball, W. W. R.—The Student's Guide to the Bar. London, 1887.
33. Ballantyne, R. M.—The Walrus Hunters. A Romance of the Realms of Ice. London, 1893.
34. Baring-Gould, S.—Guavas the Tinner. Second Edition. London, 1897.
35. Bayley, Stuart.—Speeches. Edited by R. J. Mitter. Calcutta, 1888.
36. Bellamy, Edward.—Looking Backwards. 22nd Edition. London, 1887.
37. Bengalee—or Sketches of Society in the East. 2 Vols. New Edition. Calcutta, 1843.
38. Beranger.—Songs. Translated into English Verse by William Toynbee. (Can. Po.) London.
39. Bidpai—Fables. Kalilah and Dâmnah. Translated with Notes by I. G. N. Keith-Falconer. Cambridge, 1885.
40. Binns, C. F.—The Story of the Potter. London, 1898.
41. Boccace.—The Decameron, or Ten days' entertainment. Translated from the Italian. London, 1751.
42. Book of Gems from the Poets. London, 1887.
43. Booth-Tucker.—Darkest India. A Supplement to General Booth's "In darkest England, and the way out." Bombay, 1891.
44. Brewster, Sir David.—More worlds than one. The Creed of the Philosopher and the Hope of the Christian. London, 1854.
45. Brown, James, D.—The Manual of Library Classification and Shelf Arrangement. London, 1898.
46. ———T.—School days. By an Old Boy. London, 1889.
47. Browning, Elizabeth, Barrett—Poems. (Ch. Cl.) London.
48. Bunyan, John.—The Holy War. (Ch. Cl.) London, 1887.
49. ——————The Pilgrim's Progress, from this world to that which is to come. With a Memoir of the Author. London.
50. —————— —————————— ——————New Edition. (Ch. Cl.) London.

51. ——— ———
———With a Memoir. (L. H. B. No. 41). London, 1895.

52. Burke, Edmund.—A philosophical enquiry into the origin of our ideas on the Sublime and Beautiful. With a discourse concerning taste. London, 1824.

53. ———Select Works. Edited with Introduction and Notes by E. J. Payne. 2 vols. (C. P. S.) Oxford, 1876 and 1877.

54 ———Selections from the Speeches and Writings (L. H. B. No. 52). London, 1893.

55. Burns, Robert.—Poetical Works. (Ch. Cl.) London, 1889.

56. ——— ———Edited with Introduction, Biography and Notes by Charles Kent. (L. H. B. No. 58). London, 1893.

57. Butler, Joseph.—Hudibras. With Notes and Preface by Z. Gray. London, 1890.

58. Byron, Lord.—The Poetical Works. With facsimiles of the author's hand-writing at various periods of his life. Collected and arranged with Notes. New and complete Edition. London, 1866.

59. ——— ——— (Ch. Cl.) London.

60. ———Childe Harold's Pilgrimage. A Romaunt (L. H. B. No. 29). London, 1892.

61. Caesar, Julius.—Commentaries. By A. Trollope. Edited by Rev. W. L. Collins. (A. C. E. R). London, 1870.

62. ——— ———
——— ———
And Tacitus by W. B. Donne. Edited by Rev. W. L. Collins. (A. C. E. R). Edinburgh, 1870 and 1873.

63. Campbell, Thomas.—The poetical works. With life. London.

64. ——— ———(Ch. Cl.) London.

65. Carlyle, Thomas.—On the Choice of Books, with a Life of the Author. Second Edition. London.

66. ——————Critical and Miscellaneous Essays, 7 vols. London, 1872.

67. ——————On Heroes, Hero-worship and the Heroic in History. London, 1872.

68. ——————A History of the French Revolution, 3 vols. London, 1878.

69. —————— ——————

Edited by G. T. Bettany (M. L. F. B.). London, 1898.

70. ——————(L. H. B. No. 7.) London, 1891.

71. ——————Latter-day Pamphlets. London, 1872.

72. ——————Past and Present. London, 1872.

73. ——————(L. H. B. No. 42.) London 1895.

74. ——————Sartor Resartus. London, 1878.

75. Catallus, Tibullus and Propertius. Translated by Rev. J. Davies. Edited by Rev. W. L. Collins (A. C. E. R). London, 1876.

76. Caunter, Rev. Hobart.—Romance of History. India (Ch. Cl.) London.

77. Chaucer, Geoffrey.—The Canterbury Tales. With Notes and Glossary of T. Tyrwhitt (L. H. B. No. 32). London, 1892.

78. ——————The House of Fame. Edited by Rev. W. W. Skeat (C. P. S.) Oxford, 1893.

79. ——————The Tale of the Man of Law, etc., from the Canterbury Tales. Edited by Rev. W. W. Skeat, (C. P. S.) Oxford, 1877.

80. ——————The Prioresse's Tale, Sire Thopas, The Clarke's Tale, &c., from the Canterbury Tales Edited by Rev. W. W. Skeat (C. P. S.), Second Edition. Oxford, 1877.

81. ————————The Prologue, the Knight's Tale, etc., from the Canterbury Tales. Edited by R. Morris, (C. P. S.) Second Edition. Oxford, 1869.

82. ————————————————————————Edited by A. J. Wyatt. (U. C. C. T. S.) London.

83. Cheem, Aliph.—Lays of Ind. Eighth Edition. London, 1888.

84. Chesterfield, Lord.—Letters to his Son. Edited by C. S. Carey. 2 vols. London.

85. Chrystian Lyrics.—Chiefly Selected from Modern Authors. (Ch. Cl.) London.

86. Churchill, W. L. S.—Story of the Malakand Field Force, an Episode on Frontier War. London, 1898.

87. Cicero, M. T.—and Pliny's Letters by Rev. A. Church and Rev. W. J. Brodribb. Edited by Rev. W. L. Collins. (A. C. E. R.) Edinburgh, 1871 and 1872.

88. ————————Offices. Translated by Cockman, and Cato and Laelius by Melmoth. (L. H. B. No. 76.) London, 1894.

89. Cobbett, William.—Advice to Young Men. London, 1887.

90. Coleridge, Samuel Taylor.—The Friend. A Series of Essays. London, 1875.

91. ————————————Poetical Works—(Ch. Cl.) London, 1894.

92. Confucian Analects. Translated with Notes and Introduction by W. Jennings. (L. H. B. No. 93.) London, 1895.

93. Constitutions of the Grand Lodge of Mark-Master Masons of England and Wales and the Colonies and Dependencies of the British Crown, being the regulations for the government of the Order of Mark-Master Masons and for the degree of Royal Ark Mariner. London, 1882.

94. Cook, Eliza.—The Poetical Works, Complete Edition. (Ch. Cl. London.

95. Cooper F.—The Path Finder, 1839.

96. ———W. R.—A Short History of the Egyptian Obelisks. Second Edition. London.

97. Corelli, Marie.—Barabbas. A Dream of the World's Tragedy. Twentieth Edition. London, 1896.

98. ———The Sorrows of Satan. London, 1896.

99. Courage and Candour.—The Great Plague. London, 1884.

100. Cowper, William.—Letters. Edited with introduction by Rev. W. Benham. London, 1884.

101. ———Poetical Works. Complete Edition. (Ch. Cl.) London, 1892.

102. Cox, C.—Tales of Ancient India. Bombay, 1887.

103. Crane, Stephen.—Maggie. A Child of the Streets. London, 1896.

104. Cromwell, Oliver.—Letters and Speeches with Elucidations. Edited by Thomas Carlyle, 5 vols. London, 1871.

105. Cruikshank, G.—The Travels and Surprising Adventures of Baron Munchausen. (Ch. Cl.) London.

106. Dante, Alighieri.—The Divine Comedy or the Inferno, Purgatory and Paradise. Translated into English by Frederick Pollock. London, 1854.

107. ——— ——— ———Translated by H. W. Longfellow (L. H. B. No. 60). London, 1893.

108. ———The Vision or Hell, Purgatory and Paradise. Translated by Rev. H. F. Cary. Author's corrected edition. London, 1869.

109. ——— ——— ——— (Ch. Cl.) London, 1891.

110. Darmesteter, James.—English Studies. Translated from the French, by Mary Darmesteter. London, 1896.

111. ———Selected Essays. Translated from the French, by H. B. Jastrow and edited by M. Jastrow. London, 1895.

112. Dawson, W. J.—The Makers of Modern English. A Popular Hand-book to the Greater Poets of the Century. London, 1890.

113. Day, Thomas.—The History of Sandford and Merton. Corrected and revised by C. Hartley. London.

114. Defoe, Daniel. The Life and Adventures of Robinson Crusoe. Edited by J. W. Clark. London, 1898.

115. ——————— ——————— (Ch. Cl.) London.

116. ——————— ——————— ——————— L. H. B. No. 37.) London, 1892.

117. Delectable Duchy.—Stories, Studies and Sketches. By Q. London, 1893.

118. Demosthenes—Oration upon the Crown. Translated into English with Notes by H. Brougham. Revised Edition. (L. H. B. No. 46). London, 1893.

119. Dickens, Charles—Barnaby Rudge. A Tale of the Riots of "Eighty". London.

120. ———————Bleak-House. London.

121. ———————Christmas Books, London.

122. ———————The Personal History of David Copperfield. London.

123. ——————— ——————— (L. H. B. No. 28.) London, 1892.

124. ———————Dombey and Son. London.

125. ——————— ——————— ——————— Edited by Andrew Lang. Gadshill Edition. 2 vols. London, 1897.

126. ———————Edwin Drood and Master Humphrey Clock. London, 1897.

127. ———————Great Expectations. London.

128. ———————Hard Times. London.

129. ———————The Life and Adventures of Martin Chuzzlewit. London, 1890.

130. ———————The Life and Adventures of Nicholas Nickleby. London.

131. ————The Old Curiosity Shop. London.

132. ————The Adventures of Oliver Twist. London.

133. ————Our Mutual Friend. London.

134. ————The Posthumous Papers of the Pickwick Club. London.

135. ———— ————

(L. H. B. No. 10.) London, 1891.

136. ————Reprinted Pieces. London, 1898.

137. ————Sketches by Boz. Illustrations of Every-day Life and Every-day People. London.

138. ————A Tale of Two Cities. London.

139. ————The Uncommercial Traveller, London.

140. Dilke, Sir C. W.—Two Recess Speeches. London, 1876.

141. Disraeli, Isaac.—Amenities of Literature, consisting of sketches and characters of English Literature. Edited by his son the Earl of Beaconsfield. New Edition. (Ch. Cl.) 2 vols. London.

142. ————Calamities and Quarrels of Authors. Edited by his son the Earl of Beaconsfield. New Edition. (Ch. Cl.). London.

143. ————Curiosities of Literature. Edited with Memoir and Notes by his son the Rt. Hon. B. Disraeli. 3 Vols. London, 1859.

144. ———— ————

————

3 Vols. (Ch. Cl.). London.

145. ————Literary Characters of men of genius drawn from their own feelings and confessions. Edited by his son the Earl of Beaconsfield. New Edition. (Ch. Cl.). London.

146. Dixon, William, Macneile.—A Primer of Tennyson with a Critical Essay. Lonnon, 1896.

147. Dodd, Rev. William.—The Beauties of Shakespeare (Ch. Cl.). London.

148. Dostoieffsky, Fédor—Crime and Punishment. A Russian Realistic Novel. Fourth Edition. London, 1886.

149. Dryden, John.—Select Poems. Edited by W. W. Christie. (C P. S.). Oxford, 1871.

150. ————Poetical Works. Containing the Original Poems, Tales and Translation, &c. London, 1893.

151. ———— ————(L. H. B. No. 38). London, 1892.

152. Dutt, Romesh Chander.—Lays of Ancient India. (T. O. S.). London, 1892.

153. ——Shoshee Chunder.—A Vision of Sumeru and other poems. Calcutta.

154. ——T.—Ancient Ballads and Legends of Hindustan. London, 1888.

155. Dyee, Rev. Alexander.—A Glossary to the works of William Shakespeare. London, 1876.

156. Earle, John.—A Book for the Beginner in Anglo-Saxon. Comprising a Short Grammar and some Selections from the Gospels. (C. P. S.). Oxford, 1877.

157. ————The Philology of the English Tongue. Second Edition. (C. P. S.). Oxford, 1873.

158. Eastern Tales—By Many Story Tellers. Compiled and edited by Mrs. Valentine (Ch. Cl.). London.

159. Eastwick, Captain.—Speeches on the Sinde Question, &c. London, 1862.

150. Edwards, H. Sutherland.—The Faust Legend, its Origin and Development. London, 1886.

161. Eha—The Tribes on My Frontier. Third Edition. Calcutta, 1887.

162. Eliot, George.—Adam Bede. New Edition. (L. H. B. No. 92). London.

163. Ellis, Alexander. J.—On Early English Pronunciation. With special reference to Shakespeare and Chaucer Parts I—IV. London, 1869-1875.

164. Emerson, Ralph Waldo.—Essays. (L. H. B. No. 50). London, 1893.

165. **English Poets.**—Selections. With critical introductions by various writers and a general introduction by M. Arnold. Edited by T. H. Ward. From Chaucer to Rosetti. 4 vols. London, 1891 and 1892.

166. **Epitaphiana.**—Or the Curiosities of Churchyard Literature, being a miscellaneous collection of Epitaphs with an introduction by W. Fairley. London, 1875.

167. **Eschatology.**—View and Reviews. A collection of letters, essays and other papers concerning the life and death to come by J. H. Pettengell. Yarmouth, 1887.

168. **Essays and Reviews.**—Ninth Edition. London, 1861.

169. **Euripides and Aristophanes.**—By W. B. Donne. Edited by Rev. W. L. Collins. (A. C. E. R.) Edinburgh, 1872.

170. **Every-day Book of Modern Literature.**—A Series of Short Readings from the best authors. Compiled and edited by G. H. Townsend. (Ch. Cl.) 2 vols. London.

171. **Fielding, Henry.**—The history of the life of the Late Mr. Jonathan Wilde, The Great. Edited by G. Saintsbury. London, 1893.

172. **Firdusi.**—The Epic of Kings Stories. Retold from—by H. Zimmern London, 1883.

173. **Forbes, C. J. F. S.**—A Comparative Grammar of the Languages of Further India, a fragment and other Essays. The literary remains of—London, 1881.

174. **Foster.**—Essays on Decision of Character. Madras.

175. **Fouqué, La Motte.**—Sintram and his Companions. Aslauga's Knight. (C. N. L.) London, 1887.

176. **Fraser, Sir William.**—The Words on Wellington—The Duke—Waterloo—The Ball. London, 1889.

177. **French Songs.**—The Books of—Early French Poetry and Lays of the Troubadours. Translated by J. Oxenford. (Ch. Cl.) London.

178. Froude, James Anthony.—Short Studies on Great Subjects. New Edition. 4 vols. London, 1892 and 1893.

179. Fugitive Poetry 1600-1878.—Compiled and edited by J. C. Hutchieson. (Ch. Cl.) London.

170. Garbe, Richard.—The Redemption of the Brahmin. Chicago, 1896.

181. Gems of National Poetry.—Compiled and edited by Mrs. Valentine. (Ch. Cl.) London, 1891.

182. German Ballads—Translated and Edited by Elizabeth Craigmyle. (Can. Po). London.

183. ———Literature—Beauties of. As exemplified by the works of Pichler Richter, Tschökke and Tieck. (Ch. Cl.) London.

184. ———Lyric Poets—Specimens. Consisting of translations in verse from Bürger, Goethe, Klopstock, Schiller and others. London, 1822.

185. ———Novelists—Translated from the originals with critical and biographical notices. By Thomas Roscoe (Ch. Cl.) London.

186. Gervinus, Dr. G. G.—Shakespeare Commentaries. Translated by F. E. Bunnett. New Edition revised. London, 1877.

187. Ghose, Lalmohan.—Speeches. Edited by A. Banerji. Calcutta, 1883.

188. ———Part II. Calcutta, 1884.

189. Goethe, J. D.—Faust (complete). Translated by Bayard Taylor. Edited by G. T. Bettany. (M. L. F B.) London, 1890.

190. ———Translated in the Original Metres, by B. Taylor. (Ch. Cl.) London.

191. ———The first part by John Auster. London, 1887.

192. ———By John Auster. With an Introduction by H. Morley, (L. H. B. No. 63). London, 1893

193. ——————Wilhelm Meister's Apprenticeship and Travels. Translated from German. By Thomas Carlyle. 3 vols. London.

194. Goldsmith, Oliver.—Poetical Works. With a Life of the Poet. By J. Mitford. Revised Edition by A. Dobson London, 1894.

195. ——————Poems and Plays. With the addition of the Vicar of Wakefield, Memoir, etc. (Ch. Cl.) London, 1888.

196. ——————The Vicar of Wakefield. With a Memoir by Prof. Masson. London, 1889.

197. ——————(L. H. B. No. 20), London, 1893.

198. Gouin, Francois.—The Art of Teaching and Studying Languages. Translated from French by H. Swan and V. Betis. London, 1892.

199. Gray, Beattie and Collins. The Poetical Works of—(Ch. Cl), London.

200. Gray, Thomas.—Poetical Works and Alexander Pope's Essay on Criticism, Rape of the Lock and Essay on Man. (L. H. B. Nos. 70 and 97). London, 1895.

201. Grey, Thomas.—Poetical Works. London, 1887.

202. Greek Anthology—Selections from. Edited by G. R. Tomson. (Can. Po.) London.

203. Grimm's Fairy Tales—A New Translation by Mrs. H. B. Paull. (Ch. Cl.). London.

204. Haggard, H. R.—Joan Haste. London, 1895.

205. Halcombe, Rev. J. J.—How to Speak in Public, and on the Physiology of Speech by W. H. Stone. 1891.

206. Half Hours with the Best Anthors, including Biogoaphical and Critical Notices. Edited by C. Knight. New Edition. 4 vols. (Ch. Cl.). London, 1890.

207. Hamerton, Philip Gilbert.—French and English. A Comparison, (M. C. L. S.). London, 1868.

208. ————————Human Intercourse. London, 1884.

209. ———————— The Intellectual Life. New Edition. London, 1889.

210. Hanson, C. H.—Old Greek Stories. The Siege of Troy and the Wanderings of Ulysses. London, 1887.

211. Harrison, Frederick.—The Choice of Books and other Literary Pieces. (M. C. L. S.). London, 1887.

212. Hart, James Morgan.—German Universities. A Narrative of Personal Experience. Newyork, 1874.

213. Hasan and Husain.—The Miracle Play of—Collected from Oral. Traditions by Col. Sir Lewis Pelly. 2 vols. London, 1879.

214. Hauff, William.—Tales. Translated by A. Mimdsa. London, 1886.

215. Hawthorne, Nathaniel.—Mosses from an Old Manse. (Ch. Cl.) London.

216. ————————Tanglewood Tales. A Wonder-book for Girls and Boys. (Ch. Cl.). London.

217. ————————Twice Told Tales. New Edition. (Ch. Cl.). London.

218. Hazlitt, William.—Essayist and Critic. Selections from his Writings, with a Memoir, Biographical and Critical, by A. Ireland. (Ch. Cl.). London.

219. Heber, Reginald.—Poetical Works. New Edition. (Ch. Cl.). London.

220. Hebert, George.—Works in Prose and Verse, with Memoir, Explanatory Notes, &c. (Ch. Cl.). London.

221. Heine, Heinrich.—Poems Selected from. By Kate. F. Kroeker. (Can. Po.). London.

222. Heman, Mrs.—Poetical Works. With Prefatory Memoir, Notes, &c. (Ch. Cl.). London, 1897.

223. Herodotus and Xenophon—By G. C. Swayne and Sir A. Grant. Edited by Rev. W. L. Collins. (A. C. E. R.). Edinburgh. 1870 and 1871.

224. ————Literally Translated from the Text of Baehr. With a Geographical and General Index by Henry Cary. (L. H. B. No. 1). London, 1892.

225. Hesiod—Translated by C. A. Elton. (L. H. B. No. 77). London, 1894.

226. ———and Theognis—by Rev. J. Davies. (A. C. E. R.) London, 1873.

227. ——————and the Greek Anthology—By J. Davies and Lord Neaves. Edited by Rev. W. L. Collins. (A. C. E. R.) Edinburgh, 1873 and 1874.

228. Home, W. A.—English Literature. London.

229. Homer.—Illiad.—Translated by Alexander Pope, with Notes by Rev. T. A. Buckley and F. Designs. (Ch. Cl.) London.

230. ———Odyssey—Translated by A. Pope. With Notes by Rev. T. A. Buckley and F. Designs. London.

231. ———Illiad and Odyssey—Edited by Rev. W. L. Collins. (A. C. E. R.). London, 1870 and 1871.

232. ——— ———Translated by A. Pope. Edited by Rev. H. F. Cary. (L. H. B. No. 12). London, 1891.

233. Hood, Thomas.—Poetical Works. With Memoir, Explanatory Notes, &c. (Ch. Cl.). London.

234. Hope, A. R.—A Book of Boyhoods. London, 1882.

235. Horace—The Odes, Epodes, Satires and Epistles. Translated by the most eminent English scholars and poets. London, 1889.

236. Horae Sabbaticae.—Articles contributed to the Saturday Review; a reprint by Fitz James Stephen. 3 vols. London, 1892.

237. Hugo, Victor.—Select Poems and Tragedies. Edited by G. T. Bettany. (M. L. F. B.) London, 1890.

238. ———Toilers of the Sea. Translated by W. M. Thomas. London, 1866.

239. Hume, David.—Essays. Literary, Moral and Political. (L. H. B. No. 75). London, 1894.

240. Humorous Poems of the Century.—With Notes by R. H. Caine. (Can. Po.) London.

241. Hunt, Leigh.—as a Poet and Essayist, being the choicest passages from his works. Selected and edited with a biographical introduction by C. Kent. London, 1891.

242. Ingoldsby, Thomas.—Legends or Mirth and Marvels. (Ch. Cl.) London.

243. Italian, Novelists. Translated from the originals with Critical and Biographical Notices. By Thomas Roscoe. (Ch. Cl.) London.

244. Jackson, S.—A Primer of Business. London, 1894.

245. Jaffar, Mirza.—Mardi Khasis or the Miser. A Persian Play in Five Acts. Translted into English by Mirza Mehdy Khan. Secunderabad, 1887.

246. Jesperson, Otto.—Progress in Language. With special reference to English. London, 1894.

247. Junius.—Including Letters by the same writer under other signatures. Edited by John Wade. 2 vols. London, 1890. 2 vols

248. Juvenal, Plautus and Terence. By E. Walford and Rev. W. L. Collins. Edited by the latter. (A. C. E. R. Edinburgh, 1872 and 1873.

249. Keats, John.—Poetical Works. With Memoir, Notes, &c. (Ch. Cl.) London, 1892.

250. Kent, Charles.—Modern Seven Wonders of the World. London, 1894.

251. Kingsley, Charles.—Westward Ho. (L. H. B. No. 89). London, 1895.

252. Laing, S.—A Modern Zoroastrian. Second Edition. London, 1888.

253. Lamb, Charles.—Poems and Essays. (Ch. Cl.) London.

254. ——————and Mary Lamb—Tales from Shakespeare. (Ch. Cl.). London, 1892.

255. ——————————————————
designed for the use of young people. London, 1894.

256. ——————————————————
Exhaustive Notes by Rustomjee Hoormusjee Mistri. Bombay, 1894.

257. Lancaster, H. H.—Essays and Reviews. Edited by Rev. B. Jowett. Edinburgh, 1876.

258. Lane, Edward William.—An account of the Manners and Customs of the Modern Egyptians. Edited by G. T. Bettany. (M. L. F. B.) London, 1890.

259. Lang, Andrew.—Human Origin. London, 1895.

260. ——————The Library. London, 1881.

261. Larkin, Henry.—Carlyle and the Open Secret of his Life. London, 1886.

262. Legendary Ballads of England and Scotland.—Compiled and Edited by J. S. Roberts. (Ch. Cl.) London, 1887.

263. Lesage.—Adventures of Gil Blas of Santillane. Translated from the French with Notes and Introduction. (Ch. Cl.) London.

264. Lee-Warner, W.—The Citizen of India. London, 1897.

265. Little Folks.—A Magazine for the Young, 1889.

266. Locke, John.—An Essay concerning Human Understanding. With notes and illustrations of the author, and an analysis of his doctrine of ideas. London.

267. —————— ——————————
(L. H. B. No. 72). New Edition. London, 1894.

268. Lockhart, J. G.—Spanish Ballads, and Robert Southey's Chronicle of the Cid. Translations. (Ch. Cl.) London.

269. Longer English Poems.—Edited by J. W. Hales. London, 1872.

270. Longfellow, H. W.—Selected Poetical Works. Edited by E. Hope. (Can. Po.) London.

271. ——————Poetical Works. With Notes. (Ch. Cl). London.

272. Low, W. H.—The Intermediate Text Book of English Literature. Vol. II. From the Accession of Elizabeth to the Restoration. (U. C C. T. S.). London.

273. ———— ————
Vol. III. From 1660 to 1798. (U. C. C. T, S.). London.

274. Lowell, James Russell.—Poetical Works, including the Biglow Papers. With Memoir, Notes, &c. (Ch. Cl.), London.

275. Lubbock, Sir John.—The Beauties of Nature and the Wonders of the world we live in. London, 1892.

276. ————The Pleasures of Life. Part II. London, 1892.

277. ————The Use of Life. London, 1894.

278. Lyall, Sir Alfred.—Verses Written in India. Fourth Edition. London, 1896.

279. Lytton, Lord.—The Last Days of Pompeii. (L. H. B. No. 40). London, 1893.

280. Macaulay, Thomas Babington.—Critical and Historical Essays and Lays of Ancient Rome. (L. H. B. No. 65). London, 1894.

281. ————Historical and Literary Essays. Edited by G. T. Bettany. (M. L. F. B.). London, 1891.

282. ————Lays of Ancient Rome, with Ivry and the Armada. London, 1884.

283. ————Complete Works. Edited by his sister, Lady Trevelyan. 8 vols. London, 1866.

284. Macfarlane, C.—The Romance of History. Italy. (Ch. Cl.) London.

285. Mackay, Charles.—Poetical Works. Complete in one volume.

286. ————Twenty-one days in India. London, 1890.

287. Mahmood, Syed.—A History of English Education in India. (1781-1893). Alighar, 1895.

288. Malory, Sir Thomas.—La Mort d'Arthur. The History of King Arthur and of the Knights of the Round Table. Compiled by—with Introduction and Notes by T. Wright. (L. H. B. No. 49). London, 1893.

289. Manzoni, Alessandro.—Betrothed Lovers. Edited by G. T. Bettany. London, 1890.

290. Marryat, Captain.—The Pirate and the Three Cutters. London.

291. Marsh, G. P.—The Student's Manual of the English Language. Lectures on the English Language. Edited by W. Smith. 10th Edition. London, 1885.

292. Mrvel, Ik.—Reveries of a Bachelor. London.

293. Massingham, H. W.—The London Daily Press. London, 1892.

294. Masterpieces of Foreign Literature, comprising Schiller's Tragedies translated by S. T. Coleridge, Goethe's Faust, La Fontaine's Fables, Picciola by Saintine. London, 1866.

295. Maurier, George Du.—Trilby, a Novel.

296. Mazzini, Joseph.—Essays Selected from the Writings, Literary, Political and Religious. Edited by E. Rhys. London, 1887.

297. Menon, Chandu.—Indulèka. A Malayâlam Novel. Translated into English by W. Dumergue. Madras, 1890.

298. Michael, Lord of Montaigne.—Essays. Translated by John Florio. (L. H. B. No. 14). London, 1894.

299. Mill, John Stuart.—Essay on Liberty. Second Edition. London, 1859.

300. Milton, John.—Areopagitica. A Speech for the Liberty of Unlicensed Printing. Edited by T. G. Osborn. London, 1873.

301. ———— ————Edited with Notes by John W. Hales. Second Edition. (C. P. S.). Oxford, 1878.

302. ————Poetical Works. With Notes of various authors and with some account of the authr's life and writings derived principally from original documents in Her Majesty's State Paper Office. Edited by Rev. H. J. Todd. 4 vols. 4th Edition. London, 1842.

303. ———— ————Edited with Memoir, Introduction, Notes and an Essay on the Author's English and Versification by David Masson. 3 Vols. London, 1882.

304. ———— ————with Memoir, Notes, and Biography, &c. (Ch. Cl.) London.

305. ———— ————(L. H. B. No. 62). London, 1893.

306. ————Paradise Lost. With Biographical Notice by John Bradshaw. (Can. Po.). London, 1887.

307. ————Prose Works. Vol. II. Edited with notes and preface by J. A. St. John. London, 1875.

308. Minto, William.—Characteristics of English Poets. From Chaucer to Shirley. London, 1874.

309. Mohammad, The Prophet.—Speeches and Table-Talk. Chosen and Translated with introduction and notes by Stanley Lane-Poole. London, 1882.

310. Molière.—Comedies. Edited by G. T. Bettany. (M. L. F. B.). London, 1890.

311. ————Plays. Translated by English Dramatists. With an Introduction by H. Morley. (L. H. B. No. 61.) London, 1893.

312. Montgomery, James.—Poetical Works. With Notes, &c. (Ch. Cl). London.

313. Moon, Washington.—The Dean's English. A Criticism on the Dean of Canterbury's Essays on the Queen's English. Eleventh Edition. London, 1878.

314. Moore, Thomas.—Selected Poetical Works. Edited by John Dorrian. (Can. Po.) London, 1888.

315. ————Poetical Works. With Notes, &c. (Ch. Cl). London, 1891.

316. Morell, Mrs. C.—The Mythology of Greece and Rome. London, 1875.

317. Morley, Henry.—English Literature in the Reign of Queen Victoria with a glance at the past. Leipzig, 1881.

318. ————————Shorter English Poems. Selected, edited and arranged. (L. E. L. S.) London.

319. ————————English Plays. Selected, edited and arranged. (L. E. L. S.) London.

320. ————————Shorter Works in English Prose. Selected, edited and arranged. (L. E. L. S.) London.

321. ————————Illustrative of English Religion. Selected, edited and arranged. (L. E. L. S). London.

322. ————————Sketches of Longer Works in English Verse and Prose. Selected, edited and arranged (L. E. L. S.) London.

323. Morris, Rev. Richard.—English Grammar. (L. P. S.) London, 1883.

324. ————————Historical Outlines of English Accidence. London, 1877.

325. ————————Specimens of Early English. Part I. (C. P. S.) Oxford, 1867.

326. ————————and W. W. Skeat. Specimens of Early English. Part II. A New Edition. (C. P. S.) Oxford, 1894.

327. Morrison, Arthur.—Adventures of Martin Hewitt. Third Series. London, 1896.

328. ————————A Child of the Jago. Second Edition. (M. C. L. S.) London, 1897.

329. Muir, Sir William.—Sweet First Fruits. London.

330. Murison, Alexander, F.—First Work in English. Edited by John Adam, Part I. Madras.

331. Musaeus, Tieck, Richter—Tales. Translated from the German by Thomas Carlyle. 2 Vols. London, 1874.

332. Mustafa Khan.—An Apology for the New Light. Allahabad, 1891.

333. Nazámi—Laili and Majnún. A Poem from the original Persian of—London, 1836.

334. Neele, Henry.—Romance of History. England. (Ch. Cl.) London.

335. Newnham-Davis, N.—Jadoo. An Anglo-Indian Story. London.

336. Nibelungen Lied—Lay of the Nibelung. Translated from German by A. G. Foster-Barham. (L H. B. No. 51.) London, 1893.

337. Nishîkânta Chattopadhyâya, Dr.—Lectures on Zoroastrianism. Bombay, 1894.

338. Nomani, Moulvi Shibli—An Enquiry into the destruction of the Ancient Alexandrian Library. Translated by M. G. Sayeed. Madras, 1893.

339. Odds and Ends—Being Selections from Contributions to different Anglo-Indian Journals. Hyderabad, 1894.

340. Old Old Fairy Tales. Collected and edited by Mrs. Valentine. (Ch. Cl.) London, 1890.

341. Oman, John Campbell.—Râmâyaṇa and the Mahâbhârata. (L. H. B. Nos. 98 and 99). London, 1895.

342. Omar Khayyám.—Quatrains. Translated into English Verse by E. H. Whinfield. (T. O. S.) London, 1882.

343. Palgrave, W. Gifford.—Hermann Agha. An Eastern Narrative. 2 Vols. London, 1872.

344. Penny Poets—3 Vols. (M. L. S.) London, 1895.

345. Percy Anecdotes—Edited by Reuben and C. S. Percy. With a Preface by J. W. Timbs. (Ch. Cl.) London.

346. Percy, Thomas.—Reliques of Ancient English Poetry Consisting of old heroic ballads, songs, &c. Edited by E. Walford, New Edition. (Ch. Cl.). London.

347. Phelps, Elizabeth Stuart.—Gypsy Breynton. London.

348. Pindar—Translated by Rev. F. D. Morice. Edited by Rev. W. L. Collins. (A. C. E. R.) London, 1879.

349. Plato and Lucian—Edited by Rev. W. L Collins (A. C. E. R). Edinburgh. 1873 and 1874.

350. Poe, Edgar Allan.—Complete Poetical Works and Essays on Poetry. Edited by J. H. Ingram (Ch. Cl.) London.

351. Poets of the Nineteenth Century. Selected and Edited by Rev. R. A. Willmott (Ch. Cl.). London, 1889.

352. Pool, John J.—Studies in Mahammadanism. Historical and Doctrinal. London, 1892.

353. Pope, Alexander.—Essay on Man. Edited by Mark Pattison. (C. P. S.) Oxford, 1869.

354. ————————Poetical Works. With Memoir, Notes, &c. (Ch. Cl.). London.

355. Prince of Wales, H. R. H.—Speeches and Addresses. 1863-1888. Edited by James Macaulay. London, 1889.

356. Rabelais—Works. Translated from French. Edited by G. Doré. London.

357. Râmaswâmi, P. V.—Indian Fables. Collected and Edited. London, 1887.

358. ————————Raju, P. V.—The Maid of the Mere.

359. Rawlings, G. F.—The Story of the British Coinage. London, 1898.

360. Recollections of an ex-detective of the Madras Police Force. Edited by D. S. White. Madras, 1876.

361. Reynolds, G. W. M.—The Mysteries of the Court of London. vols. (I—III).

362. Rhymes from the Russian, being translations of selections from the best Russian poets. By John Pollen. London, 1891.

363. Richardson, David Lester.—Literary Recreations or Essays, Criticisms and Poems. London, 1852.

364. Risi—A poem explaining the daily life and manners of the Risi as described in the Rig-veda Samhitâ. Poona, 1878.

365. Ritchie, Leitch.—Romance of History. France. (Ch. Cl.). London.

366. Royal Reader, No. IV., The New—Adapted to the latest requirements of the Education Department. London, 1891.

367. Ruskin, John.—The Ruskin Reader. London, 1895.

368. ————————Selections from the writings of—London, 1868.

369. ———————— The Silver Domine or Side Whispers. London, 1894.

370. Russel, W. Clark.—The Book of Authors, a collection of criticisms, &c., wholly referring to English men of letters in every age of English Literature. (Ch. Cl.). London.

371. Saint-Hilaire, J. Barthélemy.—Buddha and his religion. Translated by Laura Ensor. (L. H. B. No. 94). London, 1895.

372. Saintsbury, George.—A History of Elizabethan Literature. London, 1893.

373. Sakoontala—or The Lost Ring. Translated into English Prose and Verse by Sir. M. Monier-Williams. Seventh Edition revised. (L. H. B. No. 81). London, 1895.

374. Schiller J. C. F.—Poems and Ballads. Translated by Sir Edward Bulwer Lytton, with Memoir. (Ch. Cl.). London, 1887.

375. ——————— William Tell. Translated by Samuel Robinson. (L. H. B. No. 21). London, 1892.

376. Scotch Reciter—Scotch Poetry. 1801-1886. Edited by Alfred H. Miles.

377. Scott, Sir Walter.—Essays on Chivalry, Romance and the Drama (Ch. Cl.) London, 1867.

378. ——————— Poetical Works with Introduction and Notes. (Ch. Cl.). London.

379. ——————— ———————————— (L. H. B. No. 56). London, 1893.

380. ———————The Abbot (H. V. W.). London, 1877.

381. ——————— Anne of Geierstein, (H. V. W.). London, 1877.

382. ———————The Antiquary. (H. V. W.). London, 1877.

383. ——————— ———————(L. H. B. No. 85). London, 1894.

384. ——————— The Betrothed. (H. V. W.). London, 1877.

385. ——————— The Bride of Lammermoor, (H. V. W.). London, 1877.

386. ——————— The Fair Maid of Perth. (H. V. W). London, 1877.

387. ——————— Fortunes of Nigel. (H. V. W.) London, 1877.

388. ———————Guy Mannering. (H. V. W.). London, 1877.

389. ———————Heart of Midlothian. (H. V. W.). London, 1877.

390. ———————Ivanhoe. (H. V. W.). London, 1877.

391. ——————— ———(L. H. B. No. 25.). London, 1892.

382. ———————Kenilworth. (H. V. W.). London, 1877.

393. ———————Legend of Montrose. (H. V. W.). London, 1877.

394. ———————The Monastery, (H. V. W.). London 1877.

395. ———————Old Mortality. (H. V. W.). London, 1877.

396. ———————Peveril of the Peak. (H. V. W.). London, 1877.

397. ———————The Pirate. (H. V. W.). London, 1877.

398. ———————Quentin Durward. (H. V. W.). London, 1877.

399. ———————Redgauntlet. (H. V. W.). London, 1877.

400. ———————Count Robert of Paris. (H. V W.). London, 1877.

401. ———————Rob Roy. (H. V. W.). London, 1877.

402. ———————St. Ronan's Well. (H. V. W.). London, 1877.

403. ———————The Surgeon's Daughter. (H. V. W.). London, 1877.

404. ———————The Talisman. (H. V. W.). London, 1877.

405. ———————Waverley. (H. V. W.). London, 1877.

406. ———————Woodstock. (H. V. W.). London, 1877.

407. ———————The Lady of the Lake. With Notes. Edinburgh.

408. ———————Illustrations of The Lay of the Last Minstrel. London, 1808.

409. Seeley, J. R.—The Expansion of England. (M. C. L. S). London, 1890.

410. Servantes, M. de.—Don Quixote de la Mancha. Translated from the Spanish. London, 1842.

411. ———————— ———————————————— ————by Motteux. (Ch. Cl.). London.

412. ———————— ———————————————— ————(L. H. B. No. 35.). London, 1892.

413 Shakespeare, William.—Coriolanus. (C. N. L.) .London, 1888.

414. ——————————Hamlet, Prince of Denmark. Edited by W. G. Clark and W. A. Wright. (C. P. S.). Oxford, 1879.

415. ———————— ——————————Edited by M. Mull. London, 1885.

416. ——————————A Midsummer Night's Dream. Edited by W. A. Wright. (C. P. S.). Oxford, 1877.

417. ——————————Pericles. (C. N. L.). London 1893.

418. ——————————King Richard II. Edited by W. J. Rolfe. London.

419. ——————————The Tempest. Edited by W. A. Wright. (C. P. S.). Oxford, 1880.

420. ——————————Twelfth Night or What You Will. With notes by W. J. Rolfe. London.

421. ——————————Works. Edited by Charles Knight. London, 1875.

422. ———————— ———Containing his Plays and Poems from the Text of the Editions by C. Knight. With notes complete in one Volume. Eighth Edition. London, 1862.

423. ———————— ———12 Vols. The Avon Edition. London, 1886.

424. ———————— ———(Complete). Being the Falstaff Edition issued by Bliss Sands and Company. London, 1896.

425. ———————— ———With Life, Glossary, &c. The Victoria Edition. London.

426. ———————— ———Plays and Poems. With a Memoir, Glossary, etc. (Ch. Cl.). London.

427. ——————— ——Edited by C. Knight. (L. H. B. No. 23). London, 1899.

429. ——————— ——The Philosophy of—Delineating in 750 passages, selected from his Plays, the multiform phases of the Human Kind. London, 1857.

430. Shaw, Thomas, B.—A History of English Literature. Edited by W. Smith. Seventh Edition. London, 1871.

431. Shelley, Percy Bysshe.—Poetical Works. With Memoir, notes &c. (Ch. Cl.) London.

432. Sheridan, Richard Brinsley.—The Rivals and the School for Scandal. (C. N. L.). London, 1886.

433. ———————Plays. With an Introduction by H. Morley. (L H. B. No. 36). London, 1892.

434. Shi King.—The Old "Poetry classics" of the Chinese. A close metrical translation with annotations by W. Jennings. (L. H. B. No. 11). London, 1891.

435. Sinnett, A. P.—The Occult World. Third Edition. London, 1883.

436. Smiles, Samuel.—Character. London, 1897.

437. ———————Duty. London, 1897.

438. ———————Industrial Biography. Iron workers and tool makers. London, 1897.

439. ———————Life and Labour, or Characteristics of Men of Industry, Culture and Genius. London, 1897.

440. ———————Men of invention and Industry. London, 1897.

441. ———————Self Help. With illustrations of conduct and perseverence. London, 1897.

442. ——————————————New Edition. (L. H. B. No. 8.) London, 1894.

443. ———————Thrift. London, 1897.

444. Smith, Adam.—An Enquiry into the Nature and Causes of the Wealth of Nations. (L. H. B. No. 31.) London.

445. Sonnets of Europe—A Volume of Translations selected and arranged, with notes by Samuel Waddington. (Can. Po.) London, 1886.

446. Spanish Ballads—Translations from Spanish.

447. ———Novelists—Translated from the originals with critical and biographical notes by T. Roscoe. (Ch. Cl). London.

448. Spectator Essays—Selected with an introduction and notes by A. C. Ewald. London, 1891.

449. Spencer, Herbert.—Education. Intellectual, Moral and Physical. London, 1896.

450. Spenser, Edmund.—The Færy Queen, with Memoir, Notes, &c., (Ch. Cl.) London.

451. ——————————Disposed into 12 books to which is added his Epithalamion. (L. H. B. No. 53). London, 1893.

452. ——————————Book I. Edited by G. W. Kitchin, Ninth Edition. (C. P. S.) Oxford, 1879.

453. ——————————Complete Works. Edited by R. Morris, with a Memoir by J. W. Hales. The Globe Edition. London, 1871.

454. Stowe, H. B.—Uncle Tom's Cabin. A Tale of Life among the lowly. (Ch. Cl.) London.

455. Subjects of Examination in the English Language. Appointed by the Senate of the Calcutta University for the B. A. Examination of 1873. Calcutta, 1870.

456. Sunjana, D. D. P.—Next-of-kin marriages in old Iran. An address. London, 1888.

45 Swan, A. S.—Jack's Year of Trial. London, 1887.

458. Sweet, Henry.—An Anglo-Saxon Reader. In prose and verse. Second Edition. (C. P. S.) Oxford, 1879.

459. Swift, Jonathan.—Gulliver's Travels into several remote region of the world. (L. H. B. No. 54). London, 189

460. Swiss Family Robinson, The.—or the adventures of a ship-wrecked family on an uninhabited island near New Guinea. Translated by Mrs. H. B. Paull. (Ch. Cl.) London.

461. Syntax, Rev. Dr.—His Three Tours, in search of the Picturesque, of Consolation, and of a Wife. London.

462. Taine, H. A.—History of English Literature. Translated by H. Van Laun. With a preface by the author. 2 vols. New York, 1872.

463. Talmud, The.—Translated by H. Polano. (Ch. Cl.) London, 1890.

464. Tatler, The.—Selected Essays with an introduction and notes by A. C. Ewald. (Ch. Cl.) London, 1888.

465. Taylor, Col. Meadows.—The Confessions of a Thug. New Edition. London.

466. ——————Tara—Sixth Edition. London, 1889.

467. ——————Tippoo-Sultan.

468. Tennyson, Alfred Lord.—Works. London, 1894.

469. Thackeray, William Makepeace.—The History of Pendennis. His fortunes, and misfortunes, his friends and his greatest enemy. (L. H. B. No. 26). London, 1892.

470. ——————Vanity Fair—A novel without a hero. (L. H. B. No. 17). London, 1892.

471. Thousand Best Poems in the World, The.—Selected and arranged by E. W. Cole. London.

472. Thucydides—Edited by Rev. W. L. Collins. (A. C. E. R.) London, 1887.

473. Timbs, John.—Romance of London. Historical. (Ch. Cl.) London.

474. ——————Supernatural. (Ch. Cl.) London.

475. Todd—Complete works. New Edition, London.

476. Trevelyan, G. O.—The competition Wallah. London, 1864.

477. Trueba, Don. T. de.—The Romance of History. (Ch. Cl.) London.

478. Verses mostly written in India. By G. H. T. London, 1878.

479. Vikram and the Vampire—or Tales of Hindu Devilry. Adapted by Cap. Sir. Richard. F. Burton. Edited by his wife Isabel Burton. London, 1893.

480. Virgil and Horace.—By Rev. W. L. Collins and T. Martin. Edited by the former. Edinburgh, 1870.

481. ———Æneid——Translated by John Dryden. (L. H. B. No. 13). London, 1891.

482. ———Works—With Memoir. (Ch. Cl.) London.

83. Walton, Izaac. And Charles Cotton. The Complete Angler Edited with notes by G. C. Davies. (Ch. Cl.) London.

484. Warren, Mrs.—Comfort for small incomes. London, 1870.

485. Weismann, A.—The effect of external influences upon Development. London, 1894.

486. White, Rev. Gilbert.—The natural History and Antiquities of Selborne. Edited by Sir W. Jardine. (L. H. B. No. 9.) London, 1894.

487. ————————The natural history of Selborne and the naturalist's Calendar. Edited by G. C. Davies. (Ch. Cl.) London.

488. ————————————————(C. N. L.) London, 1887.

489. Whittier, John Greenleaf.—Poetical Works. (Ch. Cl.) London, 1891.

490. Whyte-Melville, G. J.—The Brookes of Bridlemere, London.

491. Wordsworth, William.—Poetical Works. (Ch. Cl.) London, 1891.

492. ————————————————(L. H. B. No. 68). London, 1894.

493. Wynter, Andrew.—Curiosities of Civilization. Third Edition. London.

494. Xenophon—Anabasis or Expedition of Cyrus and the Memorabilia of Socrates. Literally translated by the Rev. J. S. Watson. (L. H. B. No. 78). London, 1894.

495. Zola, Emil.—Doctor Pascal or Life and Heredity. Translated by E. A. Vizetelly, London, 1893.

496. ————Money, (L'Argent). Translated by—London, 1894.

497. ————Rome—Translated by————London, 1896.

Dictionaries.

498. Ogilvie, John.—A smaller English Dictionary. London.

499. Skeat, Rev. Walter.—A concise Etymological Dictionary of the English Language. (C. P. S.) Oxford, 1885.

500. Webster. N.—International Dictionary of the English Language. Edited by N. Porter. London, 1890.

522 Knowlson, T. Sharper – The art of thinking London 18[illegible]

523 McCarthy, J. H. – One Thousand & One days. Persian tales. 2 Vols. London. 1892 2 Vols.

524 Wilson, Anne C – After 5 Years in India or Life and work in a Panjaub District. London 189[illegible]

525. Plumptre – The Spirits in Prison.

526. International Library of Famous Literature. Edited by Dr Richard Garnett. 20 Vols. London 20 Vols 1900

527. Grant. James – Jane Seton or the King's Advocate A Scottish Historical Romance. London.

528 ———— The Captain of the Guard. London

529 ———— The King's own Borderers. A Military Romance. London

530 Smedley, Frank E – Harry Coverdale's Courtship and all that came of it. London.

531. Parker, Gilbert – The translation of a savage. London 1894 (Bell's India and Col Library Edn)

532. Hungerford. Mrs – The Honorable Mrs. Vereker a Novel. London

533. Hutchison. John C – The Pirate Junk. A story of the Sooloo Sea. London.

534. Kennard. Mrs Edward – Matron or Maid. Novel London

535. Weyman, Stanley J – Shrewsbury. A Romance. London

536. Duncan. Sara Jeannette – His Honour & a Lady London 1896

537. Harte, Bret – The Heathen Chinee with East and West Poems & Parodies. London.

N.

Biography.

1. **Abbott, Evelyn.**—Pericles and the Golden Age of Athens. (He. Na.). London, 1895.
2. **Aitchison, Sir Charles.**—Lord Lawrence and the Reconstruction of India under the Crown. (Rul. Ind.). Oxford, 1897.
3. **Ali, Syed Ameer.**—Mahomet, his Life and Teachings or the Spirit of Islam. London, 1891.
4. **Allen, Grant.**—Charles Darwin. (Eng. Wor.). London, 1885.
5. **Âpte, V. S.**—Râjasekhara, his Life and Writings. Poona, 1886.
6. **Armstrong, E.**—Lorenzo dé Medici and Florence in the Fifteenth Century. (He. Na.). London, 1896.
7. **Bain, R. Nisbet.**—Charles XII, and the Collapse of the Sweedish Empire. (He. Na.). London, 1835.
8. **Ball, Sir Robert S.**—Great Astronomers. London, 1895.
9. **Ballantine, Sergt.**—Some Experience of a Barrister Life. Sixth Revised Edition. London, 1882.
10. **Benn, Alfred William.**—The Greek Philosophers. 2 vols. London, 1882.
11. **Boswell, James.**—The Life of Samuel Johnson. With Notes. (L. H. B. No. 24.). London, 1892.
12. **Boulger, D. C.**—Lord William Bentinck. (Rul. Ind.) Oxford, 1892.
13. ———————Central Asian Portraits, the Celebrities of the Khanates and the Neighbouring States. London, 1880.
14. **Bourne, H. R. F.**—Sir Philip Sidney. Type of English Chivalry in the Elizabethan Age. (He. Na.) London, 1895.
15. **Bower, George Spencer.**—Hartley and James Mill. (Eng. Phi.) London, 1881.
16. **Bowring, L. B.**—Hyder Ali and Tipû Sultan and the Struggle with the Mussalman Powers of the South. (Rul. Ind.). Oxford, 1893

17. Bradshaw, John.—Sir Thomas Munro and the British Settlement of the Madras Presidency. (Rul. Ind.). Oxford, 1894.

18. Bright. Rev. F—Joseph II. (For. St.). London, 1897

19. ——————Maria Theresa. (For. St.). London, 1897.

20. Brooke, Stopford. A.—Milton. Edited by J. R. Green. (Cl. Wr.). London, 1879.

21. Burne, Sir. O. T.—Clyde and Strathnairn. (Rul. Ind.). Oxford, 1892.

22. Burton, Isabel.—The life of Captain Sir Richard F. Burton. By his wife. 2 vols. London, 1893.

23. Butcher, S. H.—Demosthenes. Edited by J. R. Green. (Cl. Wr.). London, 1881.

24. Compbell, Lewis.—Sophocles. Edited by J. R. Green. (Cl. Wr.). London, 1879.

25. Carlyle, Thomas.—Reminiscences. Edited by J. A. Froude, 2 Vols. London, 1881.

26. ——————The Life of John Sterling. London, 1871.

27. Caron, Frank Henri Le.—Twenty-five Years in the Secret Service. London, 1893.

28. Church, William C.—Ulysses S. Grant and the Period of National Preservation and Reconstruction. London, 1897.

29. ————A. J. and W. J. Brodribb. The Life of Tacitus. (Cl. Wr.). London, 1882.

30. Colebrooke, Sir. T. E.—The Life of H. T. Colebrooke, by his son. London, 1873.

31. Colvin, Sir Aucland.—John Russell Colvin. The last Lieutenant Governor of the North West under the Comapany. (Rul. Ind.). Oxford 1895.

32. Cotton, J. S.—Mount Stuart Elphinstone and the Making of South Western India. (Rul. Ind.). Oxford, 1896.

33. Crozier, John Beattie.—Lord Randolph Churchill. A Study of English Democracy. London, 1887.

34. Cunningham, Sir H. S.—Earl Canning. (Rul. Ind.). Oxford, 189-.

35. Düntzer, Heinrich.—Life of Goethe. Translated by T. W. Lyster. 2 Vols. London, 1883.

36. ————————Life of Schiller. Translated by P. E. Pinkerton. London, 1883.

37. Durand, H. M.—The life of Major-General Sir H. M. Durand. By his son. 2 Vols. London, 1883.

38. Elliot, Sir Charles Alfred.—Laborious days. Leaves from the Indian Record of—Calcutta, 1892.

39. Evelyn, John.—The Dairy of—from 1641 to 1705. With Memoir. Edited by W. Bray. (Ch. Cl.). London 1891.

40. Farrar, Rev. F. W.—Seekers after God. London, 1881.

41. Farrer, J. A.—Adam Smith. (Eng. Phi). London, 1881.

42. Fletcher, C. R. L.—Gustavus Adolphus II and the Struggle of Protestantism for Existence. (He. Na). London, 1895.

43. Forsyth, William.—Life of M. T. Cicero. 2 vols. London, 1864.

44. Foster, John.—Life of Charles Dickens. London.

45. Fowler, Thomas.—Francis Bacon. (Eng. Phi). London.

46. ——————Shaftesbury and Hutcheson. (Eng. Phi), London. 1882.

47. ——————W. W.—Julius Cæsar and the Foundation of the Roman Imperial System. (He. Na.). London, 1895.

48. French Literary Men—Lives of the Most Eminent Literary and Scientific Men in France. 2 vols. London, 1838 and 1839.

49. Galton, Francis.—English Men of Science. Their Nature and Nurture. London, 1874.

50. Gardner, Alice.—Julian. Philosopher and Emperor and the Last Struggle of Paganism against Christianity. (He Na.) London, 1895.

51. Gibbon, Edward.—Life and Letters. With the History of the Crusades. An Autobiography (Ch. Cl.) London.

52. Graham, Lieut-Col. G. F. I.—The life and work of Syed Ahmed Khan. London, 1885,

53. Griffin, Sir Lepel.—Ranjit Singh. (Rul. Ind.). Oxford, 1893.

54. Hameed Ullah, M.—The Life and Times of Hafiz of Shiraz.

55. Hardinge, Charles Viscount.—Viscount Hardinge. By his son and Private Secretary in India. (Rul. Ind.). Oxford, 1892.

56. Harrison, Frederic.—William the Silent. (For. St.) London, 1897.

57. Hassall, Arthur.—Louis XIV and the Zenith of the French Monarchy. (He. Na). London, 1895.

58. Hodgkin, Thomas.—Theodoric the Goth. The Barbarian Champion of Civilisation. (He. Na.). London, 1891.

59. Hume, Martin, A. S.—Philip II of Spain. (For. St.) London, 1897.

60. Hunter, Sir William Wilson.—The Marquis of Dalhousie and the Final Development of the Company's Rule. (Rul. Ind.). Oxford, 1895.

61. ——————————The Earl of Mayo. (Rul. Ind.) Oxford, 1892.

62. Hutton, William Holden.—Philip Augustus. (For. St.) London, 1896.

63. —————————— Marquis of Wellesley (Rul. Ind.). Oxford, 1893.

64. Huxley, Professor.—Hume. Edited by John Morley. (E. M. L. S.). London, 1879.

65 Irwich, W.—The Life of Oliver Goldsmith. (E. M. L. S.). London.

66. Jebb, R. C.—Life of Bentley. (E. M. L. S.). London, 1882.

67. Jehangir, Sorabjee.—Representative Men of India. A Collection of Memoirs, with Portraits of Indian Princes, Nobles, Statesmen, &c. With an introduction by Sir George C. M. Birdwood. London.

68. Johnson, Samuel.—Lives of the Most Eminent English Poets. 3 vols. London, 1896.

69. —————————— (Ch. Cl.). London.

70. Keene, H. G.—Madhava Rao Sindhia and the Hindu Reconquest of India. (Rul. Ind.). Oxford, 1895.

71. Krause, Ernst.—Life of Erasmus Darwin. Translated from German by Charles Darwin. London, 1879.

72. Kutar, Framroz Nowroji.—Life of Sir Jamsetji Jeejeebhoy. The First Parsi Baronet (in Persian.) Bombay, 1895.

73. Lane-Poole, Stanley.—Cairo. Sketches of its History, Monuments and Social Life. London, 1892.

74. Lee-Warner, William.—The Protected Princes of India. London, 1894.

75. Lethbridge, Sir. R.—Golden Book of India. London, 1893.

76. ————————The Life of Goethe. Second Edition. London, 1864.

77. Lockhart, J. G.—Memoirs of the Life of Sir Walter Scott. New Edition. Condensed and Revised. (Ch. Cl.). London, 1888.

78. Lodge, Richard.—Richelieu. (For. St.). London, 1896.

79. Macaulay, Thomas Babington.—Essay on Lord Clive. With introduction and notes by J. Cowan. London, 1891.

80. ————————————————

Essay on Warren Hastings. Edited with introduction and notes by A. D. Innes (P. P. S.). Cambridge, 1996.

81. Mahaffy, J. P.—Euripides. Edited by J. R. Green. (Cl. Wr). London, 1879.

82. Malleson, Col. G. B.—Akbar Kaiser. (Rul. Ind.). Oxford.

83. ————————Lord Clive and the Establishment of the English in India. (Rul. Ind.). Oxford, 1895.

84. ————————Dupleix. (Rul. Ind.). Oxford, 1892.

85. Masson, David.—De Quincey. (E. M. L. S.). London, 1881.

86. Max Müller, F.—Biographical Essays. London, 1884.

87. Maxwell, Sir Herbert.—Robert the Bruce and the Struggle for Scottish Independence. (He. Na.). London 1897.

88. Mijatovick, C.—Constantine. The Last Emperor of the Greeks or the Conquest of Constantinople by the Turks. London, 1892.

89. Monck, W. H. S.—Sir William Hamilton. (Eng. Phi.). London, 1881.

90. Morison, James Cotton.—Gibbon. (E. M. L. S.). London, 1878.

91. Morley, John.—Edmund Burke. A Historical Study. London, 1867.

92. ————Edited by—13 vols., (Vol. X wanting) each volume containing lives of three writers.

93.	G. Chaucer	by	A. W. Ward.
	E. Spenser	—	R. W. Church.
	J. Dryden	—	G. Saintsbury.
94.	J. Milton	—	M. Pattison.
	O. Goldsmith	—	W. Black.
	W. Cowper	—	G. Smith.
95.	C. Lamb	—	A. Ainger.
	J. Addison	—	W. J. Courthope.
	J. Swift	—	L. Stephen.
96.	S. W. Scott	—	R. H. Hutton.
	R. Burns	—	P. Shairp.
	S. T. Coleridge	—	H. D. Traill.
97.	Byron	—	J. Nichol.
	P. B. Shelly	—	J. H. Symonds.
	J. Keats	—	S. Colvin.
98.	W. Wordsworth	—	F. W. H. Myers.
	R. Southey	—	E. Dowden.
	W. S. Landor	—	S. Colvin.
99.	H. Fielding	—	A. Dobson.
	W. M. Thackeray	—	A. Trollope.
	C. Dickens	—	A. W. Ward.
100.	F. Bacon	—	R. W. Church.
	J. Bunyan	—	J. A. Froude.
	R. Bentley	—	R. C. Jebb.

101.	D. Defoe	——	W. Minto.
	R. Sterne	——	H. D. Traill.
	N. Hawthorne	——	H. James.
102.	A. Pope	——	L. Stephen.
	S. Johnson	——	————
	T. Gray	——	E. Goose.
103.	D. Hume	——	T. H. Huxley.
	J. Locke	——	T. Fowler.
	E. Burke	——	J. Morley.
104.	De Quincey	——	D. Masson.
	S. P. Sidney	——	J. A. Symonds.
	R. B. Sheridan	——	Mrs. Oliphant.

(E. M. L. S.). London, 1895.

105. Morris, William O'Connor.—Hannibal. Soldier, Statesman, Patriot and the Crisis of the Struggle between Carthage and Rome. (He. Na.). London, 1897.

106. ————————Napoleon, Warrior and Ruler and the Military Supremacy of Revolutionary France. (He. Na.). London, 1896.

107. Muhammad, Hâjî Ghulam.—Autobiography. Surat. 1893.

108. ————The Life of—Part I (in Bengalee).

109. Muir, William.—The Life of Mahomet and the History of Islam. 4 Vols. London, 1858 and 1861.

110. Nasmyth, James.—Engineer. An Autobiography. Edited by Samuel Smiles. London, 1897.

111. Noer, F. A.—Kaiser Akbar. Ein Versuch über die Geschichte Indiens. 2 vols. Leiden, 1880 and 1885.

112. Novelists and Dramatists—Lives of—(Ch. Cl.). London.

113. Oliphant, Mrs.—Jeanne D'Arc. Her Life and Death. (He. Na.). London, 1896.

114. Palmer, E. H.—Haroun Alraschid. Caliph of Bagdad. London, 1881.

115. Pepys, Samuel.—The Diary of—from 1659 to 1669 with Memoir. Edited by Lord Braybrooke. (Ch. Cl.). London.

116. Poole, S. L.—Aurangzeb. (Rul. Ind.). Oxford, 1896.

117. Plutarch—Lives. Translated from Greek with Notes, &c., and a life of the author by John Langhorne. (L. H. B No. 39). London, 1892.

118. Rammohan Roy, Rajah.—The Last Days in England of.—Edited by Mary Carpenter. London, 1866.

119. Ritchie, Anne Thackeray and R. Evans.—Lord Amherst and the British Advance Eastwards to Burma. (Rul. Ind.). Oxford, 1894.

120. Roberts, Field Marshal, Lord.—From Subaltern to Commander-in-Chief. 2 vols. London, 1897.

121. Ross-of-Bladensburg, Major.—Marquis of Hastings. (Rul. Ind.). Oxford, 1893.

122. Russell, W. Clark.—Horatio Nelson and the Naval Supremacy of England. (He Na.). London, 1895.

123. ——————Representative Actors. A Collection of Criticisms, Anecdotes, Personal Descriptions, etc., with Notes. (Ch. Cl.). London.

124. Saintsbury, G.—Dryden. Edited by J. Morley. (E. M. L. S.) London, 1881.

125. Sergeant, Lewis.—John Wyclif. Last of the Schoolmen and first of the English Reformers. (He. Na.). London, 1893.

126. Seton-Karr, W. S.—The Marquis of Cornawallis. (Rul. Ind.). Oxford.

127. Smiles, Samuel.—Lives of the Engineers. 5 Vols. London, 1874 and 1877.

128. Southey, Robert.—The Life of Nelson, (Ch. Cl.) London.

129. —————— ——————Wesley and the rise and progress of Methodism. Edited by J. H. Atkinson (Ch. Cl.). London, 1893.

130. Stephen, Leslie.—Life of Sir James Fitz James Stephen. London, 1895.

131. ————————Samuel Johnson. (E. M. L. S.). London, 1885.

132. Stephens, H. M.—Albuquerque. (Rul. Ind.). Oxford, 1899.

133. Strachan Davidson, J. L.—Cicero and the Fall of the Roman Empire. (He. Na.). London 1894.

134. Strauss, Dr. D. F.—Life of Jesus. Translated from German by George Eliot, Second Edition. London, 1892.

135. Subhân, S. A.—H. H. The Nizam of Hyderabad. (in Bengalee). Calcutta.

136. Taylor, Col. Meadows.—Story of my Life. Edited by his daughter. New Edition. London, 1882.

137. Temple, Sir Richard.—James Thomason. (Rul. Ind.) Supplementary volume. Oxford, 1893.

138. Thackeray, Miss.—Collection of British Authors. Madame De Sevigne, &c., 1881.

139. Tredwell, Daniel M.—A Sketch of the Life of Apollonius of Tyana, or the first ten decades of our era. New-york, 1886.

140. Tripâṭhi, M. S. P.—A Sketch of the Life of Gockulji Zala, and of the Vedanta. Bombay, 1881.

141. Trotter, Cap. L. J.—The Earl of Auckland. (Rul. Ind.). Oxford, 1893.

142. ————————Warren Hastings and the founding of the British administration. (Rul Ind.). Oxford, 1894.

143. Ward, A. W.—Chaucer. Edited by J. Morley, (E. M. L. S.). London, 1881.

144. White, Henry Alexander.—Robert E. Lee and the Southern Confederacy. 1807-1870 (He. Na.). London, 1897.

145. Willert, P. F.—Henry of Navarre and the Huguenots in France. (He. Na). London, 1894.

146. Williams, Montagu.—Leaves of a Life, being the reminiscences. London, 1890.

147. Wilson, G. and A. Geikie.—Memoir of Edward Forbes. Edinburgh, 1861.

148. ————Robert.—Life and Times of Queen Victoria, Empress of India, 1837-1897. London.

149. Woodall, Edward.—Charles Darwin. A paper contributed to the transactions of the Shropshire Archæological Society. London, 1884.

Dictionaries.

150. Cassell—Biographical Dictionary. London, 1895.

151. Darwin - Francis - The Life and Letters of Charles Darwin including an autobiographical Chapter - Edited by his son 3 Vols. London. 1887. 3 vols

152. Lane - Poole Stanley - Baber (Rulers of India Series) Oxford 1899.

153. Howe - Julia Ward - Margaret Fuller - London 1883. (Marchesa Ossoli) (Eminent Women series)

154. Miller - Mrs F. Fenwick - Harriet Martineau London 1884 (E. W. S.)

155. Zimmern - Helen - Maria Edgeworth. London 1883 (E. W. S.)

156. Lee - Vernon - The Countess of Albany - London 188 (E. W. S.)

157. Thomas - Bertha - George Sand - London 1883 - (E. W. S)

158 Robinson - A. Mary F. - Emily Bronte London. 188 (E. W. S.

159 Temple - Sir Richard Bart. The story of my Life 2 Vols. London - 1896 2 vols

160 Robinson - Mr Sergeant - Bench & Bar - Reminiscences of one of the last of an ancient race. London 1889

161. Jerrold - Walter - Sir Redvers H. Buller
London - 1900

162. Perry - Frederick - Saint Louis (Louis IX of France) London. 1901 (H. N. Series)

163. Green - Walford Davis - William Pitt, Earl of Chatham & the growth & Division of British Empire. 1708-1778. London 1901 (H. N. Series)

164. Perkins, James Breck - Richelieu & the growth of French Power. London. 1900 (He. Na. S.)

165. Dunlop - Robert - Daniel O'Connell. London 1900 (He. Na. Series)

166. Plutarch's Lives - Langhorne Translation. Roman Section 2 Parts. Grecian Section 2 Parts (Ch. Cl.) 4 vols.

Kingsford C. L. Henry V the typical mediaeval Hero. London 1901 (He Na.

O.

The Biblical, and other Religious Literature.

1. Apostolical Fathers.—The Genuine Epistles of the—Translated by Archbishop Wake (L. H. B. No. 44.). London, 1893.
2. Arnold, T. W.—The Preaching of Islam. A History of the propogation of the Muslim faith. Westminster, 1896.
3. Augustine, St.—Confessions. Books I—X. A revised Translation. (L. H. B. No. 87.). London, 1895.
4. Bailey, Rev. Henry Ives.—The Liturgy compared with the Bible. London, 1840.
5. Beacon of Truth, The,—or Testimony of the Koran to the truth of the Christian Religion. Translated from the Arabic by Sir William Muir. London, 1894.
6. Bettany, G. T.—A Sketch of the History of Judaism and Christianity in the light of modern research and criticism. London, 1892.
7. Bible The.—Containing the Old and New Testaments. (in Arabic.) 1811.
8. ————in Hebrew.
9. ————Holy in English. Appointed to be read in churches. Oxford, 1888.
10. ———— ———— 1890.
11. ————(L. H. B. No. 100.) London, 1895.
12. ————London.
13. ————Translated into the Telugu Language: Madras, 1881.
14. ————La Sacra. London, 1873
15. ————Sagrada.
16. ————In German. 1871.

17. Butler, Joseph.—The Analogy of Religion, natural and revealed to the Constitution and the Course of Nature. With introduction by H. Morley. (L. H. B. No. 66). London, 1894.

18. Carus, Dr. Paul.—Homilies of Science. Chicago, 1892.

19. Charities, List of.—General and Diocesan, for the relief of the clergy, their widows and families. London.

20. Clarke, Adam.—Condensed Commentary of the Holy Bible With notes by Robert Newton Young. 3 vols. London.

21. Commentary, The.—Wholly Biblical. An exposition in the very words of Scripture. Matthew to Revelation. London.

22. Cook, Joseph.—Boston Monday Lectures. Conscience, with preludes on current events. London, 1879.

23. ——— ———
Scepticism, Biology, Transcendentalism, &c. 1st Series. London, 1878.

24. ——— ———
Fourth Series. London, 1879.

25. ———Lectures on Biology, Transcendentalism and Orthodoxy. London, 1881.

26. Dale, R. W.—Protestantism, its ultimate Principle. London, 1874.

27. Davidson, Samuel.—An introduction to the Old Testament. Critical, Historical and Theological. 3 vols. Edinburgh, 1862 and 1863.

28. Genesis, The book of—and part of Exodus, in Sanskrit. Calcutta, 1843.

29. ———in Telugu. Madras, 1883.

30. ———in Hebrew. With notes by C. H. H. Wright. London, 1859.

31. Gladstone, Rt. Hon., W. E.—Collections of British Authors. Rome and the Newest Fashions in Religion. Leipzig, 1875.

32. Gospels, The.—Consolidated. With a harmonised index. Second Edition. London, 1877.

33. Gospel in many tongues. London, 1891.

34. Haarbrücker, Dr. Theodor.—Religious and Philosophical Sects. Halle, 1850.

35. Haweis, Rev. H. R.—Current Coin. London, 1876.

36. Hebrew Inscriptions—from the Valleys between Egypt and Mount Sinai in their original characters, with translations and an alphabet by Samuel Sharpe. London, 1875.

37. Hymns, Ancient and Modern.—for use in the services of the church. Complete Edition. London.

38. Isa, Abd.—The death of Christ upon the Cross. London, 1895.

39. Isaiah—in Hebrew.

40. Job, The book of.—in Hebrew.

41. Jonah—The book of—In four Semetic Versians. With notes by W. Wright. London, 1857.

42. Keble, Rev John.—The Christian Year. Thoughts in verse for the sundays and holy days throughout the year. (L. H. B. No. 64). London, 1893.

43. ———————The above. (Ch. Cl.). London.

44. Kempis, Thomas à.—On the imitation of Christ. London.

45. ——————— ——————— Translated by G. Stanhope. (L. H. B. No. 59.) London, 1893.

46. Koran, The.—Translated by E. H. Palmer. Parts I and II. (S. B E. Vols VI and IX). Oxford, 1880.

47. ———————With a discourse by George Sale. (L. H. L. No. 22.). London, 1892.

48. ———————Translated by George Sale. (Ch. Cl.) London.

49. Lenormant, François.—Chaldean Magic, its origin and development. Translated from the French of—London, 1877.

50 Modi, Jiwanji Jamshedji.—The Religious System of the Parsis. Bombay, 1893.

51. Muir, Sir William.—The apology of Al Kindy in defence of Christianity against Islam. Second Edition. London, 1887.

52. Newberry, Thomas.—The Englishman's Bible combining the "English Hebrew Bible" and the "English Greek Testament." London.

53. Oxford Essays—Contributed by Members of the University during 1855. London.

54. Paine, Thomas.—The Age of Reason, being an investigation of true and fabulous Theology. Edited by M. D. Conway. London, 1896.

55. Pascal.—Thoughts on religion. (L. H. B. No. 47).

56. Proof of Prophet Muhammad by the Holy Bible and way to Paradise for Eternal Life. Surat, 1887.

57. Psalms, &c.—in English. London.

58. ————in Hebrew.

59. Pusey, Rev.—Daniel the Prophet. London, 1892.

60. Religious Systems of the World—National, Christian and Philosophical. A collection of addresses delivered at South Place Institute. London, 1890.

61. Renan, M. Ernest.—E'tudes D' histoire Religieuse. Paris, 1862.

62. ————The Hibbert Lectures. Lectures on the influence of the Institutions, Thoughts, Culture &c., of Rome on Christianity and the development of the Catholic Church. Translated by Charles. Beard. London, 1885.

63. Sacred Books of China.—Translated by James Legge. The Texts of Confucianism and Tâoism. (S. B. E. vols. III, XVI, XXVII, XXVIII, XXXIX and XL. Parts I, II, III and IV and I and II) Oxford.

64. Saphir, Adolph.—Expository Lectures on the Epistle to the Hebrews. London.

65. Sayce, A. H.—Lectures on the origin and growth of Religion, as illustrated by the religion of the Babylonians. Hibbert Lectures. London, 1887.

66. Schaff, Rev. Dr. and M. Napolean Roussel—The Romance of M. Renan and the Christ of the Gospels. Three Essays. Newyork, 1868.

67. Sell, Rev. Edward.—The Faith of Islam. London, 1880.

68. Smith, W. Robertson.—Lectures on the religion of the Semites. The fundamental institutions. First Series. Edinburgh, 1889.

69. Spurgeon, C. H.—The Treasury of David. Vol. I. London, 1882.

70. Stanley, A. P.—Lectures on the History of the Jewish Church. 3 vols. New Edition. London, 1885.

71. ——————Sermons and Essays on the Apostolical Age. London.

72. Stone, Charles, J.—Christianity before Christ or Prototypes of our faith ond culture. London, 1885.

73. Students, The.—Commentary on the Holy Bible. Edited by J. M. Fuller. 2 vols. London, 1879.

74. —————— ——————
——————4 vols. London, 1880, 1882, 1884 and 1887.

75. Taylor, Jeremy.—The Rule and Exercises of Holy Living and Dying. Edited with introduction and notes by Revd. F. A. Malleson. (L. H. B. No. 74). London, 1894.

76 Testament, The New.—in English. With Notes by Rev. George Townsend. Vol. I. Fourth Edition. London, 1838.

77. ——————Oxford, 1869.

78. ——————Oxford, 1873.

79. ——————With a brief commentary by various authors. Fifth Edition, London, 1874.

80. ——————In Russian. London, 1869.

81. ——————Translated into Sanskrit.

82. ——————Arabic. Oxford, 1871.

83. ——————London.

84. ——————Persian. London, 1882.
85. ——————Punjabi.
86. ————The old—in English. With Notes by Rev. G. Townsend. 2 vols. Fourth Edition. London, 1836.
87. ——————Hebrew and English. Vienna, 1870.
88 ——————In Urdu with references. London. 1887.
89. ————Both New and Old. Translated into Arabic. Beroot, 1889.
90. Wilson, Rev. James.—Some Contributions to the Religious Thought of our Time. London, 1888.

Dictionaries.

91. Beeton.—Bible Dictionary. London.

P.

Works on History and Geography.

1. Allcroft, A. H. and W. F. Masom.—The Tutorial History of Rome. (U. C. C. T. S.). London.
2. Albîrûnî.—The chronology of Ancient Nations. An English Version of the Arabic Text of the Athâr-ul-Bâkiya or "Vestiges of the Past." Translated and Edited by Dr. C. Edward Sachau. London, 1879.
3. ———India. Edited with Notes by C. E. Sachau. 2 vols. (T. O. S.). London, 1888.
4. Armies of the Native States of India. Reprinted from "The Times." London, 1884.
5. Arnold, Thomas.—History of Rome. 3 Vols. Fourth Edition. London, 1848 and 1850.
6. Aschbach, Dr. Joseph.—Ommaijaden in Spanien. Wéen. 1860.
7. Aurangabad.—Gazetteer of—Published under the orders of H. H. The Nizam's Government. Bombay, 1884.
8. Australasia.—Compendium of Geography and Travel. Edited and Extended by A. R. Wallace. Second Edition. London, 1880.
9. Bartholomew, J. G.—Constable's Hand Atlas of India, under direction of—Westminster, 1893.
10. ———Thacker's Reduced Survey Map of India. With Index.
11. Bartlett, Sir Ellis Ashmead.—The Battle fields of Thessaly. With personal experiences in Turkey and Greece. London, 1897.
12. Battles of the Nineteenth Century.—Described by A. Forbes, G. A. Henty, M. A. Griffiths and other well-known writers. 2 Vols. London, 1896 and 1897.
13. Bertall.—The Communists of Paris.—1871. Types. Physiognomies and Characters. Paris, 1873.

14. Bigham, Clive.—With the Turkish Army in Thessaly. London, 1897.

15. Bilgrami, Syed Hossain, and C. Willmott.—Historical and Descriptive Sketch of H. H. the Nizam's Dominions. Compiled by—2 vols. Bombay, 1883 and 1884.

16. Bombay Presidency.—Atlas, with a Short Description. Geographical, Physical and Statistical. Bombay, 1887.

17. Bose, Pramatha Nâth.—A History of Hindu Civilisation during British Rule 2 vols. London, 1894.

18. Bretschneider, E.—Mediæval Researches. From Eastern Asiatic Sources. 2 vols. (T. O. S.). London, 1888.

19. British Islands.—Map.

20. Broughton, Thomas Duer.—Letters from a Mahratta Camp during the year 1809. Constable's Oriental Miscellany. Westminster, 1892.

21. Buckle, H. Thomas.—History of Civilisation in England. 3 Vols. New Edition. London, 1873.

22. Burke, Ulick Ralph.—History of Spain from the earliest times to the death of Ferdinand the Catholic. 2 Vols. London, 1895.

23. Calcutta.—Map.

24. Carrieres, M. Des.—L'Histoire de France. Depuis L'Etablissement de la Monarchie. London, 1856.

25. Cassell.—History of the War between France and Germany. 1870-1871. Vol. II.ond

26. Cook.—Handbook to the healthy resorts of the South of France and Riviera. London, 1893.

27. Cox, Edmund C.—A Short History of the Bombay Presidency. Bombay, 1887.

28. Croley, Henry.—Geography of the Eastern Peninsula. Ootacamund, 1878

29. Crooke, W.—The North-Western Provinces of India. Their History, Ethnology and Administration. London, 1897.

30. Danvers, Frederick Charles.—The Portuguese in India, being a history of the rise and decline of their Eastern Empire. 2 Vols. London, 1894.

31. Digby, William.—India for the Indians, and for England. London, 1885.

32. Dozy, R.—Recherches Sur L'Histoire et La Litterature de L'Espagne Pendant Le Moyen age. 2 Vols. Second Edition. Leyde, 1860.

33. Dufferin and Ava, Marchioness of.—Our Viceregal Life in India. Selections from my Journal 1884-1888. 2 vols. London, 1889.

34. Dutt, Romesh Chunder.—Ancient India. Epochs of Indian History. London, 1893.

35. Eastwick, Edward B.—Bengal Presidency. Murray's Handbook. London, 1882.

36. Edwards, H. Sutherland.—The Germans in France. London, 1887.

37. Egyptian War.—Map of the Soudan. Calcutta, 1885.

38. Elliot, Sir. H. M.—The History of India as told by its own historians. The Muhammadan period Edited from the posthumous papers of—by John Dowson. 8 vols. London, 1867 to 1877.

39. Fearenside, C. S.—The Intermediate Text Book of English History, being a longer History of England from 1485 to 1603. Vol. II. (U. C. C. T. S.). London, 1894.

40. ——————and A. Evans. A History of England from 1714-1770, being part of the Intermediate Text Book of English History. Vol. IV. (U. C. C. T. S.). London, 1895.

41. Ferishta, Mahomed Kasim.—History of the Rise of the Mahommedan Power in India till 1612. Translated from the original Persian of—By J. Briggs. 4 vols. London, 1829.

42. Firdausi.—The Shah Námeh of the Persian Poet. Translated and abridged in prose and verse by James Atkinson. Edited by the Rev. J. A. Atkinson. (Ch. Cl.). London, 1886.

43. ————The above. (L. H. B. No. 18.). London, 1892.

44. Forbes-Mitchell, William.—Reminiscences of the Great Mutiny. 1857-1859, (M. C. C. S.). London, 1893.

45. Fraser, Col. Hastings.—Memoir and Correspondence of General James S. Fraser. By his son. London, 1885.

46. ———Cap.—Our Faithful Ally The Nizam. London, 1865.

47. Freeman, Edward. A.—History of Europe. Edited by J. R. Green. Second Edition. (His. Pr.). London, 1876.

48. Gibbon, Edward.—The History of the Decline and Fall of the Roman Empire with various notes. 7 vols. (B. B. C.). London, 1853-1854.

49. ———— ————

————2 vols. (L. H. B. No. 33.). London, 1895.

50. ———— ————

————4 vols. (Ch. Cl.). London.

51. ———— ————

————the Student's Gibbon. Abridged from Gibbon's Larger History. By William Smith. London, 1866.

52. ————and S. Ockley.—History of the Saracens, and the rise and fall of their empire (Ch. Cl.). London.

53. Giekie, Professor.—Physical Geography. (Sc. Pr.). London, 1865.

54. Ghose, Loke Nâth.—The Modern History of the Indian Chiefs, Râjahs, &c. Part I. The Native States. Calcutta, 1879.

55. ———— ————

————Part II. The Native Aristocracy and Gentry. Calcutta, 1881.

56. Gilman, Arthur.—The Saracens from the earliest times to the fall of Bagdad. (S. N.). London, 1887.

57. Gramont, Le Duc de.—La France et la Prusse Avant la Guerre. Paris, 1872.

58. Grant Duff, James.—A History of the Maharattas. 3 vols. 1826.

59. Grau, Rev. Dr. R. F.—The Goal of the Human Race, or the Development of Civilisation, its origin and issue. London, 1892.

60. Green, John Richard.—A short History of the English People. London, 1876.

61. ——————— ——————— (L. H. B. No. 90.). London, 1894.

62. Gribble, J. D. B.—History of the Deccan. 2 vols. (Vol. II wanting). London, 1896.

63. Grote, George.—A History of Greece. 12 vols. London, 1869.

64. Grove, George.—Geography. (His. Pr.). London, 1877.

65. Guizot, G.—Alfred Le Grand. With notes by H. Lallemand. London, 1878.

66. Hallam, Henry.—Constitutional History of England from Edward I to Henry VII and the Constitution of England by J. L. de Lolme. (Ch. Cl.). London.

67. ——————— ———————from Henry VII to the death of George II. London, 1870.

68. Half Hours of English History.—Selected and Edited by Charles Knight. (Ch. Cl.). London.

69. Haraprasâd Śâstri.—A School History of India. Calcutta, 1899.

70. Harkness, M. E.—Assyrian Life and History. With introduction by R. S. Poole. London.

71. ———————Egyptian Life nad History. London, 1884.

72. Hind Râjasthan—or the Annals of the Native States of India. Compiled by Markand Nand Śankar Mehta and Manu Nand Śankar Mehta. Baroda, 1896.

73. Holmes, T. R. E.—History of the Indian Mutiny of 1857 and 1858. Fourth Edition. London, 1891.

74. Hübner, Otto von.—Geographisch Statistische Tabellen aller Länder der Erde. 1890.

75. Hughes, A. W.—The Country of Balochistan, its Geography, Topography, Ethnology and History. London, 1877.

76. ——————The Treasury of Geography with an Essay on Physical Geography. London, 1890.

77. Hultsch, F.—The Histories of Polybius. Translated from the Text of—By Evelyn, S. Shuckburgh. 2 vols. London, 1889.

78. Hume, David. A History of England with a short account of his Life written by himself. 6 vols. (Ch. Cl.). London.

79. —————— ——————————————

3 vols. (L. H. B. No. 71). London, 1894.

80.——————A History of England based on the History of —London, 1862.

81. Hunter, W. W.—A Brief History of the Indian People. London, 1882.

82. —————— ——————————————

Twentieth Edition. Oxford, 1893.

83. ——————England's Work in India. Madras, 1888.

84. ——————The Indian Empire. Its History, People and Products. (T. O. S.). London, 1882.

85. ——————The Imperial Gazetteer of India. 14 vols. Second Edition. London, 1885 and 1887.

86. India.—Map showing Railways with Stations.

87. ———Philips New Series of Travelling Maps. London.

88. ———Philips Popular Series of Country Maps. London.

89. Indo-China.—Essays relating to—Reprinted for the Straits Branch of the Royal Asiatic Society. 2 vols. (T. O. S.) London, 1886.

90. —— ———and the Indian Archipelago. Essays relating to—Reprinted for the Straits Branch of the Royal Asiatic Society. Second Series. 2 vols. (T. O. S.). London, 1887.

91. Irwin, H. C.—The Garden of India, or Chapters on Oudh History and Affairs. London, 1880.

92. Johnston.—Atlas world wide of Modern Geography. Third Edition. London, 1897

93. ————Map to elucidate the Afghanistan Boundary question with inset map showing the encroachments of Russia from Peter the Great in 1689 to the present time. London, 1885.

94. ————The Scripture Atlas. Edinburgh, 1875.

95. Kahlana.—Râjatarangiṇî. Kings of Kashmir, being a translation from the Sanskrit of.—by Jogesh Chunder Dutt. 2vols. Calcutta, 1879 and 1887.

96. Karim, Abdul.—Student's History of India. Calcutta, 1898.

97. Kay, H. C.—Yemen, its early History. London, 1892.

98. Kaye, Sir John.—History of the Indian Mutiny of 1857 and 1858. Edited by Col. Malleson. 6 vols. Cabinet Edition. London, 1888 and 1889.

99. ———John William.—History of the Sepoy War in India, 1857 and 1858. Fifth Edition. London, 1870.

100. Keene, Henry George.—The Fall of the Moghul Empire. London, 1876.

101. ————History of India, from the earliest times to the present day. 2 vols. London, 1893.

102. ————A Sketch of the History of Hindustan, from the first Muslim Conquest to the fall of the Moghul Empire. London, 1885.

103. ————The Turks in India. London, 1879.

104. Kinglake, A. W.—The Invasion of Crimea. 6 vols. Cabinet Edition. Sixth Edition. London, 1877.

105. Kohlrausch, F.—A book on the year 1813. With English notes by W. Wagner in German. (P. P. S.). Cambridge, 1875.

106. Lake Edward.—Journals of the Sieges of the Madras Army in the years 1817, 1818 and 1819. London, 1825.

107. ————————Plans and views illustrating the journals of the Sieges of the Madras Army in the years 1887, 1888 and 1889. London, 1825.

108. Lane Poole, Stanley.—The Moors in Spain. With the Collaboration of A. Gilman. Second Edition. (S. N.). London, 1887.

109. Lepsius, Dr. Richard.—Letters from Egypt, Ethiopia and the Peninsula of Sinai. Translated by Lëonora and Joanna B. Horner. London, 1853.

110. Lyall, Sir Alfred.—The Rise of the British Dominion in India. Second Edition. (U. E. M.). London, 1893.

111. Macdougall, Lieut.-Col. P. L.—The Campaigns of Hannibal. Arranged and critically considered by—London, 1858.

112. Mackenzie, Alexander.—How India is governed, being an account of England's Work in India. London, 1882.

113. McDermott.—British East Africa or Ibea, with Map, &c. London, 1893.

114. "Malvern Illustrated."

115. Marriott, J. A. R.—The Makers of Modern Italy. Mazzini, Cavour, Garibaldi. Three Lectures delivered at Oxford. London, 1889.

116. Maspéro, G.—Life in Ancient Egypt and Assyria. Translated by Alice Morton. London, 1892.

117. Megasthenes and Arrian.—Ancient India as described by—being translations of fragments of the Indika of Megasthenes, &c., by J. W. McCrindle. London, 1877.

118. Mirkhond.—History of the early Kings of Persia. From Kaiomars to the Conquest of Iran by Alexander the Great. Translated from the Original Persian of—with Notes, &c., by David Shea. London, 1832.

119. Mommsen, Theodor.—History of Rome. Translated by W. P. Dickson. 4 vols. London, 1894.

120. Mordacque, J.—Histoire de Napoleon Bonaparte. Fourth Edition. London, 1839.

121. Motley, Lothrop.—The Rise of the Dutch Republic. A History. 3 vols. (Ch. Cl.). London.

122. Muir, Sir William.—Annals of the early Caliphate from Original Sources. London, 1883.

123. Müller, Wilhelm.—Politische Geschichte der Neuesten Zeit. 1816-1875. Stuttgart, 1875

124. Neibuhr, B. G.—Lectures on Ancient Ethnography and Geography. Translated from the German Edition of Dr. Isler by Dr. Leonhard Schmitz. 2 vols. London, 1853.

125. ————Lectures on Ancient History. From the earliest times to the taking of Alexandria by Octavianus. Translated by Dr. Leonhard Schmitz. 3 Vols. London. 1852.

126. ————Lectures on the History of Rome from the earliest times to the death of Constantine. Edited by Dr. L. Schmitz. 3 Vols. London, 1849.

127. Nizam's Dominions, H. H. The.—Map in 5 Sheets.

128. Norvins, M. De.—Histoire de Napoléon. in French. Paris, 1844.

129. Oncken, Wilhelm.—Allgemeine Geschichte. Universal History in German. Berlin, 1878.

130. O'Reilly, M. Bernard.—Vie de Léon XIII. Edited by P. M. Brin. Paris, 1890.

131. Orme, Robert.—A History of the Military Transactions of the British Nation in Hindustan. Fourth Edition. 3 Vols. Madras, 1861 and 1862.

132. Osborn, Robert Durie.—Islam under the Arabs. London, 1876.

133. ————Islam under the Khalifs of Baghdad. London, 1878.

134. Palgrave, William Gifford.—Essays on Eastern Questions. London, 1872.

135. Pictorial Records of remarkable events in the History of the World. London.

136. Poole, Stanley D.—Cairo. London, 1892.

137. Princep, Henry T.—Origin of the Sikh Power in Punjab and Political Life of Maharâjah Runjeet Singh, with an account of the present condition, religion, laws and customs of the Sikhs. Compiled by—Calcutta, 1834.

138. Ragozin, Zenaïde A.—Assyria—from the rise of the Empire to the fall of Nineveh. (S. N.). London, 1888.

139. ——————Media, Babylon and Persia, including a study of the Zend-Avesta or Religion of Zoroaster from the fall of Nineveh to the Persian War. (S. N.). London, 1889.

140. Rawlinson, George.—Parthia. (S. N.). London, 1893.

141. Reclus, Elisee.—The Universal Geography. The earth and its inhabitants. Edited by A. H. Keane. 4 Vols. London.

142. Rees, J. D.—The Muhammadans. Epochs of Indian History. London, 1894.

143. Rose, Kinnaird.—With the Greeks in Thessaly. (M. C. L. S.). London, 1897.

144. Rowney, H. B.—The Wild Tribes of India. London, 1882.

145. Scott, James George.—Burma. As it was, as it is, and as it will be. London, 1886.

146. Schiller, Frederick.—Historical Works. Translated from German by the Rev. A. J. W. Morrison. London, 1860.

147. Sincklair, D.—Smaller Indian History for Schools.

148. Smith, Bosworth.—Carthage and Carthageneans. London, 1879.

149. ———George.—Geography of British India. Political and Physical. London, 1882.

150. Somerville, Mary.—Physical Geography. Seventh Edition. London, 1877.

151. Stanley, Arthur. P.—Sinai and Palestine—in connection with their history. New edition with maps and plans. London, 1881.

152. Tennent, Sir James Emerson.—Ceylon. An account of the Island, Physical, Historical and Topographical. 2 vols. London, 1859.

153. Thornton, Thomas Henry.—General Sir Richard Meade and the feudatory states of Central and Southern India. London, 1898.

154. Thucydides.—Peloponnesian War. Translated by William Smith. (L. H. B. No. 27).

155. Vâdhajee, Bhojajee.—Comprehensive outlines of Indian History. Ahmedabad, 1883.

156. Vaux, W. S. W.—Ancient History from the monuments. Persia from the earliest period to the Arab conquest. London.

157. Voltaire.—Histoire de Charles XII. With vocabulary by G. Masson. (H. F. C.). London, 1877.

158. ————Siecle de Louis XIV. With notes by A. Garnier. Paris, 1875.

159. ———— ————
Chapters I-XII. With notes by Victor Oger. Second Edition. London, 1879.

160. ———— ————
Part II. With notes by G. Masson and G. W. Prothero. (P. P. S.) Cambridge, 1879.

161. Wallace, Alfred Russell.—The Malay Archipelago. The land of the Orang-Utan and the Bird of Paradise. London, 1874.

162. Ward, C. B.—Twelve years work in the Nizam's dominions. 1879-1891. Bombay.

163. Wheeler, J. Talboys.—Early records of British India. A history of English Settlements in India. London, 1878.

164. ————The History of India from its earliest ages. 4 Vols. London, 1869, 1874, and 1881. 4 vols

165. With the Sirdar to Omdurman.—Letters from "The Pioneer's" Special war correspondent. Allahabad, 1898.

166. Wood, Cap. John.—Journey to the source of the River Oxus Edited by his son. With an essay on the Geography of the valley of the Oxus by Col. Henry Yule with maps. New Edition. London, 1872.

167. Zufti, Dr. Ferdinand.—An historical work in German. Berlin, 1879.

✓168 Menzies, Sutherland - History of Europe from the decadence of the Western Em[pire] to the Reformation. London 1877 (Collins series)

✓169 ——— History of the Ottoman Empire Europe for Junior Classes London 1877 (Collins School Series)

✓170 ——— History of France for Junior c[lasses] London. 1875 (Collins School S[eries])

✓171 ——— History of Germany for Junior Classes. London 1876 (Collins S[chool Series])

✓172 Pearce. W. C. History of Holland & Belgi[um] London 1877 (Collins S. S)

✓173 Reitz F. W. — A Century of wrong. Issue with Preface by W. T. Stead. Lon[don]

✓174 Fitzpatrick — The Transvaal from With[in] A Private Record of Public aff[airs] London 1899.

✓175 Wilkinson. Spencer. British Policy [in] South Africa. 2nd Edtn. Lon[don]

177. Demolins – Edmond. Boers or English. Who are in the Right:? London. 1900

178. India, Ceylon, Straits Settlements, British North Borneo, Hong Kong. London. 1899. (British Empire Series,

179. British Africa – With 4 maps. London. 1899 (British Empire Series)

180. Martineau – John – The Transvaal Trouble How it arose, being an extract from the biography of the late Sir Bartle Frere. London 1899

181 Russel Robert – Natal, the land & its story, A Geography & History with maps. London 1899

182 Ridpath – John Clark & E. S. Ellis – The story of South Africa. Illustrated copiously London

183 Our Heroes of the South African War. 16 Photos. 1899 – 1900

184 Ragozin – Zenaide A – Vedic India. As embodied principally in the Rig Veda – London – 1895

Q.

Travels and Folklore.

1. Abercromby, John.—Trip through the Eastern Caucasus. With a chapter on the languages of the country with maps, &c. London, 1889.

2. Anderson, John.—Mandalay to Moulmien. A narrative of the two expeditions to Western China with maps. London, 1876.

3. Anglo-Indian, An.—Domestic Sketch. A letter from an artist in India to his mother in England. Calcutta, 1849.

4. Arnold, Edwin.—East and West. London, 1896.

5. ——————India revisited, 1886.

6. ——————Seas and Lands. London, 1891.

7. Atkinson, James.—An expedition into Afghanistan. Notes and sketches descriptive of the country. London, 1842.

8. Baierlein, Rev. E. R.—The land of the Tamulians and its missions. Translated from the German of—by J. D. B. Gribble. Madras, 1875.

9. Balfour, Alice Blanche.—Twelve hundred miles in a waggon. London, 1895.

10. Bernier, Francis.—Travels in the Mogal Empire. Translated from the French by Irving Brock. 2 vols. London, 1826.

11. Biddulph, C. E.—From London to Samarkhand. Bombay, 1892.

12. Bishop, Mrs. Isabella L. Bird.—Journeys in Persia and Kurdistan. 2 vols. London, 1891.

13. Blennerhassett, Rose, and Lucy Sleeman.—Adventures in Mashonaland. By two hospital nurses. London, 1893.

14. Blünmer, Prof. H.—The home life of the ancient Greeks. Translated from the German of—by Alice Zimmern. London, 1893.

15. Blunt, Lady Anne.—A pilgrimage to Nejd. The cradle of the Arab race. 2 vols. Second Edition. London, 1881.

16. Boddy, Alexander, A.—To Kairwan the Holy. Scenes in Mahammadan Africa. London, 1885.

17. Bonvalot, Gabriel.—Through the heart of Asia over the Pamir to India. 2 vols. London, 1889.

18. Boy's voyage round the World, A.—Edited by Samuel Smiles. London, 1897.

19. Buchanan, Francis.—A journey from Madras through the countries of Mysore, Canara and Malabar. 2 vols. Second Edition. Madras, 1870.

20. Burnaby, Cap. Fred.—On horseback through Asia Minor. 2 vols. Second Edition. London, 1877.

21. Burton, Richard, F.—Personal narrative of a pilgrimage to El Medinah and Meccah. 3 vols. London, 1855 and 1856.

22. Caird, Sir James.—India, the land and the people. With map of India. London, 1883.

23. Calcutta to Liverpool by China, Japan and America. By H. W. N. Calcutta, 1878.

24. Chesney Lieut. Col.—The Expedition for the Survey of the River Euphrates and Tigris. 2 vols. London, 1850.

25. Chunder, Bholanauth.—Travels of a Hindu to various parts of Bengal and Upper India. 2 vols. London, 1869.

26. Comte, Louis Le.—Memoirs and observations. Topographical, Physical &c., made in a journey through the empire of China. London, 1698.

27. Cook, Cap.—Three voyages round the world with a sketch of his life. Edited by Lieut. C. R. Low. (L. H. B. No. 18). London, 1892.

28. ———————First voyage round the world. Edited by G. T. Bettany. London.

29. Cowper, H. Swainson.—Through Turkish Arabia. London, 1894.

30. Crane, Thomas Frederick.—Italian popular tales. London, 1885.

31. Day, Rev. Lâl Behâri.—Bengal peasant life. New Edition. London, 1884.

32. Elphinstone.—Cabul and its dependencies. London, 1895.

33. Elora.—A journey to the temples at.—London, 1824.

34. Emperor's Dairy of the Austro-German War—1866 and the Franco-German War.—1870 and 1871. To which is added Prince Bismarck's Rejoinder. Edited by H. W. Lucy. London, 1888.

35. Eastern Persia.—An account of the Persian Boundary commission 1870 71-72. vol. I. The Geography with Narratives by Majors St. John. Lovett, and E. Smith. Edited by Sir. F. J. Goldsmid London, 1876.

36. Fortune, Robert.—A residence among the Chinese, inland, on the coast and at sea. London, 1857.

37. Froude, James Anthony.—Oceana or England and her colonies. Leipzig, 1887.

38. Geary, Grattan.—Burma after the conquest, viewed in its Political, Social and Commercial aspects from Mandalay. London, 1886

39. ——————Through Asiatic Turkey. Narrative of a journey from Bombay to the Bosphorus. 2 vols. London, 1818.

40. Haeckel, Ernst.—A visit to Ceylon. Translated by Clara Bell. London, 1883.

41. Hooker, Joseph Dalton.—Himalayan Journals. Notes of a novelist. 2 vols. With maps. London, 1854.

42. ——————Himalayan Journals. Edited by G. T. Bettany. (M. L. F. B.). London, 1891.

43. Huc, M.—Travels in Tartary, Thibet and China. Translated from French by W. Hazlitt. 2 vols. London.

44. Humboldt, Alexander von and A. Boupland.—Personal narrative of travels to the Equinoctial regions of America. Translated and edited by T. Ross. (L. H. B. No. 86.). 3 vols. London, 1895.

45. India in the Fifteenth Century.—Being a Collection of narratives of Voyages to India from Latin, Persian, Russian and Italian sources. Translated into English. Edited with an introduction by R.H. Major. London, 1857

46. Jacquemont, Victor.—Letters from India. A Journey to the British Dominions of India, Tibet, Lahore and Cashmere. 2 vols. London, 1834.

47. James, F. L.—The wild tribes of the Soudan. An account of personal experiences and adventures with map. Second Edition. London, 1884.

48. Jennings, Samuel.—My visit to the gold-fields in the South-East Wynaad. London, 1881.

49. Keane, John F.—Six months in the Hejaz. London, 1887.

50. King, Lieut. Col. W. Ross.—The aboriginal tribes af the Nilgiri Hills. London, 1870.

51. Knight, E. F.—Where three empires meet. A narrative of recent travel in Kashmir, Western Tibet, Gilgit and the adjoining countries. Third Edition. London, 1893.

52. Layard, Austin, H.—Discoveries in the ruins of Ninevah and Babylon. London, 1853.

53. ————————The above with Travels in Armenia, Kurdistan, and the Desert. Being the result of a Second expedition undertaken for the trustees of British Museum Second Edition. New York, 1865.

54. Leared, Arthur.—Morocco and the Moors. Being an account of travels with a general description of the country and its people. Revised and Edited by Sir B. Burton. London, 1891.

55. Leitner, G. W. V.—The Hunza and Nagyr Handbook. Being an introduction to a knowledge of the Language, race and countries of Hunza, Nagyr and a part of Yasin. 2 parts. Calcutta, 1889.

56. Livingstone, David and Charles.—Narrative of an expedition to the Zambesi and its tributaries, and of the discoveries of the lakes Shirwa and Nyassa with mad &c. London, 1865.

57. ——————David.—The last journals of.—in Central Africa from 1865 to his death. With introduction, &c. by Horace Waller. 2 vols. London, 1874.

58. Margary, Augustus Raymond.—Journey. To which is added a concluding chapter by Sir Ruthford Alcock. London, 1876.

59. Marvin, Charles.—Merv, the Queen of the World; and the scourge of the man-stealing Turcomans. London, 1884.

60. Mullick, Bulloram.—Home life in Bengal. An account of the everyday life of a Hindu Home at the present day. Calcutta, 1885.

61. Nansen, Fridtjof.—Farthest North. 2 vols. (M. C. L. S.). London, 1877.

62. O'Rell, M. and Jack Allyn.—Jonathan and his continent. Translated by Madame Paul Blouët. London, 1889.

63. Palgrave, William Gifford.—Narrative of a year's journey through Central and Eastern Arabia. 2 vols. London, 1865.

64. Râmakrishna, P.—Life in an Indian village. With an introduction by the Rt. Hon. Sir. M. E. Grant Duff. London, 1891.

65. Rowe, Richard.—How our working people live. London.

66. Schamyl.—The Sultan, Warrior and Prophet of the Caucasus. Translated from the German by Wraxall. London, 1856.

67. Shah of Persia, H. M. The.—Diary, during his tour through Europe in A. D. 1873. Translated by J. W. Redhouse. London, 1874.

68. ——————————during his second tour through Europe in 1878. London.

69. Sleeman, Major General, Sir. W. H.—A journey through the Kingdom of Oude in 1849 and 1850. 2 vols. London, 1858.

70. ——————————Rambles and Recollections. London.

71. Southgate, Rev. Horatio.—Narrative of a Tour through Armenia, Kurdistan, Persia and Mesopotamia. 2 vols. London, 1840.

72. Speke, John Hanning.—Journal of the Discovery of the Sources of the Nile. London, 1840.

73. Stack, Edward.—Six Months in Persia. 2 vols. London, 1882.

74. Taine, H.—Voyage en Italie. 2 vols. Paris, 1866 and 1872.

75. Tavernier, J. B.—Travels in India. Translated from the French. By V. Ball. 2 vols. London, 1889.

76. Thomson, Sir C. Wyville.—The Voyage of the "Challenger." The Atlantic. A preliminary account of the general results of the exploring voyage of H. M. S. 'Challenger' during the year 1873 and the early part of the year 1876. 2 vols. London, 1877.

77. Vámbéry, Arminius.—Travels in Central Asia. London, 1864.

78. Visram, F.—A Khoja's Tour in Australia. Bombay, 1885.

79. Voyages of Corneille Le Brun through Russia to Persia, and India. 2 vols. (in French). Amsterdam, 1718.

80. Wallace, Alfred Russell.—A Narrative of travels on the Amazon and Rio Negro. Edited by G. T. Bettany. (M. L. F. B.). London, 1889.

81. Wylie, A. H.—Chatty Letters from the East and West. London 1879.

R.

Logic, and Mental, Moral, & Political Sciences.

1. Aristotle —Ethics. Comprising his Practical Philosophy. Translated from the Greek by John Gillies. (L. H. B. No. 43) London, 1893.
2. ——— Politics. A Treatise on Government. Translated from the Greek by William Ellis. With an Introduction by H. Morley. (L. H. B. No. 55). London, 1895.
3. Annual Administration Reports.—Divisional and District. Selections from—with the Government Resolutions on them. 1872-1873. Calcutta, 1874,
4. Application to the nobility, &c., in behalf of the Education of the Mahomedans and in aid to the M. A. O. College. Aligarh.
5. Aurelius, Marcus.—Meditations. Translated from the Greek by Jeremy Collier. With Introduction and Notes by H. Zimmern. (L. H. B. No. 3). London, 1896.
6. Bacon, Francis, Lord Verulam.—Novum Organum or True Suggestions for the interpretation of nature. (L. H. B. No. 45). London, 1893.
7. Bain, Alexander.—Mental and Moral Science. A Compendium of Psychology and Ethics. London, 1884.
8. Barbour, D.—The Theory of Bimetallism and the effects of the Partial Demonetisation of Silver on England and India. London, 1885.
9. Berkeley, Bishop.—Principles of Human Knowledge. Treatise on the nature of the material substance. With Introduction by C. Simon. (L. H. B. No. 48). London, 1893.
10. Cane, Col. Sir Edmund F. Du.—The Punishment and Prevention of Crime. (Eng. Cit.). London, 1885.
11. Chorâgh Ali, Moulvi.—Hyderabad (Deccan) under Sir Salar Jung. Four volumes in one volume. Bombay, 1885.

12. ——————The Proposed Political, Legal and Social Reforms in the Ottoman Empire and other Muhammadan States. Bombay, 1883.

13. Chesney, George.—Indian Polity. A view of the system of administration in India. Second Edition. London, 1870.

14. Cotton, J. S.—Colonies and Dependencies, Part I, India. Part II. The Colonies. By E. J. Payne. (Eng. Cit.). London, 1883.

15. Day, Alfred.—Summary and Analysis of the Dialogues of Plato. London, 1870.

16. Deussen, Dr. Paul.—The Elements of Metaphysics. Translated from the Second German Edition with the personal collaboration of the author, by C. M. Duff. (M. C. L. S.). London, 1894.

17. Education of the Muhammadan Community in British India and their employment in the Public Service generally. Selections from the Records of the Government of India, Home Department. Correspondence on the subject of—Calcutta, 1886.

18. Epictetus.—The teaching of—Trnslated from the Greek. With Introduction and Notes by T. W. Rolleston. (L. H. B. No. 4). London, 1896.

19. Fleming, William.—The Manual of Moral Philosophy. New Edition. London, 1878.

20. Fowle, T. W.—The Poor Law. (Eng. Cit.) London, 1881.

21. Fowler, Thomas.—Elements of Deductive Logic. Eighth Edition. (C P. S.). Oxford, 1883.

22. ——————Inductive Logic. Fourth Edition. (C. P. S.). Oxford, 1883.

23. Frewen, Moreton.—The Economic Crisis. London, 1888.

24. Gribble, J. D. B.—Two Native States. Hyderabad and Mysore. Madras, 1886.

25. Grote, George.—Plato and the other companions of Socrates. 3 vols. Third Edition. London, 1875.

26. Hudson, W. H.—An Introduction to the Study of Herbert Spencer. Second Edition. London, 1895.

27. Hyderabad in 1890 and 1891—Comprising all the letters on Hyderabad affairs written to the Madras "Hindu" by its Hyderabad Correspondent. Bangalore, 1892.

28. ——————Affairs—Compiled by Moulavi Syed Mahdi Ali. ! vols. Bombay, 1883.

29. Jardine, Rev. Robert.—The Elements of the Psychology o Cognition. Second Edition. London, 1884.

30. Jevons, W. Stanley.—The state in relation to labour. (Eng. Cit.) London, 1882.

31. ——————Logic. (Sc. Pr.) London, 1876.

32. ——————Money and the Mechanism of Exchange. (I. Sc. S.). Ninth Edition, London, 1890.

33. ——————Political Ecnomy. (Sc. Pr.) London, 1892.

34. Keely, Miss.—An Advanced Text Book on Domestic Economy. (M. S. S.) Madras, 1889.

35. Ladd, George, T.—Elements of Physiological Psychology. London, 1887.

36. Lakh Bribery Case.—Hyderabad. A compilation of a series of articles published in several issues of the Bangalore "Evening Mail." Bangalore, 1895.

37. Letourneau, Dr. Charles.—Sociology based upon Ethnography. Translated by H. M. Trollope. New Edition. London, 1893.

38. Lewes, George Henry.—The History of Philosophy. 2 vols. corrected and partly re-written. Fourth Edition. London, 1871.

39. ——————A Biographical History of Philosophy. (L. H. B. No. 16) London, 1894.

40. ——————Problems of Life and Mind. Third Series. The Study of Psychology, its object, scope and method. London, 1879.

41. Macgeorge, G. W.—The Ways and Works in India, being an account of the Public Works from the earliest times up to the present day. Westminster, 1894.

42. Mackintosh, Sir James.—On the Progress of Ethical Philosophy. Edited by W. Whewell. Fourth Edition. Edinburgh, 1872.

43. Mahan, Rev. Asa.—The Science of Logic or Analysis of the Laws of Thought. New York, 1873.

44. Maine, Henry Sumner.—Ancient Law, its connection with the early History of Society and its relation to modern ideas. Seventh Edition. London, 1878.

45. ——————Dissertations on early law and custom. London, 1883.

46. ——————Lectures on the Early History of Institutions. Second Edition. London, 1875.

47. ——————Village Communities on the East and West. New Edition. London, 1890.

48. Mansel, Henry.—Metaphysics or the Philosophy of Consciousness. Phenomenal and real. Fourth Edition. Edinburgh, 1883.

49. Mayor, Joseph B.—A Sketch of Ancient Philosophy from Thales to Cicero. Cambridge, 1889.

50. Mill, James.—Analysis of the phenomena of the human mind. Edited with additional notes by J. S. Mill. 2 vols. London, 1869.

51. ———John Stuart.—Considerations on Representative Government. Second Edition. London, 1861.

52. ——————A System of Logic. Ratiocinative and Inductive. 2 vols. Sixth Edition. London, 1865.

53. ——————

——————(L. H. B. No. 15.) London, 1892.

54. ——————Principles of Political Economy with some of their applications to Social Philosophy. (L. H. B. No. 6). London, 1895.

55. ——————Essays on some unsettled questions of Political Economy. Third Edition. London, 1877.

56. Narasimmaiyengar—Report on the Census of India, 1891. Mysore. Parts I and II with appendicies. Bangalore, 1893.

57. Nicholls, Sir George.—A History of the Scotch Poor Law in connection with the condition of the people. London, 1856.

58. Nizam's Dominions.—H. H. The. Administration report for 1294 Fasli. 1884-1885. Bombay, 1886.

59. ——————for 1298. Fasli, 1888-1889. Hyderabad.

60. ——————for 1303 Fasli, 1893-1894. Hyderabad, 1895.

61. —————— History of the Operations of Educational Department. For 1292, 1293 and 1294 Faslis. 1883, 1884 and 1885. By Motaman Jung. Hyderabad. 1886.

62. ——————Report on the History of the Famine in—in 1876 and 1877 and 1878. By Moulvi Syed Mahdi Ali. Bombay, 1879.

63. ——————Replies to questions contained in Chapter I of the Memorandum of the Famine Commission of—By Moulvi Mahdi Ali. Bombay, 1879.

64. ——————Annual Financial Statement of the Divani Districts for the year. 1289 Fasli.

65. ——————The above for 1292 Fasli.

66. ——————Report on the Administration of Justice for Second Quarter of 1294 Fasli in—By Mahdi Hassan.

67. ——————Memorandum on Railways. 1886.

68. ——————Report on the Working of State Railways in—from 1874 to 1885. By Sardar Diler-ul-mulk Bahadur. Hyderabad, 1888.

69. ————————Abstract of the Proceedings of H. H. The Nizam's Guaranteed State Railway from July to September 1888.

70. ————————Memorandum of the Revenue Survey Department in—by Syed Mahdi Ali for 1285-1291 Faslies. Bombay, 1882.

71. ————————Settlement of the Kulubgur and Boden Talukas. 1298 Fasli. Madras, 1891.

72. Parieu, M. E. De.—Principes de la Science Politique. (in French.) Paris, 1870.

73. Parliamentary Views.—No. I. London.

74. Plato.—Dialogues. Translated into English with Analysis and Introduction by B. Jowett. 5 vols. Second Edition. Oxford, 1875. 5 vols.

75. ———Dialogues. Containing the Apology of Socrates, Crito- Phædo, Protagoras. Translated with Introduction by H. Cary. (L. H. B. No. 34). London, 1895.

76. Ray, P. K.—A Text-Book of Deductive Logic, for the use of students. Fourth Edition. London, 1888.

77. Renan, M. Ernest.—Averroès et L'Averroïsme. Paris, 1866.

78. Spencer, Herbert.—First Principles. Synthetic Philosophy. Fifth Edition. London, 1887.

79. ————The Study of Sociology. Sixth Edition. (I. Sc. S.) London, 1877.

80. Stewart, Dugald.—The Collected Works of—Edited by Sir William Hamilton. 11 vols. Edinburgh, 1877. 11 v

81. Townsend, Calvin.—A Shorter Course in Civil Government consisting of 70 lessons. New York, 1875.

82. Traill, H. D.—Central Government. (Eng. Cit.). London, 1881.

83. Walpole, Spencer.—The Electorate and the Legislature. (Eng, Cit.). London, 1881.

84. ————Foreign Relations. (Eng. Cit.). London, 1882.

85. Whately, Richard.—Elements of Logic. London, 1867.

Dictionaries.

86. Franck, M. Ad.—Dictionnaire des Sciences Philosophiques. 2 vols. Paris, 1885.

S.

Law.

1. Agnew, W. F.—The Law of Trusts in British India. With an Appendix. (T. L. L). Calcutta, 1882.
2. Ali, Syed Ameer.—The Law Relating to Gifts, Trusts, etc. among the Mahommadans. (T. L. L.) Calcutta, 1888.
3. Amos, Sheldon.—History and Principles of the Civil Law of Rome. London, 1883.
4. ————The Science of Law. Seventh Edition. (I. Sc. S.) London, 1889.
5. Anson, Sir William, R.—Principles of the English Law of Contract, and of Agency in its relation to contract. Third Edition. Oxford, 1884.
6. Austin, John.—Lectures on Jurisprudence or the Philosophy of Positive Law. Edited by Robert Campbell. 2 Vols. Fourth Edition Revised. London, 1879.
7. ————An Analysis of—Lectures on Jurisprudence. By Gordon Campbell. Third Edition. London, 1888.
8. Baillie, Neil B. E.—A Digest of Mahomedan Law containing the doctrines of the Imameea. Code of Jurisprudence. Part Second. London, 1869.
9. ————The Mahomedan Law of Inheritance. London, 1874.
10. Beaufort, F. L.—A Digest of the Criminal Law of the Presidency of Fort William, and Guide to the Criminal Authorities therein. Part I. Second Edition. Compiled by—Calcutta, 1857.
11. ————The above. Part II. Calcutta, 1860.
12. Bhattâchârya, Krishṇa Kamal.—Notes of Lecture on Hindu Law. Calcutta, 1886.
13. Blackstone, Sir William.—The Student's Blackstone, being the Commentaries on the Laws of England. Abridged by R. M. N. Kerr. London, 1887.
14. Bombay Municipal Act of 1888, The City of.—Act No. III of 1888. Bombay, 1892.

15. Calcutta Municipal Consolidation Act.—Act III of 1888.

16. Chitty, Edward.—The Commercial and General Lawyer. A plain and practical exposition of the Law of England. Seventh Edition. London, 1851.

17. Civil Service Regulations, The.—First Edition. Calcutta, 1889

18. ——————————Corrected up to May 1892. Second Edition. Calcutta, 1892.

19. Collett, Charles.—A Manual of the Law of Torts and of the Measure of Damages. Madras, 1886.

20. Coopooswami Naicker, T. and Company.—The New Civil Cour Manual. Third Edition. 2 vols. Madras, 1893

21. ——————————The New Crimina Court Manual. Third Edition. 2 vols. Madras.

22. Cowell, Herbert.—The Hindu Law. 2 vols. (T. L. L.). Calcutta, 1870.

23. ——————————The History and Constitution of the Courts and Legislative authorities in India. Second Edition. (T. L. L.). Calcutta, 1884.

24. Cranenburgh, D. E.—The New Civil Court Manual, being the Sixth Edition of the "Civil Procedure Code and other Acts." Improved and enlarged and compiled by—Calcutta, 1883.

25. ——————————The New Code of Civil Procedure, being Act XVI of 1882, with annotations and index by—Sixth Edition, 1887.

26. ——————————The Criminal Cases of Sutherland's Weekly Reporter. 2 vols. With a general nominal index, compiled by—Calcutta, 1898.

27. Cunningham, Henry Stewart.—The Indian Evidence Act. No. I of 1872. Madras, 1883.

28. Cutler, John and E. F. Griffin.—An Analysis of the Indian Penal Code. London, 1878.

29. Field, C. D.—Introduction to the Regulations of the Bengal Code. Calcutta, 1884.

——————————The Law of Evidence in British India. Calcutta, 1884.

31. **Gaius.**—Commentaries. Translated with notes by J. T. Abdy and B. Walker. Cambridge, 1870.

32. **Gosvâmi, N.**—Transfer of Property Act. Act IV of 1882. Calcutta. 1882.

33. Goudsmit, J. E.—The Pandects. A Treatise on the Roman Law. Translated from the Dutch by R. De Tracy Gould. Reprinted. Madras, 1891.

34. Grady, S. G.—A Treatise on the Hindu Law of Inheritance. Madras, 1868.

35. Gribble, J. D. B. and P. Hehir.—Outlines of Medical Jurisprudence for Indian Courts. Third Edition. Revised and Enlarged.

36. ——————— The above. Fourth Edition. Bombay. 1898.

37. Gulam Mahamed, Munshi.—Râjkumar Law Lectures, being elementary lectures on leading legal maxims addressed to the Senior Students of the Râjkumar College, Râjkot. Râjkot, 1899.

38. Hallilay, Richard.—Digest of Examination Questions. By H.W. Purkis. Twelfth Edition. London, 1882.

39. Hanumân Prasâd and Lalla Lalita Prasâd.—Reports of the High Courts of Judicature for the North West Provinces. Agra, 1867.

40. Henderson, Gilbert. S.—The Law of Intestate and Testamentary Succession in India, including the Indian Succession Act. Act X of 1865. With a commentary. Calcutta, 1882.

41. Holland, Thomas Erskine.—The Elements of Jurisprudence Oxford, 1886.

42. Hukm Chand.—The Principles of the Law of Consent. Bombay, 1897.

43. ——————— A Treatise on the Law of Res Judicata. London, 1884.

44. Hunter. W. A.—A Systematic and historical exposition of Roman Law in the order of a Code, embodying the Institutes of Gaius and Justinian. Translated into English by J. A. Cross. Second Edition. London. 1885.

45. Indermauer, John. and Charles Thwaites.—Student's Guide to the Law of Real and Personal Property. Second Edition. London, 1889.

46. Indian Companies' Act, The.—Act No. VI of 1882 Bombay, 1882.

47. ——Law Reports, The.—Calcutta Series. Vol. I. Calcutta, 1876.

48. ——Penal Code, The.—With the First Report. (the Original Edition).

49. Jones, Sir William.—Al Sirajiyyah or. The Mahomedan Law of Inheritance with a Commentary. New Edition with improvements by Śyâmacharun Sarcar. Calcutta, 1861.

50. Justinian.—The Institutes of—with English Translation and Notes by Thomas Collett Sanders Fifth Edition. London, 1874.

51. —— ——Edited as a Recension of the Institutes of Gaius. By T. E. Holland. Second Edition. Oxford, 1881.

52. ——Student's "Auxilium" to the ——by A. H. Ruegy. London, 1879.

53. Khandekar, Ganpati Rao Hari.—The Code of Civil Procedure being Act No. X of 1877. With reference to the old Civil Procedure Code, and index. Poona.

54. Knight.—Annotated Model Bye-laws of the Local Government Board. Third Edition. London, 1890.

55. Lease of Waste Lands in Bengal, Rules for the.—Calcutta, 1880.

56. Leonards, Lord St.—A handbook on property Law in a series of letters. London, 1858.

57. Levi, Leone.—International Law with materials for a Code of International Law. (I. Sc. S.) London, 1887.

58. Macleane, C. D.—The Standing Orders of the Board of Revenue. Revised under the orders of Government. Madras, 1882.

59. Macnaghten, Sir. W. H.—The Principles of Hindu Law. Compiled by Prasanna Coomâr Sen. Serampore, 1886.

60. Macpherson. A. G.—A Treatise on the law of mortgage as administered in the Courts of Bengal and North West Provinces. Fourth Edition. Calcutta, 1865.

61. Markby, William.—Elements of Law, considered with reference to Principles of General Jurisprudence. Third Edition. Oxford, 1885.

62. Mayne, John D.—Commentaries of the Indian Penal Code. Act XLV of 1860. Twefth Edition. Revised and Enlarged. Madras, 1884.

63. Mitra, A. C.—Principles of Mahomedan Law. Calcutta, 1889.

64. Negotiable Instruments Act.—Edited by Mr. D. Chalmers. Calcutta, 1882.

65. Norton, John Bruce.—The Topics of Jurisprudence or aids to the office of the Indian Judge. Edited by J. W. Handley. Second Edition. Madras, 1870.

66. Phillips, Arthur.—The Law relating to the land tenures of Lower Bengal. (T. L. L.) Calcutta, 1886.

67. ———— H. A. D.—Manual of Revenue and Collectorate Law. With Annotations. Calcutta, 1884.

68. Prinsep, H. T.—The Code of Criminal Procedure. Act X of 1882. Seventh Edition. Calcutta, 1884.

69. Public Works Department Code.—Vol. I. General Regulations. Corrected up to 29th February 1892. Government of India. Sixth Edition. Calcutta, 1892.

70. Rattigan, W. H.—A Treatise on the Roman Law of persons. London, 1873.

71. Redman, J. H.—A Treatise on the Law relating to Railway Companies. Second Edition. London, 1880.

72. Rumsey, Almaric.—A Chart of Hindu Family Inheritance. With an Explanatory Treatise. Second Edition much enlarged. London, 1877.

73. ———— Al Sirajiyyah.—The Mahomedan Law of Inheritance. With Notes and Appendix. London, 1869.

74. Sarkâr Sâstri.—The Hindu Law of Adoption. (T. L. L.). Calcutta, 1891.

75. ——————The Hindu Law of Inheritance, and the Mahomedan Law of Inheritance according to the Sunni School. Calcutta, 1887.

76. Sing.—An Analysis of Maine's Ancient Law. Calcutta, 1890.

77. Siromaṇi, J. S.—Commentaries on the Hindu Law of Inheritance, Succession, &c. Calcutta, 1885.

78. Snel.—The Principles of Equity. An analysis thereof with Notes by E. E. Blyth. Third Edition. London, 1889.

79. Sreenivâsa Rao, P.—Legal Maxims. Illustrated with special reference to the laws in force in British India. Madras, 1873.

80. Stephen, James.—New Commentaries on the Laws of England. 4 vols. Ninth Edition. London, 1883.

81. ————James Fitz-James.—The Indian Evidence Act in British India. Act I of 1872. With an Introduction on the Principles of Judicial Evidence. Calcutta, 1872.

82. ————————A Digest of the Law of Evidence. London, 1876.

83. Stokes, Whitley.—The Indian Succession Act. Act X of 1865. With a Commentary and Notes. Calcutta, 1865.

84. Sutherland, D.—The Indian Contract Act. Act IX of 1872 and the Specific Relief Act. Act I of 1877. With a full Commentary. London, 1879.

85. Systems of land tenure in various countries. Edited by J. W. Probyn. London, 1876.

86. Tarrant, H. J.—A Digest of the decisions of the Judicial Committee and the Lords of Her Majesty's Most Honorable Privy Council. Third Edition. Madras, 1885.

87. Thomson, Reginald.—A Manual of Hindu Law. Second Edition. Madras, 1878.

88. Underhill, Arthur.—A Summary of the Law of Torts; or Wrongs independent of Contract. Fifth Edition. London, 1889.

89. West, Raymond. And J. G. Bühler.—A Digest of the Hindu Law of Inheritance, Partition and Adoption with Introduction and Notes. 2 vols. Third Edition. Bombay, 1884.

90. Wigram, H.—Selections from the Judgments of the Privy Council. Edited by—Madras, 1881.

91. Williams, Joshua. Principles of the Law of Real Property. Edited by his son T. C. Williams. Fifteenth Edition. London, 1885.

92. Woodman, Joseph, Vere.—A Digest of Indian Law Cases containing High Court Reports and Privy Council Reports of Appeals from India. 1836-1886. With an index of cases compiled under the orders of the Government of India. 5 vols. Calcutta, 1887 and 1888.

93. ——————The above 1887-1889. Calcutta, 1899.

Dictionaries.

94. Ward and Lock—Popular Law Dictionary, forming a concise Compendium of the Common and Statute Law of England and Wales. London.

T. Sciences.

I. GENERAL SCIENCE.

Bailey, James.—How to teach the babies. Second Edition, London.

2. ——————Oral Teaching in Infant Schools. London.

3. Best.—First year of Scientific Knowledge. Thirteenth Edition, London.

4. Binns, Charles F.—The Story of the Potter (L. U. S.) London, 1898.

5. British Manufacturing Industries.—Edited by G. P. Bevan. London, 1876.

6. Bornett.—Primer of Domestic Economy. London, 1892.

7. Büchner, Prof. Ludwig.—Mind in Animals. Translated from the German of—by Annie Besant. Third Revised Edition. London, 1880.

8. Carpenter, William B.—The Microscope and its Revelations. Second Edition. London, 1881.

9. Cavendish.—The Game of Lawn Tennis. Seventh Edition. London, 1886.

10. ——————The Laws and Principles of Whist. Seventeenth Edition. London, 1888.

11. Child's Guide to Knowledge.—By a Lady. London, 1892.

12. Clifford, William Kingdon.—Seeing and Thinking. (N. S.) London, 1879.

13. Clodd, Edward.—The Story of Creation. A plain account of Evolution. (L. U. S.) London, 1888.

14. ——————The Story of Primitive Man. (L. U. S.) London, 1895.

15. Cooke, J. P.—Scientific Culture and Other Essays. London, 1882.

16. Cutcrewe, Carrie.—Mem Sahib's Book of Cakes, Scones, Biscuits &c. Calcutta, 1894.

17. Darwin, Charles.—The Descent of Man and Selection in relation to Sex. London, 1877.

18. ——————The Expression of the Emotions in Man and Animals. London, 1873.

19. ——————On the Origin of Species by means of Natural Selection. London, 1860.

20. ——————The above. (L. H. B. No. 88). London, 1894.

21. ——————The Variation of Animals and Plants under Domestication. 2 vols. London, 1868. — 2 Vols

22. Fielding, T. H.—On the Theory and Practice of Painting in Oil and Water Colours. London, 1846.

23. Flower, William Henry.—Fashion in Deformity as illustrated in the customs of barbarous and civilised races. (N. S.) London, 1881.

24. Frankland, Percy Faraday.—Our Secret Friends and Foes. (R. Sc. S.) London, 1893.

25. Fuller, J. B.—An Agricultural Primer for use in Indian Elementary Schools or Classes. Allahabad, 1886.

26. Galton, Francis.—Finger Prints. London, 1892.

27. ——————Hereditary Genius. An Enquiry into its Laws and Consequences. London, 1892.

28. ——————Natural Inheritance. London, 1889.

29. Geddes, Prof. Patrick and J. A. Thomson.—The Evolution of Sex. (C. Sc. S.) London, 1889.

30. Geoghegan, J.—Silk in India. An account of the various attempts to encourage and extend Sericulture in that country. Second Edition. Calcutta. 1880.

31. Gomme, George Laurence.—The village community, with special reference to the Origin and Form of its survivals in Britain. (C. Sc. S.) London, 1890.

32. Gordon, Hugh.—Elementary Course of Practical Science. Part I. London, 1893.

33. Gray, Asa.—Scientific Papers. Selected by C. S. Sargent. Vol. I. Reviews of works on Botany and related Subjects. Vol. II. Essays and Biographical Sketches. London, 1889. — 2 vols

34. Haeckel, Ernst.—Freedom in Science and Teaching. From the German of—With preface by T. H. Huxley. London, 1879

35. ————Natürliche Schöpfungsgeschichte. Berlin, 1875.
36. ————The History of Creation. From the German of —Translated by Prof. E. Ray Lankester. 2 vols. London, 1876.
37. Haughton, Rev. S.—The three Kingdoms of Nature. Second Edition. London, 1868.
38. Hayes, M. Horace.—Riding. London, 1882.
39. Herbert.—Fifty Dinners. London, 1895.
40. Heritage, Lizzie.—Cassell's New Universal Cookery Book. London, 1894.
41. Hewitt, W.—Elementary Science Lessons, being a systematic course of Practical Object Lessons. London, 1891.
42. ————A course of simple Object Lessons for infants. London, 1891.
43. Hossain, Syed.—Scientific Nomenclature for the Vernaculars. Lucknow.
44. Huxley, Thomas Henry.—Critiques and Addresses. London, 1873.
45. ————Evidence as to Man's place in Nature. London, 1864.
46. ————Evolution, Ethics and Other Essays. London, 1894.
47. ————Lay Sermons, Addresses and Reviews. Sixth Edition. London, 1877.
48. ————On the Origin of Species or the Causes of the Phenomena of Organic Nature. A course of six lectures to working men. New York, 1871
49. ————On our knowledge of the causes of the Phenomena of Organic Nature. London, 1863.
50. ————Science and Culture and Other Essays. London, 1881.
51. ————Science and Education. Essays. London, 1893.
52. ————Science Primer Introductory. London, 1893.
53. Indian Cookery Books.—By a thirty five years' resident. Calcutta, 1891.

54. Laing, S.—Modern Science and Modern Thought. London, 1889.
55. ———Problems of the Future and Essays. London, 1890.
56. Lankester, Prof. E. Ray.—Degeneration. A chapter in Darwinism. (N. S.). London, 1880.
57. ———The Uses of Animals in relation to the Industry of Man. London.
58. Lubbock, Sir John.—Scientific Lectures. London, 1879.
59. ———On the Senses, Instincts and Intelligence of Animals with special reference to Insects. Sc. S.). London, 1888.
60. Mantegazza, Paolo.—Physiognomy and Expression. (C. Sc. S.). London.
61. Marion and Co.—Practical Guide to Photography. London, 1884.
62. Marsh, Dr. Sylvester.—Section-cutting. A practical guide to the preparation and mounting of Sections for the Microscope, special prominence being given to the subject of Animal Sections. London, 1878.
63. Miall, L. C.—Object Lessons from Nature. London, 1890.
64. Mill, Hugh Robert.—The Realm of Nature. An outline of Physiography. (U. E. M.). London, 1892.
65. Notes on Collecting and Preserving Natural History Objects. Edited by J. E. Taylor. London, 1876.
66. Patterson, Robert.—The Errors of Evolution. An Examination of the Nebular Theory, Geological Evolution, the Origin of Life, and Darwinism. Boston, 1884.
67. Pearson, Karl.—The Grammar of Science. (C. Sc. S.). London, 1892.
68. Playfair, Sir Lyon.—Subjects of Social Welfare. London, 1889
69. Pogson, Lieut. Frederick.—Manual of Agriculture for India. Calcutta, 1883.
70. Pole, William.—The Theory of the Modern Scientific Game of Whist. Sixteenth Edition. London, 1887.
71. Popular Science Review.—Edited by W. S. Dallas. London, 1880.
72. Rawlings, Gertrude Burford.—The Story of the British Coinage. (L. U. S.). London, 1898.

73. Romanes, George J.—Animal Intelligence. (I. Sc. S.). London, 1882.

74 ——————The Scientific Evidences of Organic Evolution. (N. S.). London, 1882.

75. Rundell, Mrs.—A new System of Domestic Cookery formed upon principles of Economy. London.

76. Ruskin, John.—The Elements of Drawing, in Three Letters to Beginners. London, 1859.

77. Salisbury, Marquis of.—Evolution. A Retrospect. London, 1894.

78. Science for All.—Edited by Role Brown. Illustrated. 5 vols. London.

79. Semper, Karl.—The Natural Conditions of Existence as they affect Animal Life. (I. Sc. S.). London, 1881.

80 Taylor, Isaac.—The Origin of the Aryans. An account of the prehistoric Ethnology and Civilisation of Europe. (C. Sc. S.). London, 1889.

81. Thomson, Wyville.—The Depths of the Sea. Second Edition, with Illustrations and Maps. London, 1874.

82. Vignoli, Tito.—Myth and Science. (I. Sc. S.). London, 1882.

83. Virchow, Rudolf.—The freedom of Science in the modern state. Translated from the German with the Author's sanction. Second Edition. London, 1878.

84. Wallace, Russell.—Darwinism. An Exposition of the Theory of Natural Selection with some of its applications. (M. C. L. S.). London, 1890.

85 Whitney, William Dwight.—The Life and Growth of Language. (I. Sc. S.). London, 1875.

86. Wood, Rev. J. G.—Homes without Hands, being a Description of Animals classed according to their Principle of Construction. New York, 1866.

87. Wyvern.—Culinary Jottings. A treatise in thirty chapters on reformed Cookery for Anglo-Indian Exiles based upon Modern English and Continental Principles, with thirty Menus for little Dinners worked out in detail and an Essay on our Kitchens in India. Fifth Edition. Madras, 1885.

87. Year book of Science. (Yahrbuch der Naturwissenschaften) for 1885-1886. Edited by Max Wildermann. (in German). Freiberg, 1886.

88. ——————————————— 1886-1887.

89. ——————————————— 1887-1888.

90. ——————————————— 1888-1889.

91. ——————————————— 1889-1890.

92. ——————————————— 1892.

Edited by Prof. T. G. Bonney. (in English). London, 1893.

93 Weber. J — Le Panorame des Siècles Paris 1898 (Les Livers D'or de la Science)

94 Planchut - Edm. — Les Races Jaunes les Célestes. Paris. 1898 (Les Livers D. L. Sc)

95. Aubert. L — La Photographie de l'Invisible. Paris 1898 (Les Livers D. L. Sc.)

96. Chester E — Histoire et Role du Boeuf dans la Civilisation Paris. 1898 (L. L. D. L. Sc)

97. Servant. Stéphane — La Prehistoir de la France. Paris 1898 (L. L. D. L. Sc)

98 Deschamps. Eamile — La Vie ~~d...~~ Mysterieuse des Meros. Paris 1898 (L. L. D. L. Sc.)

100 Loliée - Frederic - Tableau de l'Histoire Litteraire du Monde. Paris 1898 (L.L.D.L.

101 Michaut - L. Dr. — Pour Devenir Medecin. Paris 1899 (L.L.D.L. Se)

102 Fontenelle - Le Dr. J. De - Le Microbes et la Mor. Paris 1899 (L.L.D.L. Se)

103 Griveau - Maurice - Les Feux et les Eaux. Par 1899 (L.L.D.L. Se)

104 Richet - Charles — Les Guerres et la Paix. Paris. 1899 (L.L.D.L. Se)

105 Berthaut - Leon - La Mar les Marins et les Sauveteurs - Paris 1899 (L.L.D.L. Se)

106 D'Hurniac - L. Michaud - Les Grandes Legendes de L'Humanite. Paris 1899 (L.L.D.L. Se,

107 Darsuzz - Gesa - Les Pyrenées Francaises. Par 1899 (L.L.D.L. Se)

108 Delmer - Louis - Le Chemins de Fer - Paris 1899 (L.L.D.L.

109 Lafon - Rene - Pour devenir Avocat. Paris 1899 — " —

110 Plauzoles - Le Dr. Sicard de - La Tuberculose — " — "

111 Ruckert - C - La Photographie des Couleurs — Paris - 1900

112 Hudry - Menos - Mme - La Femme — " — " —

113 Bauel - A. D. Le - Cooperatione — " — " —

114 Toudouze - Georges - La Conquete des Mers — " — "

II. *Mathematics and Astronomy.*

1. Ball.—Story of the Heavens. Revised Edition. London, 1893.
2. Bonney.—Story of the Planets. (L. U. S.). London, 1893.
3. Brabant, F. G.—The Elements of Plane and Solid Mensuration. New Edition. London, 1889.
4. Briggs, William. and G. H. Bryan.—A Text-book of Statics. (U. C. C. T. S.). London.
5. Burgess, James.—Notes on Hindu Astronomy and the History of Our Knowledge of it. Hertford, 1893.
6. Campigneulles, Rev. V. de. and Rev. H. Josson.—The Total Solar Eclipse of January 22nd, 1898. Calcutta, 1898.
7. Chambers, G. F.—Story of the Solar System, simply told for general readers. (L. U. S.). London, 1895.
8. ————Story of the Stars, simply told for general readers. (L. U. S.). London, 1895.
9. Forbes, George.—The Transit of Venus. (N. S.). London, 1874.
10. Frome, Col.—Outline of the method of conducting a Trigonometrical Survey. London, 1862.
11. Giberne, Agnes.—The Starry Skies. First Lessons on the Sun the Moon and Stars. With illustrations. London, 1894.
12. Godfray, H.—A Treatise on Astronomy for the use of Colleges and Schools. Second Edition. London, 1874.
13. Gore, J. Ellard.—Astronomical Lessons for the use of Students and Young People. London, 1890.
14. Gregory, Richard A.—The Vault of Heaven. An Elementary Text-book of Modern Physical Astronomy. (U. E. S.).
15. Gribble, T. G.—Preliminary Survey and Estimates. (*T-B.* Sc.). London, 1891.
16. Hall, H. S. and S. R. Knight.—Algebraical Exercises and Examination Papers. Third Edition. Revised and Enlarged. London, 1890.

17. ——————————Higher Algebra. A Sequel to Elementary Algebra for Schools. Third Edition. Revised and Enlarged. London, 1890.

18. Hann, James.—A Rudimentary Treatise on Analytical Geometry and Conic Sections. New Edition. Re-written and Enlarged by J. R. Young. London, 1871.

19. Heather, J. F.—A Treatise on Mathematical Instruments. Twelfth Edition. London, 1874.

20. Herschel, Sir John F. W.—Outlines of Astronomy. New Edition. London, 1875.

21 Intermediate Mathematics.—By the Principal of the University Correspondence College. (U. C. C. T. S.). London, 1890.

22. Jackson, Major Basil.—A Course of Military Surveying, including Sketching in the Field, Plan-Drawing, Levelling and Military Reconnaissance. Second Edition London, 1841.

23. Johnston, A. K.—School Atlas of Astronomy. New and Enlarged Edition with an Elementary Survey of the Heavens by Robert Grant. London, 1877.

24. Kempe, A. B.—How to Draw a Straight Line. A Lecture on Linkages. (N. S.) London, 1877.

25. Key to the Elements of Plane Geometry in "Chamber's Educational Course." London, 1861.

26. Knox, Alexander.—Differential Calculus for Beginners. London, 1884.

27. Lock, Rev. J. B.—Trigonometry for Beginners as far as the Solution of Triangles. London, 1891.

28. Lockyer, J. N.—Astronomy. (Sc. Pr.) New Edition. London, 1879.

29. ——————Recent and Coming Eclipses, being notes on the Total Solar Eclipses of 1893, 1896 and 1898. London, 1897.

30. Merrifield, Charles W.—Technical Arithmetic and Mensuration. Second Edition. London, 1873.

Military Surveying, etc.

32. Olney, Edward.—A Treatise on Special or Elementary Geometry New York, 1876.

33. ——————A University Algebra. New York, 1876.

34. Peck.—The Constellations and how to find them. London.

35. Previous.—Containing Papers set at the Six Successive Previous Examinations ending with that of March 1871, together with Answers to the Questions on Arithmetic, Algebra, Trigonometry and Mechanics by John Dunn. Cambridge, 1871.

36. Proctor, Richard, A.—Lessons in Elementary Astronomy, containing Hints for young Telescopists. New Edition. London.

37. ——————Half-hours with the Telescope. London, 1889.

38. ——————The Moon, her Motions, Aspect, Scenery and Physical Condition. London, 1873.

39. ——————A New Star Atlas. Twelfth Edition. London, 1889.

40. ——————Star Primer, showing the Starry Sky. Week by Week in 24 Hourly Maps. London, 1886.

41. Raphael.—A Manual of Astrology or a Book of the Stars. London, 1837.

42. Sang, Edward.—Elementary Arithmetic. London, 1856.

43. ——————The Higher Arithmetic. London, 1857.

44. Tables of Heights in Sind, the Punjab, N. W. Provinces and Central India, determined by the Great Trigonometrical Survey of India. Calcutta, 1863.

45. Tate, Thomas.—The Principles of Differential and Integral Calculus. New Edition. London, 1867.

46. Todhunter, J.—A Treatise on Plane Co-ordinate Geometry as applied to the Straight Line and Conic Sections. Fifth Edition. London, 1874.

47. ——————Plane Trigonometry for the use of Colleges and Schools. New Edition. London, 1890.

48 Wood, James.—The Elements of Algebra. Sixteenth Edition. Revised and much Enlarged by T. Lund. London, 1861.

49. Young, J. R.—Navigation and Nautical Astronomy in Theory and Practice. London, 1858.

III. PHYSICAL SCIENCE.

(a) *Electricity and Magnetism.*

1. Bennett, A. R.—On the Telephoning of Great Cities. London, 1892.
2. Cook, Mary.—A First Book on Electricity and Magnetism. London, 1891.
3. Electrician Primers for the use of Students and General Readers. 2 vols. London, 1891.
4. Ferguson, Robert M.—Electricity. London, 1868.
5. Guthrie, Frederick.—Magnetism and Electricity. (C. L. Sc. S.) London, 1876.
6. Jenkins.—Electricity and Magnetism. (T-B. Sc.) London.
7. Maycock, W. Perren.—A First Book of Electricity and Magnetism. London, 1891.
8. Munro, John.—The Story of Electricity. (L. U. S.) London, 1896.
9. Podle.—The Practical Telephone Hand-book. Second Edition. London, 1895.
10. Prescott, George B.—Electricity and the Electric Telegraph. London, 1878.
11. Thompson, Silvanus P.—Elementary Lessons in Electricity and Magnetism. London, 1884.
12. Tyndall, John.—Lessons in Electricity. London, 1876.
13. ——————Notes of a course of Seven Lectures on Electrical Phenomena and Theories. London, 1873.

(b) Mechanics.

1. Barry, John Wolfe.—Railway Appliances. Third Edition. London, 1881.
2. Cotterill, James H.—Applied Mechanics. Second Edition Revised. London, 1890.
3. Goodeve, T. M.—The Elements of Mechanism. Re-written and Enlarged. New Edition. London, 1885.
4. ————.—Principles of Mechanics. Re-written and Enlarged. New Edition. London, 1885.
5. Mackay, J. C.—Light Railways of the United Kingdom, India and the Colonies. London, 1891.
6. Mitchell, C. F. and E. G. Davey.—Forty Lessons in Engineering Workshop Practice. Revised by J. Rogers. London, 1889.
7. Sells, V. Perromet.—The Mechanics of Daily Life. (U. E. S.) London, 1893.
8. Wellington, A. M.—The Economic Theory of the Location of Railways. New York, 1896.

(c) *Physics.*

1. Blanford, Henry F.—The Indian Meteorologist's Vede-Mecum. Calcutta, 1877.
2. ————A Practical Guide to the Climate and Weather of India, Ceylon and Burma. London, 1889.
3. ————Tables for the Reduction of Meteorological Observations in India. Calcutta, 1877.
4. Chambers, George F.—The Story of the Weather simply told for general readers. (L. U. S.). London, 1897.
5. Chemistry of Artificial Light. London, 1856.
6. Deschanel, A. Privat—Elementary Treatise on Natural Philosophy. Translated and Edited with extensive additions by J. D. Everett. Parts I, II and IV. London, 1877-1878. 3 vol.
7. Earl, A. G.—The Elements of Laboratory Work. A course of Natural Science. London, 1890.
8. Evers, Henry.—Steam and the Steam Engine. (C. A. Sc. S.) London.
9. Galloway, Robert A.—The Steam Engine and its Inventors. A Historical Sketch. London, 1881.
10. Ganot.—Natural Philosophy for general readers and young people. Translated by E. Atkinson. Sixth Edition. London, 1887.
11. ————Elementary Treatise on Physics. Translated by E. Atkinson. Fourteenth Edition. Revised and Enlarged. London, 1893.
12. Gibson, Frank M.—Amateur Telescopist's Handbook. London, 1894.
13. Glazebrook, R. T.—Physical Optics. (T-B. Sc.). London, 1888.
14. Goodeve, T. M.—Text Book on the Steam Engine. With a Supplement on Gas Engines. Eighth Edition Enlarged. London, 1887.
15. Guillemin, A.—The Forces of Nature. A Popular Introduction to the Study of Physical Phenomena. Second Edition. London, 1873.

16. Lardner, Dr.—A Rudimentary Treatise on the Steam Engine for the use of Beginners. Fifth Edition. London, 1857.

17. Lockyer, J. Norman.—The Spectroscope and its applications. Second Edition. (N. S.). London, 1873.

18. Marcet, Mrs.—Conversations of Natural Philosophy in which the Elements of that Science are familiarly explained. Twelfth Edition. London, 1851.

19. Maxwell, J. Clerk.—Matter and Motion. (M. E. Sc). London, 1876.

20. Mayer, Alfred M. and Charles Bernard.—Light. (N. S.). London, 1879.

21. ——————————Sound. (N. S.). London, 1879.

22. Naegeli, Prof. Carl. and Prof. S. Schwendener.—The Microscope. In Theory and Practice. Translated from the German of—London, 1887.

23. Piper, Thomas W.—Acoustics. Light and Heat. London, 1880.

24. Roscoe, Henry E.—Spectrum Analysis. Six Lectures. London, 1870.

25. Scott, Robert H.—Elementary Meteorology. (I. Sc. S.). London, 1883.

26. ——————Instruction in the Use of Meteorological Instruments. London, 1885.

27. Silliman, Benjamin.—Principles of Physics or Natural Philosophy. Second Edition. New York, 1860.

28. Spottiswoode, William.—Polarisation of Light. Fourth Edition. (N. S.). London, 1883.

29. Stallo, J. B.—The Concepts and Theories of Modern Physics. (I. Sc. S.). London, 1882.

30. Tunzelmann, G. W. De.—Electricity in Modern Life. (C. Sc. S.). London, 1889.

31. Tyndall, John.—Heat, a Mode of Motion. Fifth Edition. London, 1875.

——————Notes of a course of Nine Lectures on Light. Eighth Edition. London, 1876.

33. Walde, Frank.—Modern Meteorology. (C. Sc. S.) London, 1893.

34. Zöllner, J. C. F.—Transcendental Physics. Translated from the German by C. C. Massey, London, 1880.

Dictionaries.

Beeton.—Illustrated Dictionary of the Physical Sciences. London.

1. Bernays, A. J.—Chemistry. (M. E. Sc.) London, 1874.

2. Briggs, W. & R. W. Stewart.—Elementary Qualitative Analysis. (U. C. C. T. S.) London.

3. Cooke, Samuel.—First Principles of Chemistry. 6th Edition Revised. London, 1895.

4. —— Josiah P.—The new Chemistry. Second Edition. (I. Sc. S.) London, 1874.

5. Eltoft, T.—The combined Note book and Lecture Notes for the Use of Chemical Students. Inorganic Chemistry. London, 1876.

6. Fownes, G.—A Manual of Elementary Chemistry. Theoretical and Practical. Eleventh Edition. Revised and Enlarged by H. Watts. London, 1873.

7. Frankland, Edward.—How to teach Chemistry. Hints to Science Teachers and Students. Summarised and Edited by George Chaloner. London, 1875.

8. ——————Lecture Notes for Chemical Students. 2 vols. Seventh Edition. London, 1872 and 1876. — 2 vols

9. ——————Water Analysis for Sanitary purposes with hints for the Interpretation of Results. London. 1880.

10. ——————Percy Faraday.—Agricultural Chemical Analysis. London, 1883.

11. Fresenius, Dr. C. Remigius.—Quantitative Chemical Analysis. Vol. I. Translated from the 6th German Edition by A. Vacher. Seventh Edition. London, 1873.

12. Griffin, John Joseph.—The Chemical Testing of Wines and Spirits. London, 1872.

13. ——————First Course of Chemical Experiments. London.

14. Jago, W.—Inorganic Chemistry. Theoretical and Practical. A Manual for Students in Advanced Classes. Second Edition. London, 1890.

15. Johnston, J. F. W.—The Chemistry of Common Life. New Edition. Revised by A. H. Church. London, 1880.

16. Kingston, W.—A Brief Account of Saltpetre. Its Theory, Origin, &c. Madras, 1884.

17. Muir, Pattison.—The Story of the Chemical Elements. (L. U. S.) London, 1897.

18. Roscoe, Sir H. E. Assisted by J. Lunt.—Inorganic Chemistry for Beginners. London, 1893.

19. ——————and C. Schorlemmer. A Treatise on Chemistry. Second Edition. Vol. I & Vol. II, (Parts I & II). London, 1878-1879.

20. Valentin, William George.—A Course of Qualitative Chemical Analysis. London, 1876.

21. Vogel, Dr. H.—The Chemistry of Light and Photography in their application to Art, Science and Industry. Fourth Edition. London, 1883.

1. Allen, Grant.—The Colours of Flowers as illustrated in the British Flora. (N S.). London, 1882.
2. ————————Story of the Plants, with Illustrations. (L. U. S. London, 1895.
3. Baillon, H.—The Natural History of Plants. Translated by Marcus M. Hartog. Vols. London, 1871-1888.
4. Balfour, John Hutton.—Introduction to the Study of Palaeontological Botany. Edinburgh, 1872.
5. Beddome, Col. R. H.—Handbook to the Ferns of British India, Ceylon and the Malay Peninsula. Calcutta, 1883.
6. Bentham, G. and J. D. Hooker.—Genera Plantarum. 3 Vols. London, 1862-1883.
7. Bentley, Prof.—Botany. (M. E So.) London, 1875.
8. Bonavia, E.—The cultivated Oranges and Lemons, &c., of India and Ceylon, with Researches into their Origin and the Derivation of their names and other useful information. With an Atlas of Illustrations. London, 1888.
9. ————————The above with an Atlas of Plates, with descriptive Letter-Press. London 1890.
10. Bower, F. O. and S. H. Vines.—A course of practical instruction in Botany. Part I. London, 1885.
11. Brown, Robert N.—A Hand-book of Trees, Shrubs and Herbaceous Plants, with a Supplement by J. J. Wood. Second Edition. Madras, 1866.
12. Cameron, John.—Catalogue of Plants in the Botanical Garden Bangalore, and its Vicinity. Second Edition. Bangalore, 1891.
13. Clarke, C. B.—Compositæ Indicæ. Calcutta, 1876.
14. Class-book of Botany.—
15. Cooke, M. C.—A Manual of Structural Botany for the use of, Classes, Schools and Private Students. New. Edition. London, 1870.
16. Dalzell, N. A. and A. Gibson.—The Bombay Flora. Bombay, 1861.

17. Darwin, Charles.—The Effects of Cross and Self-Fertilisation in the Vegetable Kingdom. Second Edition. London, 1878.

18. ————————Fertilisation of Orchids. The various contrivances by which Orchids are fertilised by Insects. With Illustrations. Second Edition Revised. London, 1882.

19. ————————The Formation of Vegetable Mould through the Action of Worms with Observations of their Habits. With Illustrations. London, 1881.

20. ————————The Different Forms of Flowers on Plants of the same Species. Second Edition. With Illustrations. London, 1880.

21. ————————Insectivorous Plants. With Illustrations. London, 1876.

22. ————————Assisted by Francis Darwin. The Power of. Movement in Plants. With Illustrations. London, 1880.

23. ———Francis.—Elements of Botany. With Illustrations (C. N. Sc. M.). Cambridge, 1895.

24. Drury, Col. Heber.—The useful Plants of India, with notices of their chief value in Commerce, Medicine and in Arts. Second Edition. London, 1873.

25. Firminger, T. A. C.—A Manual of Gardening for Bengal and Upper India. Third Edition. Calcutta, 1874.

26. Gazetteer of the Bombay Presidency.—Botany. Vol. XXV. Bombay, 1886.

27. Gregg, W. H.—A Text-book of Indian Botany. Calcutta, 1883.

28. Henslow, Rev. George.—The Origin of Floral Structures through Insects and other Agencies. (I. Sc. S.). London, 1888.

29. Hooker, J. D.—Botany. (Sc. Pr.). London, 1876.

30. ————————The Flora of British India. 4 vols. London, 1875-1885. 4 vols

31. ——————and T. Thomson. Flora Indica. Being a systematic account of the Plants of British India. Vol. I. London, 1855. (Only volume published).

32. Jackson, John R.—Commercial Botany of the Nineteenth Century. London, 1890.

33. Jaffrey, Andrew Thomas.—Hints to the Amateur Gardeners of Southern India. Second Edition. Madras, 1883.

34. Kurz, Sulpiz.—Bamboo and its Use. Calcutta, 1876.

35. ——————Forest Flora of British Burma. 2 vols. Calcutta, 1877. 2 vols.

36. Lindley, John.—Introductien to Botany. London.

37. ——————School Botany. Descriptive Botany and Vegetable Physiology or the Rudiments of Botanical

38. ——————Taxological Botany, or the Classification of Plants. Part III.

39. ——————Geographical Botany, or the Geographical Distribution of Plants. Part IV.

Science. London, 1862.

40. Lubbock, Sir John.—On British Wild Flowers considered in relation to Insects. Second Edition. (N. S.). London, 1875.

41. McNab, William Ramsey.—Botany. Outlines of Morphology and Physiology. (L. Sc. L. B.). London, 1878.

42. ——————Botany. Outlines of Classification of Plants. (L. Sc. C. B.). London, 1878.

43. Morgan, Major-General H. R.—Forestry in Southern India. Edited by John Shortt. Madras, 1884.

44. Nave, Johann.—The Collector's Hand-book of Algae, Desmids, Fungi, Lichens, &c. Translated and Edited by Rev. W. W. Spicer. London.

45. Oliver, Daniel.—First Book of Indian Botany. With numerous Illustrations. London, 1869.

46. Prantl, Dr. K.—An Elementary Text-book of Botany. Translated from the German of—Revised by S. H. Vines. London, 1880.

47. ——————The above. Edited by S. H. Vines. Fifth Edition. London, 1892.

48. Rodway, James.—Story of Forest and Stream. (L. U. S.) London, 1897.

49. Roxburgh, William.—Flora Indica or Descriptions of Indian Plants. Calcutta, 1874.

50. Sachs, Julius.—Text-book of Botany. Morphological and Phsiological. Second Edition. Oxford, 1882.

51. Schlich.—Manual of Forestry. Vol. V. Forest Utilization by W. R. Fisher. With 343 Illustrations. Translated into English by Dr. Karl Gayer. London, 1896.

52. Smith, Rev. Gerard.—The Ferns of Derbyshire. Illustrated from Nature.' New Edition. London 1877.

53. Tabular View of the Vegetable Kingdom. London.

54. Taylor J. E.—The Sagacity and Morality of Plants. A Sketch of the Life and Conduct of the Vegetable Kingdom. London, 1884.

55. Thonner, F.—Analytical Key to the Natural Orders of Flowering Plants. London, 1895.

56. Voigt, J. O.—A Catalogue of the Plants which have been cultivated in the Hon. East India Company's Botanical Garden Calcutta, and in the Serampore Botanical Garden. Calcutta, 1845.

57. Wallace, Alfred R.—Island life, or the Phenomena and Causes of insular Faunas and Floras, including a revision and attempted solution of the problem of Geological Climates. London, 1880.

58. Ward, H. Marshall.—Timber and some of its Diseases. (N. S.) London, 1889.

59. Woodrow, G. M.—Hints on Gardening in India. Bombay, 1888.

VI. Zoology.

1. Aflalo, Frederick G.—A sketch of the Natural History of Australia, with some notes on sport. Illustrated by F. Seth. (M. C. L. S.) London 1896.
2. Balfour, Francis M.—A Treatise on Comparative Embryology. 2 vols. London, 1880 and 1881.
3. Barnes, Lieut. H. Edwin.—Hand-book of the Birds of the Bombay Presidency. Calcutta, 1885.
4. Bates, Henry Walter.—The Naturalist on the River Amazons. Second Edition. London, 1864.
5. Beavan, Captain R.—Hand-book of the Fresh-water Fishes of India. London, 1877.
6. Blanford, W. T.—Eastern Persia. An account of the journeys of the Persian Boundary Commission. 1870, 1871 and 1872. Vol. II. The Zoology and Geology. (For Vol. I *vide* No. 35 of Q. "Travels and Folklore"). London, 1876.
7. ——————The Fauna of British India. Mammalia. London, 1888.
8. Brehm, Dr. A. F.—Thierleben. Die Kriechthere und Lurche Leipzig, 1878.
9. Bronn, Dr. H. G.—Klassen und Ordnungen der Amphibien. Edited by C. K. Hoffman. Leipzig, 1873-1878.
10. Brown, C. Thomas.—The Taxidermist's Manual. Twenty-eighth Edition. London.
11. Buckley, Arabella B.—Life and Her Children. Glimpses of Animal Life from the Amœba to the Insects. London, 1880.
12. Butler, Capt. E. A.—A Catalogue of Birds of the Southern portion of the Bombay Presidency. Bombay, 1880.
13. Butterflies of India, Burmah and Ceylon. Calcutta.
14. Claus, Dr. Carl.—Elementary Text-book of Zoology. General Part, and Special Part. Protozoa to Insecta. Translated and Edited by Adam Sedgwick. London, 1884.

15. ——————Elementary Text-book of Zoology. Special part. Mollusca to Man. Translated and Edited by Adam Sedgwick. London, 1888.

16. ——————Kleines Lehrbuch der Zoologie. Marburg, 1880.

17. ——————Grundzüge der Zoologie. 2 vols. Marburg, 1880 and 82.

18. Coues, Prof. Elliott.—Hand-book of Field and General Ornithology. A Manual of the Structure and Classification of Birds. Illustrated Edition. London, 1890.

19. Day, Francis.—The Fishes of India. Text and Atlas. 2 vols. London, 1878 and 1888.

20. Ewart, Joseph.—The Poisonous Snakes of India. London, 1878.

21. Faber, G. L.—The Fisheries of the Adriatic. London, 1883.

22. Flower, William Henry.—An Introduction to the Osteology of the Mammalia. Second Edition Revised. London, 1876.

23. Foster, M. and F. M. Balfour.—The Elements of Embryology. London, 1874.

24. Gervais, Paul—Bibliothèque des Sciences Naturelles. Zoologie. Reptiles Vivants et Fossiles. Paris, 1869.

25. Greenwood, Major.—Aids to Zoology and Comparative Anatomy. London, 1883.

26. Günther, Albert C. L. G.—An Introduction to the Study of Fishes. Edinburgh, 1880.

27. ——————The Reptiles of British India. (The Ray Society). London, 1864. (Very rare).

28. Hartmann, Robert.—Anthropoid Apes. (I. Sc. S.) London, 1885.

29. Hume, Allan.—The Indian Ornithological Collector's Vade Mecum. Calcutta, 1881.

30. ——————List of the Birds of India. Calcutta, 1879.

31. ——————My Scrap Book or Rough Notes on Indian Oology and Ornithology. Calcutta, 1869.

32. Huxley, T. H.—An Introduction to the Classification of Animals. London, 1869.

33. ———————The Crayfish. An Introduction to the Study of Zoology. (I. Sc. S.) London, 1880.

34. ———————A Manual of the Anatomy of Vertebrated Animals. London, 1871.

35. ——————— ——————————Invertebrated Animals. London, 1877.

36. ———————Assisted by H. N. Martin.—A Course of Elementary Instruction in Practical Biology. Second Edition Revised. London, 1876.

37. Jerdon, T. C.—The Birds of India. Vol. I and Vol. II, Parts I and II. Calcutta, 1877. (Very rare).

38. ———————Illustrations of Indian Ornithology. Vols. III and IV. Madras, 1846-1847.

39. ———————The Mammals of India. London, 1874.

40. Keane, A. H.—Ethnology in 2 parts. 1. Fundamental Ethnical Problems. 2. The Primary Ethnical Groups. Cambridge, 1896.

41. Letourneau, Dr. Charles.—Biology. Translated from the French. New Edition. London, 1890.

42. Life of an Insect —London.

43. Lubbock, Sir John.—Ants, Bees and Wasps. A Record of Observations on the Habits of the Social Hymenopetra. (I. Sc. S.). Fourth Edition. London, 1882.

44. ———————On the Origin and Metamorphoses of Insects. (N. S.). Second Edition. London, 1874.

45. Marshall, Cap. G. F. L.—Birds' Nesting in India. Calcutta, 1877.

46. ———————and L. de Niceville.—The Butterflies of India, Burmah and Ceylon. Calcutta, 1882.

47. Mivart, St George.—The Cat. An Introduction to the Study of Backformed Animals esp. Mammals. London, 1881.

48. ———————The Common Frog. (N. S.) London, 1874.

49. Morris, Rev. F. O.—A History of British Butterflies. London, 1853.

50. Moseley, H. N.—Notes by a Naturalist on the "Challenger." London, 1879.

51. Nicholson, Edward.—Indian Snakes. An Elementary Treatsie on Ophiology with a Descriptive Catalogue of the Snakes found in India and the adjoining Countries. Second Edition. Madras, 1874.

52. Owen, Richard.—Odontography or a Treatise on the Comparative Anatomy of the Teeth. Text and Atlas. 2 vols. London, 1840 and 1845.

53. Packard, A. S.—Zoology for High Schools and Colleges. Second Edition Revised. New York, 1880.

54. Parker, T. Jeffrey.— A Course of Instruction in Zootomy. Vertebrata. London, 1884.

55. ———W. K.—On Mammalian Descent. London, 1885.

56. ————and G. T. Bettany.—The Morphology of the Skull. London, 1877.

57. Rennie, James.—Insect Architecture. London, 1857.

58. Report of the Scientific Results of the Exploring Voyage of H.M.S. "Challenger" during the years 1873-76 Zoology. Vols. III and IV, prepared under the superintendence of Sir. C. Wyville Thomson. London, 1881-82.

59. Romanes, G. J.—Jelly-fish, Star-fish and Sea-Urchins. (I. Sc. S.) London, 1885.

60. Royal Natural History, The —Edited by Richard Lydekker. With preface by P. L. Sclater. 12 vols. London, 1894-1896.

61. Salter, J. W. and H. Woodward.—Chart of Fossil Crustacea. With descriptive catalogue. London.

62. ————————A descriptive catalogue to accompany the Chart of Fossil Crustacea. London.

63. Starcke, C. N.—The Primitive Family in its Origin and Development. (I. Sc. S.) London, 1889.

64. Sterndale, Robert A.—Natural History of the Mammalia of India. Calcutta, 1884.

65. Swainson, William.—Exotic Conchology. Second Edition. London, 1841.

66 Theobald, William.—A Descriptive Catalogue of the Reptiles of British India. Calcutta, 1876.

67. Topinard, Dr. Paul.—Anthropology. With Preface by Paul Broca. Translated from the French. New Edition. London, 1890.

68. Tweedie, Major-General W.—The Arabian Horse, His Country and People, with Portraits of typical or famous Arabians and Other Illustrations. London, 1894.

69. Tylor, Edward B.—Anthropology. London, 1881.

70. Vagrancy Acts.—By A. C. McM. Secunderabad, 1895.

71. Whymper, F.—The Fisheries of the World. London.

72. Wilson, Andrew.—Students' Guide to Zoology. London, 1884.

73. Woodward, S. P.—A Manual of Mollusca. London, 1875.

1. Ainslie, W.—Materia Medica of Hindoostan, and Artisans' and Agriculturists' Nomenclature. Madras, 1813.

2. Ally, Meer Safder.—Hygiene, or the Principles of Sanitation. Hyderabad, 1888.

3. Althaus, Julius.—The Functions of the Brain. A popular essay. London, 1880.

4. Anatomical Remembrancer.—Seventh Edition. London, 1872.

5. Ashby, Henry.—Notes on Physiology. Second Edition Revised. London, 1880.

6. Bæhr, Bernard.—The Science of Therapeutics according to the principles of Homœopathy. Translated and Enlarged by Charles J. Hempel. 2 vols. Philadelphia, 1883.

7. Baker, Morrant.—Hand-book of Physiology. Ninth Edition. London, 1879.

8. Bartholow, Roberts.—A Practical Treatise on Materia Medical and Therapeutics. New and Enlarged Edition. London, 1878.

9. Bell, F. Jeffrey.—Comparative Anatomy and Physiology. London, 1885.

10. Brunton, T. Lauder.—Disorders of Digestion. Their Consequences and Treatment. London, 1888.

11. Burt, W. H.—Characteristic Materia Medica. Second Edition. New York, 1873.

12. Campbell, Harry.—The Causation of Disease. An Exposition of the Ultimate Factors which induce it. London, 1889.

13. Chadwick, Sir Edwin.—National Health. Abridged from "The Health of Nations." A review of the works of—By Benjamin Ward Richardson. London, 1890.

14. Chaumont, Francis S. B. François—The Habitation in relation to Health. (M. E. Sc.) London, 1879.

15. Clark, F. de Gros.—Physiology. (M. E. Sc.) London, 1873.

16. Clarke, John A.—The Prescriber. A Dictionary of the New Therapeutics, Second Edition. London, 1886.

17. Conn, H. W.—Story of Germ Life. (L. U. S.) London, 1897.
18. Cooley.—Cyclopædia of Practical Receipts. Revised and greatly Enlarged by Richard V. Tuson. 2 vols. Sixth Edition. London, 1880.
19. Davidson, Andrew.—Geographical Pathology. An Enquiry into the Geographical Distribution of Infective and Climatic Diseases. 2 vols. London, 1892.
20. Davis, Ainsworth.—Elementary Physiology, 1895.
21. Dhanakoti Raju, W. E.—The Elements of Hygiene or Easy Lessons on the Laws of Health. Madras, 1875.
22. Duke, Joshua.—How to get thin or Banting in India. Second Edition. Calcutta.
23. Dymock, W.—A Catalogue of Indian Drugs. Bombay, 1883.
24. Fayrer, Sir J.—On Preservation of Health in India. London, 1894.
25. Fearnley, William.—A Course of Elementary Practical Histology. London, 1887.
26. Fellow.—Hypophosphites. Quinine, Strychnine, Iron, Lime, Potassa and Manganese. A few remarks upon.—For the Medical Profession. Fourth Edition. London, 1881.
27. Foster, M.—Physiology. (Sc. Pr.). London, 1874.
28. ———A Text-Book of Physiology. Second Edition. Revised and Enlarged. London, 1878.
29. ———and J. N. Lanley.—A course of Elementary Practical Physiology. London, 1876.
30. Gegenbaur, Carl.—Elements of Comparative Anatomy. Translated by F. Jeffrey Bell. London, 1878.
31. Gill, John Beadnell.—Indigestion. What it is; What it leads to; and a New Method of Treating it. London, 1880.
32. Gooday, Harry.—The Text-Book of Veterinary Homœopathic Practice. Edited and Revised with Notes and Additions by H. J. Surmon. London.
33. Gribble, J. D. B.—Outlines of Medical Jurisprudence for Indian Criminal Courts. Madras, 1885.

34. Hahnemann, Dr. Samuel.—The Chronic Diseases. Their Specific Nature and Homœopathic Treatment. Translated and Edited by Charles J. Hempel, with a Preface by C. Hering. New York, 1845.

35. Hebra, Ferdinand, and M. Kaposi.—On Diseases of the Skin including the Exanthemata. London, 1880.

36. Hebir, Patrick.—Alcohol. Its Moral, Physical and Social Effects. Second Edition. Madras, 1891.

37. ——————A Catechism of Hygiene and Sanitary Science. Part I. Water. (H. S. Sc. S.). Calcutta, 1894.

38. ——————Hygiene of Water and Water Supplies. Calcutta, 1890.

39. ——————Opium. Its Physical, Moral and Social Effects. London, 1894.

40. ——————The Rudiments of Sanitation for Indian Schools, with a Section on Diseases and Injuries and Accidents. Calcutta, 1891.

41. Hendley.—Personal and Domestic Hygiene. Calcutta, 1893.

42. Homœopathic Medicines.—The Sixteen Principles. London, 1880.

43. Hughes, Richard.—A Manual of Pharmacodynamics. Being the course of Materia Medica and Therapeutics delivered at the London School of Homœopathy. Fourth Edition. London, 1880

44. ——————A Manual of Therapeutics. London, 1877.

45. Husband, H. Aubrey.—Medical and Surgical Examination Questions. New Edition. London, 1876.

46. Huxley, Thomas Henry.—Lessons in Elementary Physiology. New Edition. London, 1879.

47. ——————and J. Youmans. Elements of Physiology and Hygiene. A Text-book for Educational Institutions. New York, 1872.

48. Jahr.—Pocket Dictionary and Concordance of Homœopathic Practice. A Clinical Guide and Repertory. Translated by C. J. Hempel and Edited with complete Glossary and Index by J. Laurie. London, 1850.

49. Kellogg, J. H.—The Home Hand-book of Domestic Hygiene and Rational Medicine. Illustrated. London, 1891.

50. ————————Ladies' Guide in Health and Disease. Illustrated Edition. London, 1894.

51. Kemp, D. S.—Companion to the Medicine Chest for India. Third Edition. Bombay, 1884.

52. Kirby, Edmund A.—On the value of Phosphorus as a Remedy for Loss of Nerve Power and Functional Disorders of the Nervous System induced by Overwork. London, 1881.

53. Lane, James, R.—Lectures on Syphilis. Second Edition. London, 1881.

54. Latham, Mr. P. M.—Collected works. Edited by Robert Martin. Vol. II with Index. Clinical Medicine, London, 1878.

55. Laurie, Dr.—Homœopathic Guide for Family Use. Revised by R. S. Gutteridge. Ninety Seventh Edition. London, 1881.

56. Malan.—Family Guide to the Administration of Homœopathic Remedies. New York.

57. M'Alpine.—Elementary Physiology. London, 1883.

58. Mayne, R. G.—A Medical Vocabulary. London, 1881.

59. Meyer, George Hermann von.—The Organs of Speech, and their Application in the Formation of Articulate Sounds. (I. Sc. S.). London, 1883.

60. Miall, L. C. and F. Greenwood.—Anatomy of the Indian Elephant. London, 1878.

61. Mivart, St. George.—Lessons in Elementary Anatomy. London, 1873.

62. Moore, George Lennox.—Supplement to the Domestic Practice of Homœopathy. London, 1858.

63. ————Sir William.—A Manual of Family Medicines and Hygiene for India. Sixth Edition. London, 1893.

64. Morgan, William.—The Homœopathic Treatment of Indigestion, Constipation and Hæmorrhoids. Second Edition. London, 1856.

65. Murrell, William.—Massotherapeutics, or Massage as a mode of Treatment. Fifth Edition. London, 1890.

66. Narayaniah, A. Y.—A Manual of Medical Jurisprudence. Madras, 1890.

67. Parkes, Edmund, A.—A Manual of Practical Hygiene. Fifth Edition. London, 1878.

68. Philips.—Anatomical Model with Descriptive Text by Dr. Schmidt. Illustrated. London.

69. Pilley, John, J.—Hygiene. Third Edition. London, 1888.

70. Pocket Gray or the Anatomist's Vede Mecum. Compiled especially for Students. London, 1879.

71. Prescriber's Pharmacopœia containing all the Medicines in the British Pharmacopœia. Revised and Edited by N. Tirand. London, 1886.

72. ——————————. Second Edition. Bombay, 1891.

73. Proctor, Richard, A.—Strength. How to get Strong and keep Strong. London, 1889.

74. Ray, D. N.—Cholera and its Preventive and Curative Treatment, with an Introduction by T. F. Allen. New York, 1884.

75. Repertory of the Materia Medica Pura, vol. II of the Pathogenetic Cyclopædia. London, 1859.

76. Ruddock, E. Harris.—The Diseases of Infants and Children and their Homœopathic Treatment. London, 1876.

77. ——————————. The Ladies' Manual of Homœopathic Treatment. London, 1875.

78. Russell, Dr. Rutherford.—The Treatment of Rheumatism, Epilepsy, Asthma and Fever. Clinical Lectures. London, 1865.

79. Schäfer, E. A.—The Essentials of Histology, Descriptive and Practical, for the use of Students. London, 1885.

80. Schieiber, J.—A Manual of Treatment by Massage and Methodical Muscle Exercise. Translated by W. Mendelson. Edinburgh, 1887.

81. Smellie.—Treatise on the Theory and Practice of Midwifery. Edited with Annotations by Alfred H. McClintock. Vol. III with Index. London, 1878.

82. Smith, Thomas and W. J. Walsham.—A Manual of Operative Surgery on the Dead Body. Second Edition. London, 1876.

83. Sutton, J Bland.—Evolution and Disease. (C. Sc. S.). London, 1890.

84. Teste, Alph.—A Homœopathic Treatise on the Diseases of Children. Translated from the French by E. H. Coté, Revised by J. H. Pulte. Fifth Edition. Philadelphia.

85. Thompson, Henry.—Clinical Lectures on Diseases of the Urinary Organs. Fifth Edition. London, 1879.

86. Tibbits, Edward T.—Muscles, Mind and Morals or Hints on the Prolongation of Life. London.

87. Traveller's Surgical and Medical Guide. London, 1888.

88. Virchow, Prof. Rudolph.—Infection-Diseases. Translated by John James. London, 1879.

89. ————————Post Mortem Examinations. Translated from the German by Dr. T. P. Smith. London, 1880.

90. Wakefield.—Lessons on Living. London, 1896.

91. Waring, Edward John.—Remarks on the Uses of some of the Bazaar Medicines and common Medical Plants of India. Third Edition. London, 1875.

92. ————————Bibliography of Therapeutics chiefly in reference to Articles of Materia Medica. 2 vols. London, 1878-1879.

93. Whittaker, J. Travis.—Student's Primer on the Urine. London 1880.

94. Wilson, Erasmus.—The Anatomist's Vede Mecum, a System of Human Anatomy. Edited by G. Buchanan and assisted by H. E. Clark. Ninth Edition. London,

95. Wyld, George.—Diseases of the Heart and Lungs. Their Physical Diagnosis and Homœopathic and Hygienic Treatment. London, 1860.

Yeo, Gerald, F.—A Manual of Physiology for the use of junior students of Medicine. London, 1884.

1. Bauerman, Hilary.—Text-book of Descriptive Mineralogy. London, 1884.
2. ————Text book of Systematic Mineralogy. London, 1881.
3. Bloxam, Charles, L.—Metals, their Properties and Treatment. New Edition. London, 1885.
4. Bristow, Henry William.—A Glossary of Mineralogy. London, 1861.
5. Cotta, Bernhard von.—Die Gesteinslehre. Freiberg, 1862.
6. Dana, Edward Salisbury.—A Text-book of Mineralogy. New York, 1885.
7. ——, J. D.—Manual of Mineralogy and Lithology. London, 1885.
8. Emanuel, Harry.—Diamonds and Precious Stones. London, 1885.
9. Jewesbury, F. Noel.—Mineralogical Tables. London, 1873.
10. Jordon, James B.—Elementary Crystallography. London, 1876.
11. Lasaulx, Dr. A. Von.—Elemente der Petrographie. Bonn, 1875.
12. Nicol, James.—Elements of Mineralogy. Second Edition. Edinburgh, 1873.
13. Pepper, J. H.—Play Book of Metals. London.
14. Ross, Lieut. Col. W. A.—The Blowpipe in Chemistry, Mineralogy and Geology. London, 1889.
15. Rutley, Frank.—Rock-forming Minerals. London, 1888.
16. ————The Study of Rocks. An Elementary Text-book of Petrology. London, 1879.
17. Scheerer, Theodore.—An Introduction to the use of the Mouth Blowpipe. Third Edition. London, 1895.
18. Story-Maskelyne, N.—Crystallography. A Treatise on the Morphology of Crystals. Oxford, 1894.

Streeter, Edwin.—Precious Stones and Jems. Fifth Edition. London, 1892.

20. Woodward, C. J.—Crystallography for Beginners. London, 1896.

21. Zirkel, Dr. Ferdinand.—Die Mikroskopische Beschaffenheit der Mineralien und Gesteine. Leipzig, 1873.

1. André, George G.—A Practical Treatise on Coal Mining. 2 vols. London, 1876. 2 vol.
2. ——————Rock Blasting. London, 1878.
3. Bauerman, Hilary.—A Descriptive Catalogue of Geological, Mining and Metallurgical Models in the Museum of Practical Geology. London, 1865.
4. ——————A Treatise on the Metallurgy of Iron. London, 1874.
5. Bowie, Aug. J.—A Practical Treatise on Hydraulic Mining in California. Third Edition. New York, 1889.
6. Burgoyne, Lieut.-Genl. Sir John.—Rudimentary Treatise on the Blasting and Quarrying of Stone. Second Edition. London, 1852.
7. Catalogue of the Michigan Mining School. 1892-1894. Houghton, 1894.
8. ——————1894-1896. Houghton, 1896.
9. Chambers, T. G.—Register of the Associates and Old Students of the Royal College of Cambridge, the Royal School of Mines and the Royal College of Science. London, 1896.
10. Collins, J. H.—Principles of Metal Mining (C. E. Sc. S.) London, 1875.
11. Eissler, M.—The Metallurgy of Gold. London, 1889.
12. —————— ——————of Silver. London, 1889.
13. Galloway, Robert, L.—A History of Coal Mining in Great Britain. London, 1882.
14. Greenwood, W. H.—A Manual of Metallurgy. 2 vols. (C. A. Sc. S.) London, 1875-1877. 2 vol.
15. Hunt, Robert.—British Mining. A Treatise on the Metalliferous Mines of the United Kingdom. London, 1884.
16. Kirkpatrick, T. S. G.—The Hydraulic Gold Miner's Manual. London, 1890.
17. Landauer, J.—Blowpipe Analysis. London, 1879.

18. Lock, C. G. W.—Miner's Pocket-book. London, 1892.

19. ——————Practical Gold Mining. London, 1889.

20. Lottner, Heinrich.—Leitfaden Zur Bergbaukunde. Berlin. 1873.

21. Lupton, Arnold.—Mining. London, 1893.

22. Martin, Edward, A.—The Story of a Piece of Coal. (L. U. S.) London, 1896.

23. M'Dermott, Walter. and P. W. Duffield.—Losses in Gold Amalgamation. Second Edition. London, 1890.

24. Morgans, William.—Manual of Mining Tools, with an Atlas of Engravings to illustrate it. 2 vols. London, 1871.

25. North, Oliver.—The Practical Assayer. containing easy methods for the Assay of the principal Metals and Alloys. London, 1874.

26. Pamely, Caleb.—The Colliery Manager's Hand-book. London, 1891.

27. Percy, C. M.—The Mechanical Engineering of Collieries. Vol. 1. Third Edition. London, 1885.

28. ——John.—Metallurgy of Lead including Desilverization and Cupellation. London, 1870.

29. Phillips, J. Arthur.—Elements of Metallurgy. New Edition. Revised and Enlarged by the Author and H. Bauerman. London, 1887.

30. Plattner.—Manual of Quantitative and Qualitative Analysis with the Blow-pepe. Edited by T. H. Cookesley. London, 1889.

31. Randall, P. M.—The Quartz Operator's Hand-book. New York, 1880.

32. Reports of the Director of the Michigan Mining School for 1890-1892.

33. Roberts-Austen, W. C.—An Introduction to the Study of Metallurgy. (G. Sc. T. B.) London, 1891.

34. Sawyer, Arthur Robert.—Accidents in Mines. London, 1886.

35. Smyth, Warington W.—A Rudimentary Treatise on Coal and Coal-Mining. Second Edition. Revised and Corrected. London, 1872.

36. Swindell, John George.—Rudimentary Treatise on Well-digging, Boring and Pump Work. London, 1877.

37. Syllabus, and full description of the lessons by correspondence established for preparing candidates for the Colliery Manager's Examination, 1st and 2nd Classes in every District of the United Kingdom. Sixth Edition. 1893.

38. Watt, Alexander.—The History of a Lump of Chalk, its family circle and their uses. London, 1883.

39. ———————The History of a Lump of Coal, from the Pit's Mouth to a Bonnet Ribbon. London, 1882.

———————The History of a Lump of Iron, from Mine to the Magnet. London, 1884.

1. Ball, V.—The Diamonds, Coal and Gold of India, their Mode of Occurrence and Distribution. London, 1881.

2. Beche, Sir Henry T. de la.—The Geological Observer. Second Edition Revised. London, 1853.

3. Blanford, W. T.—Observations on the Geology and Zoology of Abyssinia made during the progress of the British Expedition to that Country in 1867-68. London, 1879.

4. ———— A Sketch of the Geology of India. Calcutta, 1879.

5. Bonney, T. G.—Geology. (M. E. Sc.) London, 1874

6. Calvert, John.—The Gold Rocks of Great Britain and Ireland. London, 1853.

7 Carter, Henry J.—Geological Papers on Western India with Atlas. Bombay, 1857.

Cole, Grenville, A. J.—Aids in Practical Geology. London, 1891.

Cooke, T.—An Elementary Manual of Geology for Indian Students. Bombay, 1871.

Croll, James.—Discussions on Climate and Cosmology. Edinburgh, 1885.

Darwin, Charles.—Geological Observations on the Volcanic Islands and Parts of South America visited during the voyage of H. M. S. "Beagle." London, 1876.

———— Journals of Researches in the Natural History and Geology of the Countries visited during the Voyage of H. M. S. "Beagle" round the world. London, 1879.

———— The above. (L. H. B. No. 2). London, 1891.

———— Structure and Distribution of Coral Reefs and Geological Observations on the Volcanic Islands and Parts of South America. (M. L. F. B.) London, 1890.

————————

Third Edition. London, 1899.

Dawkins, W. Boyd.—Cave Hunting. Researches on the Evidence of Caves respecting the early Inhabitants of Europe. London, 1874.

17. ——————Early Man in Britain, and his Place in the Tertiary Period. London, 1880.

18. Dawson, J. W.—The Chain of Life in Geological Time. A Sketch of the Origin and Succession of Animals and Plants. Second Revised Edition. London, 1885.

19. ——————Fossil Men and their Modern Representatives. London, 1880.

20. Evans, John.—The Ancient Stone Implements, Weapons and Ornaments of Great Britain. London, 1872.

21. Falconer, Hugh.—Palæontological Memoirs and Notes. Compiled and Edited by Charles Murchison. 2 vols. London, 1868.

22. Forbes, Prof. E.—Memoirs of the Geological Survey of Great Britain. London, 1856.

23. Geikie, Archibald —Class Book of Geology. London, 1887.

24. ——————Geological Sketches at Home and Abroad. London, 1882.

25. ——————Outlines of Field Geology. Second Edition Revised and Enlarged. London, 1879.

26. ——————Physical Geography. (Sc. Pr.). London, 1885.

27. ——————Text-book of Geology. Second Edition. London, 1885.

28. ——————James.—The great Ice Age, and its relation to the Antiquity of Man. London, 1874.

29. Geology.—Descriptive Catalogue of Rock-Specimens in the Lithological Collection. Madras, 1867.

30. ————, The. of Bombay.

31. ————of India—A Manual of the, with Map chiefly compiled by H. B. Medlicott, W. T. Blankford, V. Ball and F. R. Mallet. 5 vols. Calcutta, 1879-1887 (rare).

32. Goodrich, Frank B.—The History of the Sea. Illustrated, Sydney.

33. Gurvelle.—Geology in Systematic Work and Tables. London, 1898.

34. Heer, Prof.—The Primæval World of Switzerland. Edited by James Heywood. 2 vols. London, 1876.

35. Herschel, Sir John F. W.—Physical Geography of the Globe. Fifth Edition. Edinburgh, 1875.

36. Hull, Edward.—The Coal-fields of Great Britain, their History, Structure and Resources. London, 1881.

37. Huxley, T. H.—Physiography. An Introduction to the Study of Nature. London, 1877.

38. Judd, John W.—The Geology of Rutland, being Memoirs of the Geological Survey of England and Wales. With an Introductory Essay on the Classification and Correlation of the Jurassic Rocks of the Midland District of England. London, 1875.

39. ————————Volcanoes. What they are and what they teach. (I. Sc. S.). London, 1881.

40. Jukes, J. Beete.—The School Manual of Geology, Edited by Alfred J. Jukes-Browne. Third Edition. Revised and Enlarged. Edinburgh, 1876.

41. King, W. and T. A. Pope.—Gold, Copper and Lead in Chota Nagpore and the Adjacent Countries. Calcutta, 1891.

42. Lyell, Sir Charles.—Elements of Geology. Sixth Edition. London, 1865. (rare)

43. ————————Principles of Geology, or the Modern Changes of the Earth and its Inhabitants. 2 vols. Twelfth Edition. London, 1875.

44. ————————The Student's Elements of Geology. Second Edition. Revised and Enlarged. London, 1874.

45. Mantell, G. A.—Geological Excursions round the Isle of Wight. Third Edition. London, 1854.

46. Maury, M. F.—The Physical Geography of the Sea and its Meteorology. Twelfth Edition. London, 1866.

47. Meldola, Raphael.—Coal and what we get from it. A romance of Applied Science. (R. Sc. S.) London, 1891.

48. Memoirs of the Geological Survey of India. Palæontologia Indica. Vol. I. Calcutta, 1870.

49. ——————————Vol. XVIII. Calcutta, 1881.

50. Murchison, Sir Roderick J.—Siluria. A History of the Oldest Rocks in the British Isles and Other Countries. Fifth Edition. London, 1872.

51. ——————————Figures of the Silurian Fossils to illustrate. With a map Fifth Edition. London, 1872.

52. ——————————E. de Verneuil and Count Alexander von Keyserling. The Geology of Russia in Europe and the Ural Mountains. 2 vols. London, 1845. (very rare)

53. Nicholson, Henry A. and Richard Lydekker.—A Manual of Palæontology for the Use of Students. 2 vols. Third Edition. London, 1889.

54. Owen, Richard —Palæontology, or a Systematic Summary of Extinct Animals and their Geological Relations. Second Edition. Edinburgh, 1861.

55. Penning, W. Henry —A Textbook of Field Geology, with a Section on Palaeontology by A. J. Jukes-Browne. Second Edition. London, 1879.

56. Phillips, J. Arthur.—A Treatise on Ore Deposits London, 1884.

57. Prestwich, Joseph.—Geology. Chemical, Physical and Stratigraphical. 2 vols. Oxford, 1886-1888.

58. Records of the Geological Survey of India. 6 vols. from 1868-1889. Calcutta. (rare)

59. Scrope, G. Poulett.—The Geology and Extinct Volcanoes of Central France, with Map. London, 1858.

60. Seeley, H. G.—The Story of the Earth in past Ages. (L. U. S.) London, 1895.

61. Shaler, N. S.—Aspects of the Earth. A popular account of some familiar Geological Phenomena. London, 1890.

62. Small, E. W.—The Earth. An Introduction to the Study of Inorganic Nature. London, 1894.

63. Somerville, Mary.—Physical Geography. Seventh Edition. Revised. London, 1877.

64. Tabular View of Characteristic British Fossils, Stratigraphically arranged. London.

65. Thornton, John.—Advanced Phisiography. London, 18?0.

66. Tyndall, John.—The forms of Water, or Clouds, Rivers, Ice and Glaciers. Fifth Edition. (I. Sc. S.). London, 1875.

67. Woodward, Horace, B.—The Geology of England and Wales. With Map, &c. London, 1876.

68. Young, John.—Physical Geography. (C. A. Sc. S.). London, 1874.

1. Badger, G. Percy.—A guide to Malta and Gozo. Malta, 1881.
2. Baedeker, K.—La Suisse et les parties limitrophes de L'Italie, de la Savoie et du Tyrol. Manuel du Voyageur. Coblenz, 1864.
3. ——————Lower Egypt and the Peninsula of Sinai. Hand-book for Travellers. London, 1895.
4. ——————Upper Egypt and Nubia as far as the Second Cataract. Hand-book for Travellers. London, 1892.
5. ——————Greece. Handbook for Travellers. London, 1894.
6. ——————Palestine and Syria. Hand-book for Travellers. London, 1894.
7. ——————Switzerland and the Adjacent Portions of Italy, Savoy, and the Tyrol. Hand-book for Travellers with Maps &c. 12th Edition. Leipsic, 1887.
8. ——————Manual. The Traveller's Manual of Conversation in Four Languages—English, French, German and Italian. With Vocabulary, short questions, &c., London.
9. Baness, J. F.—Index Geographicus Indicus. London, 1881.
10. Bartlett, John.—Familiar Quotations, being an attempt to trace to their source, Passages and Phrases in Common use. London.
11. Beale, Thomas William.—An Oriental Biographical Dictionary. New Edition. Revised and Enlarged by H. G. Keene. London, 1894.
12. Beeton.—Universal Information. The Dictionary of Geography, History, Biography, Mythology and Chronology. New and Enlarged Edition with Maps. London.
13 Boulillet, M. N.—Dictionnaire Universel D'Histoire et de Geographie. New Edition. Paris, 1859.
14. Bradshaw.—Continental Railway, Steam Transit, and General Guide, for Travellers through Europe. London, 1899.
15. Brewer, Rev. E. Cobham.—Dictionary of Phrase and Fable. Twelfth Edition. London.

16. ———————— Reader's Hand-book of Allusions. References, Plots and Stories. London, 1896.

17. Calendar.—Oxford University for 1899. Oxford.

18. ————London University for 1885-1886. London.

19. ———— ————for 1891-1892 (Part II). Examaination Papers. 1890-1891. London.

20. ———— ————for 1892-1893. (Part II). London.

21. ———— ————for 1893-1894 (Part I). Charters, Regulations, Lists, &c. London.

22. ———— ————for 1897-1898 and the Revised Regulations for 1899. London.

23. ———— University Correspondence College for 1893-1894. The London Matriculation Directory. London.

24. ———— ————for 1897-1898. The London Matriculation Directory. London.

25. ————University College of Wales 1897-1898. Twenty-Sixth Session. Manchester.

26. ————Tokio Kaisei—Gakko, or Imperial University of Tokio for 1876.

27. ————Allahabad University for 1889. Allahabad.

28. ————Bombay University for 1889-1890. Bombay.

29. ————Calcutta University for 1880-1881. Calcutta.

30. ———— ———— for 1883-1834. Calcutta.

31. ———— ———— for 1889. Calcutta.

32. ———— ———— for 1890. Calcutta.

33. ———— ———— for 1891. Examination Papers. Calcutta.

34. ———— ———— for 1893. Calcutta.

35. ———— ———— for 1894. Calcutta.

36. ———— ———— for 1895. Calcutta.

37. ———— ———— for 1897. Calcutta.

38. ————Madras University for 1892-1893. Madras.

39. ———— ———— for 1895-1896. Madras.

40. ————College of Engineering for 1896. Madras.

41. ————Thomason Civil Engineering College for 1895. Roorkee.

42. ——— ——————— for 1897. Roorkee.

43. ———Hyderabad Middle School for 1898. Madras.

44. ———Royal Indian Engineering College. Cooper's Hill for 1898-1899 containing a Syllabus of the Courses of Study. London.

45. ———Birkbeck. Literary and Scientific Institution. Session 1897-1898. Syllabus of Schemes of Work. Particulars of Examinations, Scholarships, Prizes, Associates, Examination Papers, &c. London.

46. Cassell.—Miniature Cyclopædia. Compiled by W. L. Clowes. London, 1888.

47. ———New Popular Educator. A Complete Encyclopædia of Elementary and Advanced Education. London, 1890-1892.

48. Chamber, Robert.—Cyclopaedia of English Literature. Revised by Robert Carruthers. 8 Vols. (Vols. I, V and VIII are wanting). Third Edition. New York, 1879.

49. Colliery Manager's Pocket Book, Almanac and Diary for 1887. Edited by W. Fairley. London.

50. English, French, Turkish and Russian Vocabulary for the use of the Army, Navy and Travellers. London, 1855.

51. Enquire within upon Everything. 76th Edition. Revised. London, 1887.

52, Godwin, Rev. G. N.—A Guide to the Maltese Islands. Malta.

53. Guide de L'Etranger dans Paris et ses environs. Sixth Edition. Paris, 1876.

54. Guide de Bruxelles et de Ses environs Souvenir des Hotels de Belle-vue and de Flandre. Edited by E. Dremel. 1887.

55. Hand-book for Homeward bound travellers for India, Australia and the East, 1892.

56. Hand-book to the Special Loan Collection for the South Kensington Museum of Scientific Apparatus. London, 1876.

57. Hazell.—Annual for 1889. A Cyclopædic Record of Men and Topics of the Day. Edited by E. D. Price. London, 1889

58. Hyderabad Almanac and Directory for 1889. Compiled by M. T. Davasigamoney Moodelliar. Madras.

59. ———————————for 1890.——————— ——————————— Madras.

60. India, Burma and Ceylon. Information for Travellers and Residents with 4 Maps. London.

61. Liverpool and its Environs.—A Pictorial and Descriptive Guide to—Seventh Edition. Revised and Re-illustrated. London.

62. Lockwood.—A Dictionary of the Terms used in the Practice of Mechanical Engineering. Second Edition. London, 1892.

63. Misra, Madhura Prasâd.—Trilingual Dictionary. English, Hindustani and Hindi. Benaras, 1865.

64. Orient Line Guide.—Chapters for Travellers by Sea and by Land. Edited by W. J. Loftie. London, 1894.

65. Palmer, Rev. A. Smythe.—Folk Etymology. A Dictionary of Verbal Corruptions, &c. London, 1882.

66. Pocket Dictionary of Technical Terms. English, French and German. 3 vols. London, 1872.

67. ——————————, A new.—English, French and German. Compiled by Dr. F. E. Feller. 3 vols. Leipzig, 1877.

68. Prendergast, Thomas.—Hand-book to the Mastery Series. Fourth Edition. London, 1877.

69. Reference Catalogue of Current Literature, containing the full titles of books now in print and on sale with the prices at which they may be obtained of all booksellers and an Index containing upwards of 53,000 References. London, 1885.

70. Roget, P. M.—The Thesaurus of English Words and Phrases. Classified and arranged by——.New Edition. London, 1886.

71. Routledge, Edmund.—Book of the year 1897. A chronicle of the Times, and a Record of Events. Compiled by ———. London, 1898

72. Royal Academy of Arts Exhibition for 1876, 1878 and 1879. 3 vols. London.

73. Royal Road to Foreign Languages. French, German, Spanish and Italian. Being the first twelve numbers of "Foreign Languages made easy." London, 1894.

74. Russell, W. Clark.—Sailor's Language. A Collection of Sea Terms and their Definitions. London, 1883.

75. Thacker.—Indian Directory for 1893. Calcutta.

76. ——— ——— for 1898. Calcutta.

77. ——— ——— for 1900. Calcutta.

78. "Times of India."—Calendar and Directory for 1894. Bombay.

79. ——— ——— for 1895. Bombay.

80. ——— ——— for 1897. Bombay.

81. ——— ——— for 1898. Bombay.

82. ——— ——— for 1899. Bombay.

83. ——— ——— for 1900. Bombay.

84. Vincent, Benjamin.—Haydn's Dictionary of Dates and Universal Information relating to all ages and nations. 21st Edition. London, 1895.

85. Vocabulary in five languages.—English, Portuguese, Goanese, Marâthi and Hindustâni. Printed in the Roman character. Satara, 1878.

86. Weale, John.—A Dictionary of the terms used in Architecture, Building, Engineering, Mining, Metallurgy, Archæology, the Fine Arts, &c. Edited by Robert Hunt. Sixth Edition. London, 1891.

87. Whitaker, Joseph.—Almanac for 1890. London.

88. ——— ——— for 1895. London.

89. ——— ——— for 1899. London.

90. ——— ——— for 1900. London.

91. ——— Peerage for 1900. London.

92. ———Naval and Military Directory for 1898. London.

93. ———————— Naval and Military Directory and Indian Army List for 1900. London.

94. Who's Who for 1899.—An Annual Biographical Dictionary. Edited by Douglas Sladen. London, 1899.

1. Bengali Magazine, A.—XI Nos.
2. Charter, Supplemental Charter, By-Laws, and List of Members of the Institution of Civil Engineers for 1887, 1891 and 1893, London.
3. Contemporary Review, The.—February 1886, London.
4. Engineering.—An Illustrated Weekly Journal. Edited by W. H. Maw and J. Dredge. Vols. 17—23 bound. Vols. 27, 28, 30, 31, 36—42, 45—47, 49, 50, 59 and 60 unbound. London, 1874—1895.
5. ————Magazine. Vol. XV. 2 Nos. 1898.
6. Geological Literature added to the Geological Society's Library during the year ended 31st December 1895. Compiled by the Asst. Librarian. London, 1896.
7. Geological Magazine, The.—Edited by Henry Woodward. (Vol. for 1882 wanting). London, 1879—1888.
8. Hardwicke's Science Gossip. Edited by J. E. Taylor. Vols. XVI—XXII. (Vol. XVII wanting). London, 1880—1886.
9. Imperial and Asiatic Quarterly Review and Oriental and Colonial Record. Vol. II, No. 4. Vol. III, No. 5 and Vol. VII, Nos. 13 and 15. 1891—1894. London.
10. Index to the Transactions of the Literary Society of Bombay. Vols. I—III and to the Journals of the Bombay Branch of the Royal Asiatic Society. With a Historical Sketch of the Society by G. K. Tivarekar. Vols. I—XIII Bombay.
11. Indian Journal of Education. A Monthly Review. From July 1894 to Decr. 1899. (Nos. for Novr., Decr. 1894, Feb., Aprl., May 1895, Novr. 1897. Nov., Dec. 1899, are wanting). Madras.
12. Indische Studien.—Edited by Dr. A. Weber. Vols. I—XVII 1850—1885. (Vol. III, is wanting). For Vols. VI and VII, *vide* A. I. No. 63 and for Vols. XI and XII *vide* A. I. No. 111 of the Catalogue.
13. Journal Asiatique. Ou Recueil de Mémoires. (In French) 1856—58. Vols. VII—XII and 1886—1889. Vols. VII—XIV. Paris.

14. ——— of the Bombay Branch of the Royal Asiatic Society. Vol. XIV, 2 Nos,. Vol. XV, 1 No. Vol. XVI, 2 Nos, Vol. XVII, 2 Nos., Vol. XVIII, 1 No., Vol. XIX, 2 Nos., Vol XX, 1 No. Extra number containing Prof. Peterson's Report on Sanskrit Manuscripts Vol. XVI, Vol. XVII, 2 Nos. and Vol XVIII, 1 No. 1880-1865, Bombay.

15 ——— of the Bombay Natural History Society. Edited by H. M. Phipson, Vol. VI, 3 Nos. Vol. VII, 4 Nos. Vol. VIII, 5 Nos. Vol. IX, 4 Nos. Vol. X, 2 Nos. Vol. XI, 1 No. and Vol. XII, 1 No. Bombay, 1891-1898.

16. ——— of the Royal Microscopical Society. Edited by Frank Crisp. 2 Vols. London, 1878-1878.

17. ——— of the Asiatic Society of Bengal, 1885-1900. (Vol. LX, wanting). Calcutta.

18. ——— Natural History, conducted by John M'Clelland. 6 Vols. Calcutta, 1841-1846. (very rare)

19. Knowldge.—An Illustrated Magazine of Science. Conducted by Richard A. Proctor. 3 Vols. (bound). London, 1883-1885.

20. List of Members of the Institution of Civil Engineers. January 1879, London.

21. ——of Geological Society of London, for 1891, 1892 and 1896, 3 Vols. London.

22. Nadras Review.—Published quarterly. November 1895, May 1896-1900.

23. Minutes of Proceedings of the Institution of Civil Engineers with other selected and abstracted papers. Edited by James Forrest, Vols. 81-104. London, 1885 (Vol. 91 is wanting).

Science.—A monthly Review of Scientific Progress, 1895-1898 and 9 Nos. of 1899. (Nos. 59 and 60 for January and February 1897 are wanting). London.

25. Nature.—A Weekly Illustrated Journal of Science. 1876-1887 and 1895 till June 1899. Vols. XIV-XXXV. London. (Vols. XVIII, XVIV, XXV and XXVI and Nos. 1317, 1339, 1340, 1353, 1364, 1432, 1487, 1486 are wanting).

26. Nouvelle Bibliotheque Populaire, Paris.

27. Official Report of the Calcutta International Exhibition of 1883-1884. Calcutta, 1885.

28. Proceedings of the Asiatic Society of Bengal, 1898-1900. 18 Nos. Calcutta.

29. Quarterly Journal of the Geological Society of London. 1859-1896. Vol. XV—LII. (Vols. XXXII, XXXV-XXXVII, XXXIX and XLII are wanting). London.

30. ——————of the Microscopical Science. Edited by E. Ray Lankester. Vol. XX. London, 1880.

31. Report on the British Collection of Antiquities from Central Asia prepared by the Survey of India. With Plates. 1899.

32. Royal School of Mines Magazine.

33. Rules of the Asiatic Society of Bengal. Calcutta, 1899.

34. Theosophist, The—A Magazine of Oriental Philosophy, Art, Literature and Occultism. Conducted by H. P. Blavatsky. Vol. VII, No. 76. Madras, 1886.

35. Transactions of the Federated Institution of Mining Engineers, 1892-1897. Vol. III, Vol IV, 4 parts. Vol. V. 4 parts. Vol. VI, 4 parts. Vol VII, 4 parts. Vol. VIII, 3 parts. Vol. IX, 3 parts Vol. X, 3 parts. Vol. XI, Vol. XII, 4 parts. Vol. XIII, 3 parts.

36. Washington, J. W. P.—Fifteenth Annual Report of the United States Geological Survey for 1893-1894.

37. Wissenschafticher Jahresberlicht uber die Morgenlandischen Studien. Von. E. Kuhn and A. Socin. Leipzig, 1876-1880.

38. Zeitschrift der Deutschen Morgenländischen Gesellschaft. Transactions of the German Oriental Society. Vols. I—XLII und Register. 2 vols. Leipzig, 1847-1889.

FINIS.